P9-AQX-756

WITHDRAWN

Gramley Library
Salem College
Winston-Salem, NC 27108

Paul Valéry Revisited

Twayne's World Authors Series

French Literature

David O'Connell, Editor

Georgia State University

TWAS 850

Gramley Library
Salem College
Winston-Salem, NC 27108

PAUL VALÉRY IN 1894.
Photograph by Pierre Louÿs
(Courtesy of Madame Agathe Rouart-Valéry.)

Paul Valéry Revisited

Walter Putnam

University of New Mexico

Twayne Publishers • New York
Maxwell Macmillan Canada • Toronto
Maxwell Macmillan International • New York Oxford Singapore Sydney

Twayne's World Authors Series No. 850

Paul Valéry Revisited
Walter Putnam

Copyright © 1995 by Twayne Publishers
All rights reserved. No part of this book may be reproduced or transmitted in any form or by any means, electronic or mechanical, including photocopying, recording, or by any information storage and retrieval system, without permission in writing from the Publisher.

Twayne Publishers   Maxwell Macmillan Canada, Inc.
Macmillan Publishing Company   1200 Eglinton Avenue East
866 Third Avenue   Suite 200
New York, New York 10022   Don Mills, Ontario M3C 3N1

Library of Congress Cataloging-in-Publication Data

Putnam, Walter C.
    Paul Valéry / Walter Putnam.
        p.   cm.—(Twayne's world authors series ; TWAS 850. French literature)
    Includes bibliographical references and indexes.
    ISBN 0-8057-8291-5
    1. Valéry, Paul, 1871–1945—Criticism and interpretation. I. Title. II. Series:
Twayne's world authors series ; TWAS 850. III. Series: Twayne's world authors series.
French literature.
PQ2643.A26Z732   1994   94-12619
841'.912—dc20   CIP

The paper used in this publication meets the minimum requirements of American National Standard for Information Services—Permanence of Paper for Printed Library Materials. ANSI Z3948–1984.∞ ™

10 9 8 7 6 5 4 3 2 1 (hc)

Printed in the United States of America

For my parents

Contents

Preface

A lire Valéry on acquiert cette sagesse de se sentir un peu plus sot qu'avant.

Gide

This volume, like others in the Twayne World Authors Series, aims at providing a literate, nonspecialist audience with a reliable introduction to one of the world's foremost literary figures. The case of Paul Valéry is particularly interesting now that he seems to have survived the half-century purgatory following his death in 1945. It has been a daunting task to be entrusted with presenting to an American public a thinker and writer of Valéry's stature. I can think of no other figure in modern times who has inspired the kind of awe and respect that Valéry commands. He provides a lesson in humility or, as noted in the above quotation by his close friend, André Gide, "Reading Valéry gives one the wisdom that comes with feeling a bit less intelligent than before."[1]

Indeed, one can hardly avoid the word *intelligent* in reference to Valéry—a man who was the most widely admired poet of his day after having given up poetry for 20 years due to his own dissatisfaction with his verse; a man who religiously spent several hours every morning consigning his thoughts to paper, leaving a mass of over 26,000 pages in his private notebooks; finally, a man who epitomized the French intellectual, at least of the pre-*engagé* sort, neither a stodgy academic nor a fashionable media celebrity, but rather one whose entire life and work were guided by constant, conscious attention to himself and to the surrounding world.

It is hardly surprising that Valéry's reputation has unfortunately discouraged firsthand knowledge of his work by nonspecialists. It seems that there have evolved two attitudes towards Valéry: on the one hand, that of the reverential scholar for whom Valéry exemplifies the superlative qualities that one admires in a writer; on the other hand, that of the vast majority of readers who remain daunted by the breadth and depth of his work and wonder even where to begin. While I hope that this book will be of some interest to the former, it is addressed primarily to the latter. This might be seen as contradicting Valéry's own wish that he be read several times by one person rather than one time by several people.[2] I would nevertheless like to suggest that Valéry can be read and appreciated by anyone who has an interest and desire to explore the heart, mind, and soul of a great writer.

My own knowledge and understanding of Valéry have been significantly enriched by the work of the numerous scholars who have thought and written about him. Roland Barthes once defined culture as what one learns from others, and I would be remiss in not recognizing those whose work will inevitably be echoed in this brief study. Valéry is fortunate to have fostered the admiration and dedication of the likes of James Lawler, Pierre-Olivier Walzer, Christine Crow, Jean Hytier, Judith Robinson, Jean Bellemin-Noël, Suzanne Nash, and Jacques Duchesne-Guillemin, to mention but a few of the more prominent figures. Interested readers can consult the Selected Bibliography for fuller details and further reading.

Dealing with a French writer for whom language was revered to the point that it was often spelled with a capital *L,* it has been necessary to devise a system that will facilitate access to the writings. While it is probable that the majority of readers will be students of French literature, I have made no presumption of linguistic proficiency. I have therefore chosen to translate most of the prose quotations into English, with the appropriate reference allowing for direct consultation back to the original. Poetry will be cited in French, followed by a very literal translation that will allow anyone with at least some knowledge of the language to appreciate the exceptionally rich sounds of Valéry's verse. This is very much in keeping with Valéry's own oft-stated belief that poetry cannot be summed up in everyday words but is rather grounded in the language that it creates and that creates it.

In order not to overtax the reader with extended quotations that break the flow of the text, I have refrained from providing more than a few words or lines at any one time. This means, on the other hand, that it will be necessary in most cases to refer back to the original text of the work under examination. My interpretations, summaries, and observations are not meant to be a substitute for the words of Valéry himself. It is my hope that every reader of this book, whether from idle curiosity or scholastic necessity, will become acquainted with the range and variety of Valéry's writing and will go on to read even more of his work.

Albuquerque
January 1994

Acknowledgments and Note on the References

No undertaking of this nature could reach fruition without the help of many people, at least some of whom I wish to single out for recognition. For her kind authorization and words of encouragement, I wish to thank Madame Agathe Rouart-Valéry. The University of New Mexico also accorded me a sabbatical leave that facilitated the research and writing of this book. I would also like to express my gratitude to the students in my graduate seminar, Ausra, Quannah, Florence, Lisa, Joseph, and Edouard, who agreed to spend a semester exploring Valéry with me and whose comments and reactions were always enlightening. My interest in French literature would certainly not exist without the guidance of two exemplary professors, Wallace Fowlie and Claude Pichois, who will find here only a small expression of my appreciation. My thanks also go to David O'Connell, whose editorial assistance and advice have made the writing of this book a pleasurable experience. Anne Kiefer and her staff at Twayne have been extremely helpful and efficient in turning my manuscript into a book. My parents deserve many heartfelt thanks for their love and support over the years. Finally, I could never have finished this project without the patience and encouragement of my wife, Valérie, and my daughter, Anna.

In order to simplify the system of notes, the following abbreviations are included directly in the body of the book and refer to the Pléiade editions of Paul Valéry's writings as indicated in the Selected Bibliography:

ŒI—*Œuvres I*
ŒII—*Œuvres II*
CI—*Cahiers I*
CII—*Cahiers II*

I hope that no readers will be offended by the preponderant use of *man* throughout this study. The choice is dictated by the need to respect Valéry's own language and incorporate it into my style. I trust that anyone who knows me and anyone who reads Valéry will know that the term carries no intended bias.

Chronology

1871 Ambroise Paul Toussaint Jules Valéry born 30 October in Cette (since spelled Sète), second son of Barthélémy Valéry and Marianne-Françoise-Alexandrine Grassi.

1876 Enters *onzième* (first grade) in school run by Dominican friars.

1878 Enters *neuvième* (third grade) at the Collège de Cette, now Collège Paul-Valéry.

1884 In January, writes first verse in a notebook with the insignia "Collège de Cette"; asks older brother to buy him a dictionary of rhymes. In fall, family moves to Montpellier where Paul enters *troisième* (ninth grade) at the Lycée de Montpellier. Meets Gustave Fourment, closest friend and confidant in coming years. Paul escapes the boring rhythm of school through reading, painting, theater, or swimming and hiking.

1887 Father dies in March; older brother, Jules, becomes legal guardian. In July, passes the written part of the *baccalauréat* with an essay on Nicolas Boileau. Vacations in Genoa where he swims and writes numerous sonnets. The prelude to *Lohengrin* is a revelation.

1888 Passes the second part of his baccalauréat and enrolls in law school at Montpellier.

1889 Discovers Edgar Allan Poe. First published poem, "Rêve," appears. Abandons law school for one year to enroll in the 122nd Infantry regiment stationed in Montpellier. Writes more than 80 poems in spare time.

1890 Meets Pierre Louÿs, beginning a long, fruitful, and sometimes turbulent friendship; Louÿs copies by hand 30 lines from Stéphane Mallarmé's *Hérodiade*. Valéry sends Mallarmé two poems and receives an encouraging response. Resumes law school in October. In December, meets André Gide, who will remain his lifelong friend and correspondent; their walks in the botanical gardens at Montpellier seal a rare, literary friendship.

1891   Publishes "Narcisse parle," which draws the admiration of Mallarmé; writes "La Fileuse," which he sends to Gide. Visits Paris with mother and brother; meets Joris-Karl Huysmans, whose *A rebours* had been a decisive influence on his early years. Louÿs introduces him to Mallarmé.

1892   During the night of 4–5 October, undergoes a serious emotional and intellectual crisis while on vacation in Genoa; renounces poetry.

1894   Settles in Paris in an austere room in the rue Gay-Lussac; frequent visits with Gide, Henri de Régnier, and Louÿs. Begins *La Soirée avec Monsieur Teste* and *Introduction à la méthode de Léonard de Vinci*. Begins the first of his 261 *Cahiers,* which he writes every morning over the next 51 years.

1896   Visits London on highly secret business concerning South Africa; writes *La Conquête allemande. Monsieur Teste* published. Attends the premiere of Alfred Jarry's *Ubu-roi*.

1897   Mallarmé gives him the corrected proofs of *Un Coup de dés*; Valéry participates in homage to the *"Maître."* Continues study of mathematics while working at the War Ministry.

1898   Meets Jeannie Gobillard, his future wife, at a musical evening attended by Pierre-Auguste Renoir, Edgar Degas, and Mallarmé. Mallarmé dies; an emotional funeral service follows.

1900   Marries Jeannie Gobillard. Obtains a position as personal secretary to André Lebey at the Agence Havas.

1900–1914   Numerous visits with Gide, Louÿs, Claude Monet, Degas, Renoir, Odilon Redon, Claude Debussy, Jean Cocteau, Breton, and others.

1902   Attends the premiere of *Pelléas et Mélisande*; moves to 40, rue de Villejust, now rue Paul-Valéry (in the 16th *arrondissement* of Paris).

1903   Birth of first son, Claude.

1906   Birth of first daughter, Agathe.

1912   Gide and Gaston Gallimard persuade Valéry to publish a volume of his early works; begins *La Jeune Parque* (finished in 1917). Meets Alexis Léger (Saint-John Perse), future Nobel Prize-winning poet.

1916   Birth of second son, François.

1917   Publishes *La Jeune Parque*, which brings him immediate fame and numerous invitations to attend gatherings of high Parisian society. Family visits Gide's estate in Normandy.

1918   Divides time between Paris, which is frequently bombed by the German Bertha, and Brittany, where his family has taken refuge. Publishes "Au Platane."

1919   Publishes "La Pythie"; advises Breton and Soupault on the title of the first surrealist review, *Littérature,* in which "Cantique des colonnes" soon appears. Meets Anna de Noailles. Gallimard publishes *Monsieur Teste* and *L'Introduction à la méthode de Léonard de Vinci.*

1920   "Le Cimetière marin" appears in the *Nouvelle Revue Française.* Original edition of the *Album de vers anciens* is published. Begins a love affair with Catherine Pozzi.

1921   Finishes *Eupalinos* and *L'Ame et la danse.* A survey in *Connaissance* names Valéry the greatest living poet.

1922   Death of Edouard Lebey leaves Valéry without a stable job. First edition of *Charmes* is published. Numerous homages and articles appear as well as frequent requests for lectures. Visits Joseph Conrad in England.

1923   Named *Chevalier de la Légion d'honneur.*

1924   Meets Rainer Maria Rilke, Gabriele D'Annunzio, Ortega y Gasset; has conversations with Benito Mussolini, Henri-Louis Bergson. First edition of *Variété* appears. Death of Anatole France, whom Valéry succeeds as president of Pen Club.

1925   Elected to the Académie française in the place of Anatole France. Pierre Louÿs dies. Debate over pure poetry rages at the Académie française.

1926   Writes numerous prefaces, essays, articles. Lecture in Berlin attended by Albert Einstein. Augmented editions of *L'Album de vers anciens* and *Charmes* are published.

1927   Valéry's mother dies in Montpellier. His acceptance speech at the Académie française creates a scandal when he omits the name of Anatole France.

1928   Gustave Cohen delivers commentary on "Le Cimetière marin" at the Sorbonne.

1929   Alain's commentary on *Charmes* appears.

1931   Valéry awarded a doctorate *honoris causa* from Oxford. *Regards sur le monde actuel* published. Invited to deliver numerous lectures around Europe. *Amphion* premieres at the Paris Opera.

1932   "Discours en l'honneur de Goethe" delivered at the Sorbonne. Reads *L'Idée fixe* to Gide; published in March.

1933   Named head administrator of the Centre Universitaire Méditerranéen de Nice.

1934   *Sémiramis* premieres, with music by Arthur Honegger, at the Paris Opera.

1936   *Variété III* and *Degas, Danse, Dessin* are published.

1937   Appointed Professor of Poetics at the Collège de France, where he will lecture regularly until his death. Named Doctor *honoris causa* at the University of Coïmbra, Portugal.

1938   Jules Valéry dies. *Variété IV* is published.

1939–45 War years divided between Paris lectures, courses at the Collège de France, and visits with his family in the provinces.

1940   Writes two acts of *Mon Faust*.

1941   Delivers memorial speech for Bergson at the Académie française. Removed from his role as director of the Centre Universitaire Méditerranéen in Nice (restored after the war). *Tel Quel* appears.

1942   Germans refuse paper for *Mauvaises pensées et autres*, wondering why he doesn't write good ones!

1944   *Variété V* appears. Attends gala evening to celebrate the liberation of Paris at the Comédie-Française alongside General de Gaulle. Delivers *Discours sur Voltaire* in the grand amphitheater at the Sorbonne.

1945   Dies 20 July at 9:00 A.M. General de Gaulle orders a state funeral. Valéry's body lies in state between the two wings of the Palais de Chaillot; 24–25 July, ceremony and speeches are followed by an all-night procession. Buried on 27 July in the "cimetière marin" overlooking the port of Sète.

Chapter One

Valéry as Himself: A Biographical Sketch

Il faut entrer en soi-même armé jusques aux dents. (One must enter into oneself armed to the teeth.)

Cahiers II, 1406

Ambroise Paul Toussaint Jules Valéry was born on 30 October 1871 in the Mediterranean port city of Sète (spelled *Cette* at the time).[1] His father was of Corsican origin and worked as a customs officer; his mother, née Grassi, descended from a prominent northern Italian family. Although not prone to expand on his past, Valéry would later make clear his attachment to the Mediterranean and to its way of life in his "Inspirations méditerranéennes," a moving text of personal recollections and impressions.

> . . . I shall make this naive observation that I was born in one of those places where I would have chosen to be born. I feel fortunate to have been born in a place where my first impressions were those one receives facing the sea and living amidst human activity. There is no sight for me worthier than what one can observe from a terrace or balcony overlooking a port. (*ŒI*, 1084)

Paul Valéry grew up surrounded by the vibrant Mediterranean nature, basking from his earliest years in the ambiance of classical civilization, absorbing a sense of clarity and rigor that he would later make into his personal credo. The deities that presided over his youth were named Sea, Sky, and Sun (*ŒI*, 1092). This natural world molded his being and contributed to his sense of a universal self that linked the intense, outer world of sensation and the limitless, inner world of thought. Except for almost drowning in a pool in the public park when he was three, his childhood was rather carefree, harmonious, and happy, with long hours spent on the docks watching ships come and go and frequent family vacations spent in Genoa at the home of his relatives.

As a child, young Paul was a contemplative, sensitive boy who didn't engage in rough games. He already preferred the infinitely richer world of his own mind:

> I began at the age of nine or ten to make my mind into a sort of island and, despite the fact that I was sociable and easily communicative, I reserved an increasingly greater part of myself for a very secret garden where I could cultivate those images that seemed to be all mine, that could belong only to me. (*ŒI*, 14)

After two years in a school run by Dominican friars, Paul entered the Collège de Cette, a lower school overlooking the port and which now bears his name. His "Inspirations méditerranéennes" or "Discours prononcé à l'occasion de la distribution des prix du collège de Sète" contain fond memories of those early years. He recalls the smell of new notebooks and ink, or the spectacle of a sailing vessel ablaze in the port below. An avid swimmer and student of the marine world, he even dreamed of a naval career. This dream was not to come about due to his insufficient training in math, surprising in light of his future preoccupation with mathematics and science. The sea nevertheless constitutes a major force in the poetry of Valéry, and one cannot imagine lines such as these from "Le Cimetière marin" (The Seaside cemetery) written by someone without such a strong attachment to the sea: "Une fraîcheur, de la mer exhalée, / Me rend mon âme . . . O puissance salée! / Courons à l'onde en rejaillir vivant!" (A freshness, from the sea exhaled, / Renders me my soul . . . O briny potentate! / Let us run to the wave and reemerge in life!).

When Paul turned 13, his family moved to nearby Montpellier where he entered the *lycée*. The adjustment was difficult, and he vehemently objected to the rigid scholastic regimen imposed on young minds. In a 1907 note from the *Cahiers,* he deplores how naturally curious children are placed in schools that cure them of their curiosity by a good dose of boredom.[2] The *baccalauréat,* with its emphasis on acquired knowledge rather than critical thinking, was the culprit. His modest successes at school were obtained reluctantly and without the joy and excitement of discovery and understanding that would characterize his intellectual life as an adult. Paul's own readings—Victor Hugo, who died in 1885, Théophile Gautier, and Charles Baudelaire—became increasingly important in those adolescent years.

At the age of 14, he asked his older brother, Jules, for a dictionary of rhymes and shortly thereafter began writing his first poems. Especially revealing is a parody in the manner of Victor Hugo of the educational system he had come to despise. This attitude did not keep him from obtaining first prize in French composition that year. This bright, sensitive boy also discovered a passion for architecture, diligently reading and copying works by Eugène-Emmanuel Viollet-le-Duc and Owen Jones. With his father and older brother, Paul enjoyed outings to the theater, the beach, and the countryside, all the while filling up notebooks with his own observations, drawings and thoughts. His father passed away in March 1887, only three months before Valéry succeeded in the first part of his *baccalauréat* exams. He completed the exams the following year with honorable mention.

During a family visit to Genoa that summer, he continued to swim, paint, read, and write, including this most revealing line from a sonnet that announces his future direction: "Et je jouis sans fin de mon propre cerveau" (*ŒI,* 1588; And I feel endless exaltation from my own mind). Valéry was already intrigued by the study of his own intellectual functioning, and this was to become his main preoccupation over the next half century.

He enrolled in the law school at the Université de Montpellier in 1888, a situation that left him ample free time to develop his newfound passion for mathematics, physics, and music while continuing to read. *A rebours* (Against the grain) by Joris-Karl Huysmans as well as the poetry of Paul Verlaine and Stéphane Mallarmé all came to exert a significant impact on his literary sensitivity in a short period of time. That year, Valéry wrote 19 poems. Although he volunteered to do his military service in the 122nd Infantry regiment in Montpellier, he still managed to devote a great deal of time and energy to his intellectual endeavors, writing and revising over 80 poems in 1889.

Writers, especially aspiring ones, can sometimes be judged by the company they keep. In May 1890, Valéry attended a banquet celebrating the 600th anniversary of the Université de Montpellier where he met quite by chance one of the young literary figures of the day, Pierre Louis (who soon changed the spelling of his last name to Louÿs). The two young writers immediately became close friends. In an autobiographical "autopsy" that he sent to Louÿs in September 1890, Valéry depicts himself as attracted by religion and poetry, mystified by women, and repulsed by work. He writes poetry in spite of himself and with the realization that it could cost him a future career.[3]

In response to a request from his provincial friend, Louÿs sent him 30 lines of Mallarmé's *Hérodiade* that he had copied out by hand. Valéry then wrote his first letter to Mallarmé, who quickly supplanted all other influences, providing the model against whom he would measure all subsequent work, including his own. Later that year, he sent Mallarmé two poems to which the master answered, "The gift of subtle analogy along with adequate music are already yours and they are all that count . . . As for advice, only solitude will give you that . . . " (*ŒI,* 18). Despite his impressive beginnings, Valéry was soon to apply his mentor's advice in dramatic fashion.

Louÿs also served as the go-between in another capital encounter, this one with André Gide, who came to Montpellier to visit his uncle Charles, a noted law professor at the university. The friendship between Gide and Valéry would last until the latter's death in 1945, leaving one of the truly remarkable literary correspondences of the twentieth century. During their walk through the botanical gardens of Montpellier, they spent much time discussing around the tombstone of the daughter of the English poet Edward Young. Her name, Narcissa, suggested the character of Narcissus that was so crucial to poets in the latter years of the nineteenth century. In March 1891, Louÿs published Valéry's most significant poem to date, "Narcisse parle," in *La Conque,* a short-lived literary journal that would nevertheless prove to be a venue for several important writers of his generation. The aspiring poet was especially pleased to receive this appreciation from Mallarmé: "Your 'Narcisse parle' charms me . . . Conserve that rare tone . . . " (quoted in *ŒI,* 19).

While moving forward with his legal studies, Paul accompanied his mother on a visit to Paris in September and October 1891. During their stay, he managed to visit his two literary idols, Huysmans and Mallarmé, the former in his office at the Ministry of the Interior, the latter at his apartment on the rue de Rome, where he held the regular Tuesday literary soirées so important to the symbolist poets of the day. Despite the fact that he continued to publish his poems and despite the lure of aestheticism and even dandyism that surrounded him in the personages of Louÿs and Gide, Valéry was not entirely satisfied with his work nor with his life.

These tensions came to a head in the fall of 1892 while young Valéry was on vacation in Genoa. On the one hand, he had suffered an emotional setback that summer in the form of his unrequited passion for a mysterious stranger, Madame de R[ovira]. Almost 50 years later, Valéry would recall how he drove himself mad and suffered years of unhappiness for a woman to whom he had never even spoken a word (*CII,* 534). On the other hand, his writings to that point failed to satisfy the exigencies he attached to the artistic process, especially as exemplified by the discovery of the poetry of Mallarmé.

The night of 4–5 October became such a turning point for Valéry that it is commonly referred to as the "nuit de Gênes" (Genovese night). With a thunderstorm raging outside, an equally violent inner tumult rocked the young poet: "My entire destiny was played out in my head. I am between myself and myself" (*ŒI,* 20). It is difficult to say exactly what Valéry saw when he looked into himself, when he became his own observer: "I had transformed myself into a gaze" (*ŒI,* 20). In part as a refusal to fall prey to his emotional self, in part in response to his dissatisfaction with his work to date and in answer to his increased demand for control of his own intellectual powers, Valéry experienced a turning point in his life and career, a "revolution of the mind," as he would later call it (*CI,* 154).

As a consequence of this illumination, he reached an important decision—to renounce poetry writing and to dedicate himself to seeking knowledge and control of his intellect, which was to become his life's work for the next half century. It had never been his real aim to become a poet, but only to develop the *potential* to become one (*CI,* 178). Instead of focusing his efforts on the fabrication of a product of his mind, he decided to devote himself to the construction of the mind itself. This prolonged period of silence would occasionally be broken, as in 1896 when two of his poems, "Eté" and "Vue," were published in the first issue of an influential review, *Centaure.*

It was also at that time that he adopted as a measure of the value of his mind what he called "mathematical thought" (*CI,* 106), suggesting a high degree of self-consciousness and self-control according to the most rigorous of standards. As a symbol of this rupture or "coup d'état," as he called it, he even went so far as to sell off most of his personal library.

Thus began in earnest the intellectual quest that would become his obsession for over 50 years—the exploration and possession of the intricate workings of his own mind freed from emotional, affective influences. The struggle to cultivate his intellect should not be taken to mean that Valéry refused the physical or material world around him. As we shall see, many of his poems have a sensual quality that heightens their impact on the reader. Indeed, he can be credited with incorporating the natural world into his poetry at a time when symbolists were scorning the outside world in favor of their inner selves. Besides the sensual, erotic poetry that he wrote throughout his life, one need only read *La Jeune Parque* to realize that, while an intellectual poem, it is anything but a piece extolling ascetic virtues. Valéry had nevertheless faced his demons that night in Genoa and struggled to overcome them. He resolved never again to yield to the seductive voices of passion and poetry, never again to worship false gods.

In a step towards redefining his existence, Valéry moved to Paris in early 1894 and took a small room on the rue Gay-Lussac near the Latin Quarter. His only decorations were a chalkboard on which to carry out his mathematical investigations and a reproduction of Ligier Richier's skeleton to remind him of the vanity of all knowledge. Mathematics were to become his opium, as he would later comment (*Œl, 32*). He continued to see Gide, Pierre Louÿs, and Henri de Régnier, as well as José María de Heredia and, of course, Mallarmé. He shared with Mallarmé an interest in the poetic ideas of Edgar Allan Poe that had been so influential in France since Baudelaire's translations in the 1850s and 1860s. According to their demanding aesthetic, poetry is not just a product of the mysterious forces of inspiration as the Romantics had propounded. It also results from craft and work when submitted to the greatest degree of consciousness and the highest standard of composition. In other words, poetry could be as much a science as a religion.

Although Valéry almost ceased all personal production, he nevertheless continued to think about poetry. This indefinable, immeasurable period of maturation and aging is too often minimized by Valéry's critics, who understandably look to the poems already written or those yet to come for a measure of his genius. He was, nevertheless, to spend the next 20 years without any preconceived literary goal and with little to show for his efforts other than the knowledge that he was following his own path.

Despite the fact that he had no literary ambitions or projects in mind, Valéry was anything but inactive. He read works of mathematics and physics and attended the weekly Lamoureux concerts that provided the musical education for many poets of the day. Valéry also became a regular at the Tuesday gatherings at Mallarmé's apartment on the rue de Rome where most of the aspiring writers met and listened to the master expound on poetry and art. None of this, of course, helped Valéry's material well-being. At one point, he considered taking a teaching job at the Armenian school in Constantinople and unsuccessfully applied for a position as *secrétaire* at the *Revue de Paris*. During this transition period, he continued to seek employment while leading a frugal existence and writing occasional articles, prefaces, and other short pieces.

By 1894, he had also begun to keep the *Cahiers,* the private notebooks that would ultimately include over 26,000 pages of thoughts, queries, sketches, and observations. Almost every day until his death in 1945, Valéry would arise before dawn, have coffee, and smoke cigarettes as he filled up notebook after notebook with his meditations on a wide range of subjects. The *Cahiers,* whether the facsimile edition in 29 volumes or the two-volume Pléiade edition, can rightly be considered the most revealing and most modern of his writings. Although not intended for publication, they are his masterpiece, representing the sum of over 50 years of thoughts and observations by one of our century's greatest minds.

But Valéry had not completely relinquished writing for an audience and, by the end of 1894, had begun two of his most important early works, *La Soirée avec Monsieur Teste* and the *Introduction à la méthode de Léonard de Vinci.* Monsieur Teste stands as a hypothetical being who lives as pure, lucid intelligence vis-à-vis the material, social world around him. Da Vinci provided Valéry with a perfect example of an individual equally at home in the artistic and scientific worlds and whose motto, "Hostinato rigore" (Obstinate rigor), he could easily adopt as his own. Both pieces represent excursions into the ideal mind and the power of the intellect, the workings of which so fascinated Valéry.

This cursory portrait should not lead us to conclude that Valéry was completely removed from worldly affairs. To the contrary, he cultivated friendships with diligence, tact, and grace. He was appreciated as a witty, charming guest whose conversation enlivened and enlightened many salons and dinner gatherings. Faced with the necessity of earning a living, Valéry followed the advice of Huysmans and took a civil service exam to join the War Ministry. The official report describes him as " . . . a cloudy mind, a common decadent, a Paul Verlaine which the administration can do without" (*ŒI,* 23). He was nevertheless accepted and later even recommended for a promotion. A keen observer of the world scene, Valéry wrote political pieces on the Sino-Japanese conflict, German expansionism, and the role of Europe in the world. These articles would later be collected under the title *Regards sur le monde actuel.* He also made a top secret trip to London in 1896 to translate some sensitive articles on South Africa. Like others of his generation, Valéry was drawn into some of the heated debates surrounding the Dreyfus affair.

Alfred Dreyfus, a French military officer of Alsatian Jewish background, had been wrongly convicted in 1894 of treason in smuggling documents to the Germans. The succeeding controversy polarized French society, pitting the Left against the Right in one of the longest and most bitter political crises in modern French history. Contrary to most writers and intellectuals and perhaps because of his job at the War Ministry, Valéry did not support the revision of the guilty verdict against Dreyfus, who was eventually acquitted and returned to his functions in 1906. In general, his political opinions were conservative, at least in the sense that he wished to conserve some of the better traits of a society undergoing radical changes.

Despite his retreat from literature, Valéry continued to live in close contact with the literary and cultural world, attending the premiere of Alfred Jarry's *Ubu-roi* in 1896, reading the poetry of Anna de Noailles and Francis Jammes, discovering and appreciating the music of Richard Wagner, Claude Debussy, Christoph Gluck, and Carl Maria von Weber. Not at all a recluse, Valéry was frequently a guest at dinners and gatherings with all the prominent literary and artistic figures of the day. The rich cultural and social life of Paris at the turn of the century placed him in contact with painters such as Claude Monet, Pierre-Auguste Renoir, and Edgar Degas; musicians such as Maurice Ravel, Claude Debussy, and Gabriel-Urbain Fauré; writers such as Jean Cocteau, Alexis Léger (the future Saint-John Perse), and the founding group of the *Nouvelle Revue Française*. Besides Gide, he knew Henri Ghéon, Jacques Copeau, and Gaston Gallimard; the latter, along with Gide, would be instrumental in convincing Valéry to return to poetry in 1912.

La Soirée avec Monsieur Teste was published in October 1896, followed three months later by his piece on German expansionism, *Une Conquête méthodique,* published in the *New Review* in England. Valéry wanted to dedicate his *Monsieur Teste* to Degas, the painter he most admired of the contemporary generation, but Degas refused the honor twice. Despite this disappointment, the two men became rather close friends and Valéry was one of the painter's most fervent admirers. Degas would also play an important role in Valéry's private life, for the painter introduced the poet to his future wife, Jeannie Gobillard, a niece of Berthe Morisot and a relative of the painter Edouard Manet. When married in 1900, Valéry wrote that Mallarmé had wanted to unite him with that milieu—now the deed was done (*Œl, 26–27*). The couple would have three children—Claude, born in 1903, Agathe in 1906, and François in 1916.

Among those to whom Valéry remained the most devoted, special mention must be made of Mallarmé. Besides being a regular visitor at the famous "mardis de la rue de Rome," where most of the symbolist poets gathered to hear the "Maître," Valéry became a close family friend and literary and spiritual successor to Mallarmé. As proof of their profound mutual understanding, it was to Valéry that Mallarmé gave the corrected proofs of his great poetic work "Un Coup de dés," asking his young disciple if he didn't think that he was mad to have attempted to push poetry so close to the limits of silence and self-destruction. Valéry would later declare his admiration for his "paternel, suprême ami" in the several articles that he wrote about him as well as in a poem titled "Valvins." At Mallarmé's funeral in 1898, Valéry was so overcome with emotion that he could not finish his oration. After Mallarmé's death, he and Gide would periodically provide financial assistance to his widow and daughter.

The husband and soon-to-be father nevertheless had to earn a living since he did not have a personal fortune on which to draw. He therefore decided to leave the War Ministry and, in July 1900, accepted a position as personal secretary to Edouard Lebey, one of the chief executives of the Agence Havas, a financial conglomerate located in Paris. Monsieur Lebey was paralyzed, and for over 20 years Valéry would spend a few hours a day reading to him and discussing world affairs and business decisions. He learned a great deal about the world of high finance and politics. But, more importantly, his job left him ample time to pursue his own intellectual and artistic interests.

Although Valéry had officially turned his back on poetry, the years prior to the outbreak of World War I were filled with literary encounters and sporadic publications. Besides a renewed admiration for modern poets since Baudelaire and including Arthur Rimbaud, Paul Verlaine, and Mallarmé, Valéry's readings went beyond the strictly literary to include Friedrich Nietzsche and scientific and mathematical works by the likes of Henri Poincaré or Georges Cantor. He continued, as always, to carry on with his *Cahiers* the internal dialogue that would only grow richer with time. In addition to these more intellectual pursuits, Valéry led a rather full family life with periodic trips and frequent dinners with relatives and friends, as well as visits to the numerous artists and writers that he knew quite well.

The year 1912 marked the beginning of Valéry's return to literature as a public practice. Five years later, with the publication of *La Jeune Parque,* he attained the type of overnight fame that few poets of our century have enjoyed. Gaston Gallimard and Gide encouraged him throughout most of the year to gather and edit his earlier writings with a view to publishing a volume of collected poems. In a letter to Gide, he wonders if the publication of his works wouldn't provide a sort of "con-sécration" to the very deep-felt reasons that he had relinquished poetry in the first place.[4]

Going over his past writing proved a difficult experience. After much coaxing, Valéry finally yielded and, in late July, agreed to give Gallimard and Gide his manuscripts. He asked for some time to touch up some of his older poems and to write a 30- or 40-line poem to round out the col-lection. This latter piece, which he envisaged as a "récitatif d'opéra à la Gluck," would slowly expand to 512 lines and take over four years and some 800 pages of notes to complete. The result was *La Jeune Parque,* published by Gallimard on 28 April 1917. It was to become arguably the most outstanding long poem of our century, one which would be recited in literary salons as well as in the trenches of World War I, a poem that would make Valéry famous in all of Europe.

Although Valéry soon became a regular guest at social functions such as the salon of Madame Mühlfeld where Paris high society, intellectuals, and diplomats gathered, this newfound celebrity was not entirely to his taste. He said of his own poem, "Its obscurity puts me in the spotlight: neither one, nor the other were the result of my wishes" (*Œl,* 39). But Valéry was once again a poet and, as such, wrote and published regular-ly until the mid-1920s. "Le Cimetière marin" and the *Album de vers anciens* in 1920 were followed by the important collection *Charmes,* pub-lished in 1922. After this, his productive career as a poet was virtually over, and he would spend the next 20 years as France's unofficial poet laureate. So great was the public reputation of Valéry that a 1921 survey in *Connaissance* elected him the most important living French poet.

In a curious chapter in literary encounters, it is interesting to note that André Breton, the charismatic leader of the surrealist movement, admired Valéry early on in his career, even seeking out his advice. The Valéry that he admired was the one who had written *Monsieur Teste,* of which Breton knew large parts by heart, as well as the Valéry that had turned his back on literature, as Rimbaud had. It was Valéry who sug-gested the title *Littérature* given by Breton and Philippe Soupault to the first major surrealist review in 1919. Breton even asked Valéry to be his *témoin* (best man) at his wedding in 1921, a sign of deep friendship and trust. Their collaboration was nevertheless to be short-lived, since Breton took a much more radical stand than Valéry in matters of poetry, politics, society, and morals. Their break would lead Breton to hold Valéry up to public ridicule, while the elder poet tried his best to ignore the antics of his younger admirer. A few passages in the *Cahiers* suffice, however, to show how much Valéry disapproved of surrealism in general and Breton in particular.

The First World War provided a test of Valéry's ideas on the modern world. His 1896 article on "La Conquête allemande" was reprinted in 1915, expressing fears that Europe, which had made such progress in science and technology, would prove to be its own agent of destruction. Valéry held a clearly European view of the future, advocating unity among European nations as requisite to survival in an expanding, modern world. He feared a decline in European importance as a result of its own self-destructive competition and conflict. Valéry was not called up for active duty, but he followed the war closely and tended to Monsieur Lebey as well as to his family, who had to flee Paris when the Germans unleashed Bertha on the French capital. Although he was a former infantryman, he felt helpless and useless while the world around him went to war: "In every tragic period in humanity, there has always been a man sitting in a corner trying to perfect his writing and stringing pearls" (Rouart-Valéry, 75). He was clearly referring to the painstaking labor of composing *La Jeune Parque* against such a savage and chaotic background.

After the armistice, Valéry wrote an article for John Middleton Murry's *Atheneum* titled "La Crise de l'Esprit," the prophetic opening line of which has remained famous: "Our civilizations know now that they are mortal" (*ŒI*, 988). Valéry's analysis and commentary in his quasi-political essays remained steadfastly Eurocentric, warning that the continent that had played such a role in shaping the modern world was in danger of becoming a second-rate power. His recognition of the random, transitory, noncyclical nature of historical change strikes us as especially modern and frighteningly pessimistic.

The period of the *entre-deux-guerres* was one of official consecration for Valéry, who received numerous honors: president of the Pen Club in 1924, member of the Académie française in 1925, Doctor *honoris causa* at Oxford in 1931, Administrator of the Centre Universitaire Méditerranéen de Nice in 1933, and Professor of Poetics at the Collège de France from 1937 until his death in 1945. In his acceptance speech to the other members of the Académie, Valéry created something of a scandal by refusing to mention the name of his predecessor, Anatole France. It is generally believed that this was his revenge for France's refusal to publish

Gramley Library
Salem College
Winston-Salem, NC 27108

Mallarmé's *L'Après-midi d'un faune* in *Le Parnasse contemporain* in 1874. Valéry was widely sought out for lectures and speeches at venues ranging from his beloved Collège de Sète to the Hungarian Academy of Sciences. Some of these speeches are collected in volume one of his *Œuvres* in the Pléiade edition. A more exhaustive listing can be consulted in Agathe Rouart-Valéry's biographical introduction. Valéry's travels also brought him in contact with writers such as Conrad, T. S. Eliot, James Joyce, Rabindranath Tagore, and H. G. Wells in England, Rainer Maria Rilke and Stefan Zweig in Germany, Luigi Pirandello and Gabriele D'Annunzio in Italy. His contacts extended well beyond the literary world and included political leaders such as Aristide Briand and Léon Blum, military leaders such as Philippe Pétain and Ferdinand Foch, mathematicians and physicists such as Louis de Broglie and Nils Bohr. When Albert Einstein paid him a visit in Paris in 1929, Valéry took him to visit another friend who was hospitalized at the time, Henri Bergson.

Who else but the "official spokesman of the Third Republic," as he ironically referred to himself, would have been asked in 1935 to compose the four inscriptions that still adorn the Palais de Chaillot? They announce the approach to an artistic haven, a museum: "It depends on he who passes by here / Whether I be tomb or treasure / Whether I speak or remain silent / This depends only on you / Friend, do not enter without desire" (*ŒII*, 1585). Valéry accepted these honors and distractions, in part because since the death of Edouard Lebey in 1922 he was without a stable job and source of income. Poets, even of the stature of Paul Valéry, had a difficult time living from their pen. This busy schedule occasionally took its toll on both his work and health, as he described in this letter of 1927 addressed but never sent to Gide:

> I get up between five and six to face an avalanche of obligations, stupid promises, duties, so I toil without reprieve on these boring tasks that people have ordered. At eight o'clock, the cursed mailman. The correspondence of a government official, but without offices, without secretaries. If I had started to get a bit excited by my writing jobs, this mail shock just hits me over the head and crushes my spirits. At ten o'clock, visits begin. Until one o'clock, I greet people and talk, talk, talk. I'm dead by lunch time. Then I have to run errands—one must make a "living"—and I dash from editor to library, etc. I am *finished* by then and it matters little that I go socializing. That's about all I am good for by the time evening comes. (*Corr. Gide–Valéry*, 530)

Robert Mallet, in his introduction to the Gide–Valéry correspondence, points out an interesting paradox: Valéry, who poured so much energy and thought into the denial of literature, was the one who became an almost archetypal literary figure with celebrity, acclaim, and honors, whereas Gide, who never hid his literary vocation, managed to remain relatively free of many of the traps and trappings of a public literary figure (*Corr. Gide–Valéry,* 17). This could have been because Gide had a personal fortune that allowed him to be free of all material worries. In one of their earlier exchanges, Gide had said that he would kill himself if deprived of the ability to write, to which Valéry responded that he would kill himself, too . . . if forced to write! (*Corr. Gide–Valéry,* 34).

Although Valéry's poetic career was virtually finished after the augmented edition of *Charmes* in 1926, he continued to write essays, articles, and Socratic dialogues as well as continuing the "daily exercise" of keeping his *Cahiers.* Among the more notable of his essays and dialogues are *Note et Digression, Eupalinos,* and *L'Ame et la danse* in which he moves ever so slightly in the direction of a more earthly and human dimension to his quest for intellectual purity. After so much attention paid to the cerebral functions, we discover a Valéry turning to dance and architecture as expressions of the pure self in the real world. He seems to wish to answer his own challenge launched at the end of "Le Cimetière marin": "Le vent se lève, il faut tenter de vivre." (The wind is picking up, one must try to live). Like one of his emblematic heroes, Robinson Crusoe, cast away on a desert island of his own making, Valéry strove not just to survive in a hostile world but also to control that world in thought and deed. This constant questioning coupled with an incisive wit and a scathing sense of irony and even sarcasm made him a formidable critic of society and the modern world and, ultimately, a lucid critic of himself. The aphoristic style of *Tel Quel* or the more developed essays in the five volumes of *Variété* contain enough of the classical, French moralist and the modern skeptic to make them timeless pieces.

In addition to operatic librettos such as *Amphion* and *Sémiramis,* both put to music by Arthur Honegger and staged at the Paris Opéra, Valéry also tried his hand at theater with *Mon Faust* in 1940. Indeed, the only genre that he categorically refused to consider was the novel, which he dismissed as a concession to naturalistic concerns about banal, daily lives of sentimentalized characters. In this rejection, Valéry follows Mallarmé and other symbolists of his younger years. His example of a sentence that he could never bring himself to write, "La marquise demanda sa voiture et sortit à cinq heures" (The marquise called for her carriage and went out at five o'clock), is a hasty dismissal of a complex problem. His negative reaction and scathing criticism seem to aim at the more popular, less polished works, particularly of the nineteenth century.

Paradoxically, Valéry would later be much admired by writers and theorists of the novel, especially the *noveau roman*. Among the many literary essays that he wrote, he expressed interest or admiration most often for Stendhal, perhaps because the latter is closer in spirit to the eighteenth century. This does not mean that Valéry did not read novels, but rather that he did not consider them worthy of the same respect and interest as poetry, theater, science, or opera.

The private side of Paul Valéry remains something of a mystery in contrast to his public persona, which was affable, witty, and urbane in the best sense of the term. As we have said, he jealously cultivated friendships, and both his conversations and letters radiate a deep sense of complicity and passion. Except for Pierre Louÿs with whom he quarreled, Valéry had friendships that lasted his entire life. Indeed, he later recognized how much he owed to his friends.

> I realize that friendship will have been the great passion of my life. I despise the public, crowds and humanity proportionally to the pleasure I feel with small groups and the happy few. I should not complain. I have had happy friendships.[5]

We also know that he was a devoted father who took time to invent stories and poems, draw pictures, and stage puppet shows for his children, grandchildren, nieces, and nephews. In time of war, or illness such as befell his wife, Valéry put the well-being of his family above all. While his relationship with Jeannie was harmonious and affectionate on the whole, we also know that his search for an ideal, passionate woman led him to have at least three mistresses.

The most famous of these was an eight-year liaison with Catherine Pozzi, herself a gifted poet and intellectual with similar interests in sciences and mathematics.[6] Valéry often referred to two crucial dates in his life, 1892 and 1920, the second being the beginning of his turbulent affair with Pozzi. Indeed, their relationship was as much a meeting of two exceptional minds as it was a realization of their physical passion. Although Valéry fled any expression of pathetic sentimentalism, especially since the 1892 *nuit de Gênes,* he showed himself to be capable of deep feelings. A note from the *Cahiers* summed up his feelings: "I cast a lightning bolt on what I was in '92. 28 years later, it has fallen back down on me—from your lips" (*CII,* 460).

Their relationship was tumultuous, as might be expected of the union of two such extraordinary personalities. It was also carried on in the greatest secrecy so as not to jeopardize their public lives. Their final rupture took place in 1928 and Pozzi, who suffered from tuberculosis, passed away in 1934. Shortly after her death, five sealed boxes containing several thousand letters from her illustrious lover were burned by her order. One could not be more mistaken than to reduce Valéry to the polarized image of a mind without a body, a head without a heart. There was a warm, tender side to him that is too often obscured by considerations of a loftier, more formal nature.

At the outbreak of the Second World War, Valéry took his family to safe haven in the provinces. The keen observer of world affairs would note,

> This Monday, September 3, we woke up to war. Man is the enemy of humankind . . . I wonder if Europe and all will not end up in a state of dementia or generalized mush. WHEN THE CLOCK STRIKES FOUR, it will be the end of the world. (Rouart-Valéry, *Paul Valéry* 176)

Distressed by the absurd fury that he witnessed and by his incapacity to change the course of events, Valéry would even declare that he wished he had not lived to see that day. During those trying years, he returned periodically to Paris on business or to continue his lectures at the Collège de France on such subjects as Poe, rhythm, grammar, and poetry. It is a great shame that no substantial trace of those lectures has survived to our day, except for his own inaugural address. In January 1941, he pronounced the funeral oration in honor of Bergson before the Académie française, declaring him to be "the last great name in the history of European intelligence" (*ŒI*, 886). Although the text of Valéry's talk went largely unnoticed in France, it was widely read abroad, from England to South America. The exiled actor, Louis Jouvet, read it before a standing-room-only crowd in Bogotá. Was it because Bergson was Jewish or was it Valéry's general attitude of defiance that led the Vichy regime to remove him from his position as administrator of the Centre Universitaire Méditerranéen de Nice? The following year, the Germans would refuse to provide paper for the publication of his *Mauvaises pensées et autres* under the pretext that he would do better to write down his good thoughts!

The war years weighed heavy on Valéry's sense of nationalism and his belief that the type of civilization represented by France was in danger of disappearing altogether. At the Liberation, Valéry would write in *Le Figaro*, "Freedom can be felt. It can be breathed. The idea that we are free dilates the future contained in every moment" (*ŒII*, 1157). His attitude all along had been, however, not to assign blame nor to incriminate those responsible for the disaster. This led him to sign the petition sponsored by François Mauriac in favor of leniency for those who were to be executed as punishment for their wartime activities and sympathies. In a curious gesture that irritated many people and pleased others, Valéry intervened personally in favor of Charles Maurras, Robert Brasillach, and Henri Bérard, all accused of collaboration with the enemy during the occupation. This position should not be interpreted to mean that Valéry felt or demonstrated any sympathy toward the Nazi ideology; nothing could be further from the case. He rather thought that the future stability and survival of France and Europe lay in healing old wounds as quickly as possible. General de Gaulle would subsequently return Valéry to his position at the Centre Universitaire de Nice, and, despite failing health, he continued his lectures at the Collège de France.

In early May 1945, the ailing Valéry felt well enough to attend a luncheon in the company of Gide and T. S. Eliot, one of his most fervent admirers outside of France. But at the end of that same month, suffering from cancer, he noted, "I have the feeling that my life is over; by that I mean that I see nothing at present that requires a tomorrow" (*CII*, 388). When Valéry died on 20 July, General de Gaulle ordered that he be honored by a state funeral. The coffin, draped in the French colors, was placed in the central esplanade of the Palais de Chaillot where admirers and friends filed by all night. The Pantheon was the only public building in Paris to remain lit that night. On 27 July, his remains were fittingly laid to rest in the "Cimetière marin" overlooking Sète, and these words from his celebrated poem were inscribed on his tomb:

> O récompense après une pensée
> Qu'un long regard sur le calme des dieux.

> What a reward after thought
> Is a long look over the calm of the gods.

Chapter Two
Poetics: The Making of an Art

Parce que la forme est contraignante, l'idée jaillit plus intense.
(Because the form is constraining, the idea emerges with greater intensity.)

Baudelaire

Valéry has become as well known and influential for his ideas on poetry as for his poetic production proper. It is no coincidence that the avantgarde literary review *Tel Quel* took its title from one of his collections of thoughts on literature and language. Both a theoretician and a practitioner, Valéry speaks with a powerful voice about the challenges and ambitions of modern poetry. Indeed, his poetics lie at the intersection of European modernism, going back to Poe and Baudelaire, moving up through Mallarmé and symbolism and, finally, attracting the attention of such prominent structuralist and post-structuralist critics as Gérard Genette, Tzvetan Todorov, Jacques Derrida, and Roland Barthes.

Scholars of poetry typically lump under the term *poetics* the numerous rules and precepts governing the art of writing and reading verse. In Valéry's case, he stresses the etymological origin of the word, which comes from the Greek *poïein* (to make). He thereby emphasizes the goal of capturing the nascent poetic moment and crafting it into a work of art. Of particular interest to him are those productions where language is both the means and the substance (*ŒI*, 1441). The two volumes of *Œuvres* in the Bibliothèque de la Pléiade contain in convenient form the major articles and lectures, whether texts such as *Variété* and *Tel Quel,* transcriptions of important speeches such as his inaugural address to the Collège de France, or the critical essay titled "Poésie et pensée abstraite." In addition, the two Pléiade volumes of *Cahiers* contain many valuable insights into Valéry's poetic theory, and the two rubrics titled "Poïétique" (*CII,* 987–1056) and "Poésie" (*CII,* 1059–1142) are included here rather than in my specific discussion of the *Cahiers.*

Even during those years when he distanced himself from the writing of poetry, Valéry continued to devote much thought to the art of writing verse. Many of his theories of poetry date from that early period or from the 1930s when he was a much sought-after lecturer in France and around Europe. Valéry's own tastes in poetry can serve as an introduction to his poetics. From Edgar Allan Poe, he inherits the lucidity and artistic consciousness that are grounded in craft as opposed to inspiration. The American poet, revered by many French writers from Baudelaire onward, attempts to establish a conscious, psychological effect between text and reader. In Valery's first letter addressed to Mallarmé in 1890, he qualifies Poe as "perhaps the most subtle artist of the century" (*ŒI,* 1582). Poe's lucidity vis-à-vis his art, his striving for greater consciousness of the mind as well as his interest in the physical and mechanical laws of the universe could only excite Valéry's intelligence. He gives Poe credit for having been the first to lay the foundations for a pure theory of the literary work. The others would be Mallarmé and Valéry himself (*CII,* 1208). The Romantics are summarily dismissed as being prey to excessive, uncontrollable forces that blur their vision and powers of analysis, thus leading them away from an art of composition and more towards an overflow of expression. He does not have a moment of remorse and pity for Vigny, who is a "detestable poet" born in the worst of times (*CII,* 1129). Baudelaire stands as the turning point in the evolution of French poetry towards a conscious, analytical approach that transcends Romantic ideas of inspiration and applies Poe's poetic principle to the search for aesthetic beauty in verse.

In Valéry's opinion, the crucial years of 1845–1885 (the year of Victor Hugo's death) saw the appearance of over three-fourths of the most beautiful poetry written in French (*ŒII,* 1088). As a direct inheritor of that period, Valéry cannot fail to judge the aspirations and accomplishments of his predecessors and contemporaries. His own literary beginnings, as we know, coincide with the symbolist movement in the last two decades of the nineteenth century, a movement that required a quasi-religious status for poetry.

While he admires the vision of Rimbaud and the delicate musicality of Verlaine, it is Victor Hugo and Stéphane Mallarmé who provide an ideal terrain for contrasting Valéry's ideas on poetry. Hugo, one of the earliest beacons in Valéry's poetic education, remains a great poet who does not always submit his genius to the control of his reason. For Valéry, this leads to a grandiose body of work in which one finds the best and the worst, leading him to qualify Hugo as a millionaire, but not a prince (*CII,* 1071).

Mallarmé, whom Valéry knew and admired above all others, is the most demanding poet since he has mastered the internal musicality of the French language through endless effort and tireless work (*CII,* 1095). Contrary to Hugo, for whom everything can be expressed poetically,

Mallarmé has the "natural sterility" of a poet who cannot say anything that is not verse. Hugo is fecund while Mallarmé is sterile (*CII,* 1067). The overwhelming verbalism of Hugo contrasts with the calculated refusal of Mallarmé to accept anything less than absolute perfection. This leads Valéry to conjecture that Mallarmé would certainly have discarded 85 percent of what Hugo wrote. His apparent sterility does not suggest that Mallarmé did not have as many ideas as Hugo, but simply that he would have refused to accept those that did not correspond to his high ideal of poetry (*CII,* 1067). The consciousness of Mallarmé places him at the extreme limit of the literature that he sought to renew by ridding it of its parasitical, impure elements. Valéry is also aware that the strict application of Mallarmé's precepts might also lead to the self-destruction of poetry itself. Poetry is, in a way, capable of perfecting itself out of existence.

Valéry's prolonged silence between the *nuit de Gênes* (1892) and *La Jeune Parque* (which he wrote between 1912–1917 and which resulted in some 800 pages of notes) was devoted in large part to trying to find a way to continue to write poetry in light of the problematic situation in which Mallarmé had left the art of verse. While retaining and pursuing the complex musicality of his mentor, Valéry conceives of poetry as a less pure activity that can incorporate a physiology of the body and the mind. Poetry should aspire to "a state of perpetual invention," he says (*CII,* 1077), confirming the need for a sense of discovery, especially by the poet as he is writing his verse. As for his contemporaries, Valéry generally criticizes their lack of rigor and clear direction since their main goal would appear to be to produce an effect on the reader at all costs and by any means available (*CII,* 1023).

The two greatest literary events of his time, Valéry writes in 1911, have been the increased awareness of the properties of language and music (*CII,* 1159). He even comments in 1926–27 that he does not always believe in the future of poetry (*CII,* 1110), suggesting that there might be other areas of study and creation that procure greater challenges and rewards for the mind.

Rather than attempting the unfair practice of confronting Valéry's poetry with his many theoretical pronouncements on the subject, I shall respect his fundamental belief that poetry is first and foremost an art based on *Langage* (which he often spelled with a capital *L*). Indeed, a poem that can be paraphrased in words other than those of the poet is doomed to lose its poetic charge. Ambiguity and abstraction are the pillars of poetry since the poet is using such an impure medium as language

(*CII*, 1081). A poem always hovers between sound and sense; however, as soon as its meaning can be translated into common language, the poem has lost its attraction for the mind.

Valéry would undoubtedly have shared Robert Frost's opinion that poetry is what is lost in translation, as he states in almost identical terms in 1915 (*CII*, 1069). This unique quality is due, of course, to the fact that poetry is inextricably grounded in rough language. The poet, through his deliberate construction, attempts to express the inexpressible by means of words, which have a plurality of possible meanings. The activation of one of the significations of a linguistic sign constitutes the essence of poetry (*CII*, 1123). Poetry cannot render its meaning, or at least not so readily, without sacrificing the very quality that makes it poetry. As we shall see, Valéry always defers to the reader in conferring meaning to a poem.

Contrary to many poets of the symbolist persuasion, Valéry does not worship poetry as a sacred art with divine powers to open up new worlds. He objects vehemently to being cast in the public eye as the representative of French poetry when, as he put it to Gide in a moment of exasperation, he doesn't give a damn about poetry.[1] Verse is only one of the many manifestations of the life of the mind, constituting for Valéry an endless subject of fascination and inquiry, the means and end of which are founded in Language. It tends, however, to raise more questions than it provides answers. Poetry is just one possibility among others in his quest to understand and explain complex mental processes: "I do not like literature, but rather the acts and exercises of the mind," he declared in 1918 (*CI*, 249).

In that light, we can better understand how Valéry considers that a poem should be a "feast for the Intellect" (*Tel Quel I, OII*, 546), suggesting the way in which a poem excites the mind and stimulates it to react to the poem as a whole. This does not mean that Valéry's poetry is "intellectual" in the sense that it only appeals to the mind and not to the entire physical being. It is rather the subtle mixture of insistence on formal perfection and attention to the sensuous quality of experience that best characterizes his poetry. Poetry is what emerges from "the struggle between sensations and language" (*CII*, 1064). No one who reads "Les Grenades" can ever see or taste a pomegranate in the same way, just as it is impossible after reading "Le Cimetière marin" to view life, death, the sun, and the sea as before.

Valéry considers poetry to be an art of composition more than of expression. Indeed, he deplores the fact that so few poems in French are "composed" in the sense of every part being governed by purely poetic considerations (*CII*, 1096). One of the long poems from *Charmes*, "La Pythie," caricatures the raving, uncontrolled utterances emitted by the Pythia, a Greek priestess through whom the oracle speaks. The poem nevertheless ends on an elevated note when the "Saint LANGAGE" overtakes the obscure, irrational sounds of her other-worldly voice. Valéry makes his point quite clearly: "I would rather write a weak piece in full consciousness and complete lucidity than to give life to the most beautiful masterpiece thanks to a trance that takes me out of myself" (*ŒI*, 640).

The craft of poetry should not *use* language to reveal the inner state of the poet. Such a Romantic approach had led to great lyrical movements of pure subjectivity based on intense emotion. As Valéry put it later in life, a poet should never say that it is raining; he should make it rain (*CII*, 1120). Simple inspiration is, however, gratuitous for Valéry. Achieved without effort, it is without value (*ŒII*, 550). "Beautiful verses reach maturation on the day after inspiration" (*ŒII*, 1069), and only after the poet has recognized their potential. Valéry shares equal scorn for the surrealists, whose "écriture automatique" relies on random words that are never subjected to the critical control of the artist. The "inspired" poet who is prey to the excesses of his art cannot be lucid, for "Enthusiasm is not a conducive state for the writer" (*ŒI*, 1205).

While Valéry's poetry is rich in images and figures of speech, it relies less on metaphors than does most other poetry of our century. A metaphor is "shapeless" and "fluid" (*CII*, 1060) instead of having the hard, cutting quality that he so values. Unbridled invention was not Valéry's goal, and we find only an occasional obscure word, colloquial expression, or invented term. On the other hand, he often uses words in their etymological sense and never loses sight of the polysemantic quality of language.

Rather than a self-indulgent tool for expressing oneself, poetry is for Valéry an *act* in that it allows the intellect to function in full awareness of its actions. Poetry is not only self-reflexive. It is self-conscious. Valéry conceives of poetry more as a game of chess than as a game of roulette. The former involves maneuvering pieces with prescribed attributes on a board with a set number of squares, while the latter relies on pure, random luck for winning. The virtually endless permutations and combinations in a chess game, like the limitless arrangements of words to compose a poem, provide enough latitude for the poet without embracing unbridled liberty, which can quickly turn to formless nonsense.

The combination of words and signs in a given linguistic environment, or what Gérard Genette refers to as a "jeu combinatoire" (a combining game),[2] is one of the cornerstones of Valéry's poetic theory and practice. The formal quality figures among his earliest preoccupations if we refer back to a 1902 definition of poetry as consisting of "the arrangement of arbitrary *formality*" (*CII,* 1059). This quest is comparable to the rigorous complexity of mathematics, and Valéry suggests numerous analogies between the two areas of inquiry, especially in terms of arriving at a geometry of the mind. Literature, as he reminds us in the dedication to *La Jeune Parque,* is an *exercice,* the aim of which is to heighten the poet's awareness of his own inner self.

This formal, linguistic approach to poetry makes language, and not the poet, the real motor to the poem. A good heart does not lead to good verse, he says, adding that poetry serves not to move the writer but the reader of the work (*CII,* 1004). Such careful attention to the formal aspect of a poem supposes an arduous task for the poet, who must be a critic and craftsman in the transformation of rough words into a work of art.

This emphasis on composition does not mean that Valéry denies the possible worth of poetry that results from chance or accident. In this context, he tells a long, exemplary tale in "Poésie et pensée abstraite" about how a certain rhythm found its way into his head one day as he was walking through the streets of Paris (*ŒI,* 1322–24). Wondering as to the origin of this rhythm, he is led to conclude that it could only come from the harmonious conjunction of three components: the outside world, his own body, and his mind. This tripartite division is a fundamental element of Valéry's "system" and is called *C.E.M.* (Corps, Esprit, Monde = Body, Mind, World).

In his anecdote, he insists that such "found" verses were "gifts of the gods" to be subjected to the rigors of the poetic process that would craft them into poetry: "There are those verses one finds. The others, one must make. One must perfect those that are found" (*ŒII,* 591). A poet, like an architect, must work with the raw materials at his disposal. A true writer, according to Valéry, is one who must search for his words and, in the process of searching, finds them (*CII,* 987). Far from being the invention of words, poetry allows the poet to discover and activate selected riches that he has stored within his mind and body.

Since pure invention falls short of aesthetic perfection, the artist must also be a critic. The critical acumen of the poet is what will allow him to *make* his poem a work of art and not simply let it remain a vague, random assembling of words. The author, in the process of discovery and critical examination, is "written" by the work that he composes, even against his strongest resistance. Valéry's criticism of most twentieth-century poetry is that he doesn't feel their "resistances" (*CII*, 1138). The true pleasure for a writer is not so much to express his thoughts as to discover that he had such thoughts. The poem has its greatest impact on the person who creates it (*CII*, 1006).

In order to provide a framework for his activity as a poet, Valéry makes an aesthetic principle out of the numerous constraints that the poet imposes upon his craft. These formal constraints define the terms by which the poet will seek to fashion his work. In a phrase reminiscent of the epigraph placed at the head of this chapter, Valéry declares that it is the works with the greatest constraints that also contain the greatest freedom of mind (*CII*, 1017). In *Autres Rhumbs,* he provides an extreme example of a poet's task: find a feminine word made up of two syllables, containing a *p* or *f,* ending in a mute sound, synonymous with "breaking" or "falling apart" and neither rare, nor scholarly. Six conditions, he gloats (*ŒII*, 676)! These formal constraints aim primarily at organizing language so that it produces sound and not simply noise. Unlike the musician who composes and plays in a specific musical language designed for that very purpose, the poet must avail himself of the most common of raw materials—language, and especially, the spoken word.

Like Mallarmé, Valéry is deeply aware that the use and abuse of language through daily discourse has made it an impure medium (*ŒI*, 657). The task of the poet will therefore consist of arranging words above all so that they attract the interest of the ear at least as much as they appeal to the mind (*ŒI*, 207). Rather than conceiving of poetic language as a vehicle to transmit a message or to state a position, Valéry always seeks to use words for their sonority as much as for their sense. Sound is at least as essential to the poem as is meaning since it is the vibration of the words that will strike a chord in both the poet and the listener or reader.

Considerations of voice become especially important in this context, leading Valéry to state that the most beautiful poetry has for him the voice of an ideal female named "Mlle Ame" (Miss Soul) (*CII*, 1076). That inner voice tells the poet if a word reflects his true self. The meaning to be attributed to that word will be decided as it dialogues with the listener of the poem. We also might remember that Valéry expressed several times his desire to have a professional singer or actor *perform* his works in order to gain another appreciation of their vocal quality.

In an eloquent image, Valéry compares prose to walking and poetry to dancing: both use essentially the same body parts, yet walking supposes a direction and a destination whereas dancing is an activity in and of itself that leads nowhere (*ŒI,* 1330). It is beauty of movement without the mirage of progress. This distinction allows him to restore a balance between form and substance, between sound and sense, between language and meaning.

Realizing that words, even those that seem to have no stable, definable meaning, will inevitably be interpreted by listeners and readers, Valéry makes it clear in his poetic theory that transmitting a preconceived meaning is not for him the goal of a poem. On the contrary, a poem invites and challenges its reader to become actively involved in the mental exercise of bestowing upon the poem some significance. A poet should refrain from trying to express ideas through verse when prose is a much more appropriate vehicle (*CII,* 1089). A prose work, like walking, tends to lead somewhere in order to show something to a reader. Along the way, the reader passes over words whose general meaning is taken in but whose intrinsic value as words is immediately forgotten in favor of the general thrust of the plot and characters. Prose thus serves a utilitarian function in the transmission of a message, the exact words of which are usually of little or no importance.

The poet works otherwise. He attempts to keep the language of poetry alive beyond the immediate understanding of the reader by making words resistant to our tendency to digest and discard their meaning. The conscious inscription of difficulty in poetry is more than a defiant act of seeking obscurity for obscurity's sake. In his belief that what is difficult is always new (*ŒII,* 517), Valéry underscores the aesthetic value of returning constantly to the text in order to rediscover its many unknown facets.

This is not to suggest that the words of poetry appeal only to some higher mental functions. Valéry criticizes the novel for using language in such a way as to alienate the reader from his body by making him believe in another reality, another setting peopled with other characters. We become so absorbed in a novel, especially of the escapist variety, that we forget who we are. Prose therefore separates the reader from himself and the world around him, whereas poetry encourages contact and presence. Indeed, it appeals to the profound unity of the physical being through rhythms and harmony that engage our total self (*ŒI,* 1374).

Could this purely physiological difference be what Roland Barthes had in mind when he declared, "There is a body in Valéry that we do not know well"[3]? Valéry makes it very clear, as we shall see, that *La Jeune Parque* was to be, among other things, a poem about the physiological dimension of consciousness. This emphasis on physical sensation and bodily presence saves Valéry's poetry from becoming an arid exercise in form alone.

Since poetic language is not so readily transformed into meaning (i.e., understood in order to be forgotten), it lingers on in the reader's mind where the plurality of meanings creates a dilemma. Since words rarely mean just one thing, since signifiers can have many significations, a poem cannot be reduced to a single idea or meaning. Indeed, invention is made possible only because of the "plurality of possible functions of an object" (*CII*, 1001). It is, according to Valéry, the worst parts of a literary work, those where the ideas are most apparent, that make up its subject (*ŒII*, 679).

Sound is our first contact with the poem, and it is through the ear that we first capture the familiar sounds, even if often in unfamiliar surroundings. In the context of the Cratyllic belief that there is an intrinsic connection between sound and sense, Valéry responds categorically that they are two separate entities (*ŒI*, 1328). The whole poem, and not just its various elements, lives by its form, which carries it and allows it to survive in the reader's voice. Valéry posits a pendulum-like movement that goes from sound to sense and back again, making poetic form a part of the poetic effect (*ŒI*, 1332). The reception of the poem is as important as the poem itself. Even in a quasi-political essay on the state of intelligence, Valéry reaffirms his belief that, for the true poet, sound is at least as important as meaning (*ŒI*, 1079). The poet's aim, rather than using language to express his own state of mind or his own personal drama, consists of attempting to create a poetic state in the reader (*ŒI*, 1337). This objective is quite modern and anticipates a linguistic approach to literature as well as one of the basic principles behind reader-response criticism. Rather than affirming the existence of only one valid interpretation, Valéry willingly recognizes that a published work belongs as much to its audience as to its author.

In his "Commentaire de *Charmes*," Valéry asserts that it is the very nature of poetry *not* to have a single meaning predetermined by the poet. As he cogently puts it, "Mes vers ont le sens qu'on leur prête" (*ŒI*, 1509; "My verses have the meaning that are given them"). The process by which a poem's meaning emerges is a result of the conjunction of poet, text, and reader. Valéry declares in a 1916 passage from the *Cahiers* that the right to confer meaning rests squarely with the reader. It is the poet's role to construct a sort of "verbal body" that has both the solidity and the ambiguity of an object (*CII*, 1074).

This is not to suggest, of course, that any reader has the right to assign any meaning to any poem. In the previous reference to the "Commentaire de *Charmes,*" Valéry is reacting to the commentary of his own poetry by the philosopher Alain, who makes many astute and ingenious remarks about what he thinks a certain word, verse, or poem means. Valéry's objection goes beyond specific "good" or "bad" interpretations, "right" or "wrong" meanings. He recognizes the interpreter's liberty to state what a poem means once it has left the poet's hands and has become an object of public curiosity and debate. The commentary of a poem supposes, however, a prose translation of poetic language, which, as we know, can only be a vague approximation of the poem's subject matter.

Valéry makes it clear on numerous occasions that the subject of a poem is only of secondary importance and that poetry should not be a vehicle for ideas. The form of the poem is, for him, what constitutes the interest and value of the work since the sounds and rhythms of the words are combined in a way that cannot be summarized or altered without damaging the integrity of the poem itself. The form of the poem is its substance, he confirms (*ŒI*, 1456). Any critical and analytical discourse that attempts to discuss poetry, including what I am attempting here, goes against Valéry's objections to scholarly discussion of poetry in unpoetic terms. The highly codified practice in French schools of textual commentary and explication stands contrary to his higher conception of what poetry does. He also warns against the "vice of interpretation" that errs by considering the poem to be a finished, polished product instead of taking into account the way in which it has evolved as a series of instants in time (*CII*, 1054).

A poem can thus be defined as a "prolonged hesitation between sound and sense" (*ŒII*, 637). Instead of saying what he feels to a hypothetical reader, who may or may not understand fully, the true poet attempts to make that reader feel, see, or understand for himself. Words and poems do not hold any predetermined meaning in and of themselves. They take on meaning as they meet the consciousness of the reader, who resists, wonders, and repeats until he is satisfied that he has appreciated the many dimensions of the poem.

Given the above, it is hardly surprising that Valéry was, in spite of himself, a key figure in one of the more interesting literary debates of his day—the question of pure poetry. Indeed, he is widely credited with having made the term popular in the early 1920s, and certainly it has been utilized often since then in reference to his work. He writes in 1916, for instance, that *poésie pure* leads the poet to reject those words and subjects that are not in accord with his inner voice (*CII*, 1076).

The public debate erupted in 1925 when the abbé Brémond, an Académicien and author of a multivolume work *Histoire littéraire du sentiment religieux en France*, delivered a highly official lecture to a joint session of the five academies on the subject. Without ever clearly defining what he meant by "pure poetry," the abbé Brémond made it clear that he considered poetry to follow a quasi-mystical path, believing that it results from a sort of divine inspiration that the poet attempts to recreate through words. Pure poetry is, by this definition, unexplainable. Marcel Proust, in *Du côté de chez Swann*, had hailed this verse from Jean Racine's *Phèdre*, "La fille de Minos et de Pasiphaé" (The daughter of Minos and Pasiphaë), stating that it was all the more beautiful because it meant strictly nothing.

Valéry, while trying not to get drawn into the animated debate that occupied much of the literary scene well into the following year, nevertheless had much to say about a subject so central to his own concerns. As we already have seen, he would have differed from the abbé Brémond by the importance that he attaches to the poet's craft instead of reliance on the inspiration of the muses or the gods. In his notes for a 1927 lecture on *Poésie pure*, Valéry clearly takes the position that pure poetry is an ideal objective that, while laudable, is impossible to achieve (*ŒI*, 1457). Like Brémond, he does believe that poetry gains in purity to the extent that it distances itself from prose. He recommends using the term *poésie absolue*, not only to avoid the suggestion of moral purity but also to underscore his belief that poetry appeals to our sensitivity, which is governed by language (*ŒI*, 1458). Rather than comparing the poetic process to musical composition or mystical inquiry, Valéry points out the numerous aspects of language that make poetry such a complex art: phonetics, metrics, rhythm, logic, semantics, rhetoric, and syntax (*ŒI*, 1462). Even if the poet masters all of these elements, he still does not control the interpretation that a reader might assign to his work. Pure poetry exists perhaps as an idealized concept against which to measure the success of a poet's undertaking. It is, however, impossible to realize. With an implicit awareness that the goal of pure poetry might well result in the abolition of the poetic voice, that purity might lead to sterility, Valéry kept a rather low profile in the public debate and continued his own investigations, both creative and critical.

Chapter Three
Album de vers anciens: The Past as Prologue

Voici quelques vers commis en province par un provincial loin du grand brasier de Paris.
(These few verses penned in the provinces by a provincial far from the bright fires of Paris.)
Valéry to Charles Boès, 1889, *Œuvres I,* 1577

Valéry's return to poetry after a self-imposed silence of practically 20 years followed a long, sinuous path, culminating in a brilliant succession of works from *La Jeune Parque* (1917) to *Charmes* (1922). This revived effort at poetic production came under the impetus of André Gide and Gaston Gallimard, who approached Valéry in 1912 asking him to assemble his best poems from the 1890s with a view to a volume of collected verse. This volume was to be published by the new Editions Gallimard, quickly to become the most prestigious French publishing house of the twentieth century. We know how *La Jeune Parque* grew out of this undertaking and, in many ways, overshadowed the initial project.

Valéry's decision to publish *La Jeune Parque* separately and in the midst of the war signaled his conviction that his long poem held a special place and could not figure alongside the previous poems, even revised. The publication of the works turned out to be contrary to his original intent. He gave *La Jeune Parque* to the Gallimard publishing house, whereas the 16 poems contained in the 1920 edition of the *Album de vers anciens* were published by Adrienne Monnier whose Amis des Livres bookshop was a nexus of literary activity at the time.

The composition of the successive editions of the *Album de vers anciens* is a complicated topic that would lead us away from our purpose here. It is important to keep in mind, nevertheless, that Valéry considered a poem or a collection never to be cast in its definitive form. This led him to constant revisions of individual poems, even after they had been published, and to the redistribution of poems between collections.

It is worth pointing out, in this context, that editions of the *Album* in 1926 and 1927 contained new poems. Other poems were revised and transferred to the 1922 and 1926 editions of *Charmes*. The monumental collected volume of *Poésies* published in 1929 resulted in a total of 21 poems in the standard edition of the *Album* and the same number in *Charmes,* thus producing a symmetry that undoubtedly pleased Valéry's sense of proportion and architecture. They were chosen from among the range of poems that had appeared during the last decade of the nineteenth century in a multitude of small, ephemeral literary reviews: *La Conque, Le Centaure, La Syrinx, L'Ermitage, La Plume,* to mention but a few.[1]

It is not an unusual event to have a poet edit and revise his earlier work after some years. Only a naive reader could believe that a poet creates the definitive version of a work in one dash of the pen. Such a romantic notion hardly prevailed by the time that poets after Baudelaire privileged work and craft over inspiration, divine or other. Most poems undergo successive versions until that decisive moment when they are consigned to print. Indeed, Valéry incorporated constant revision into his poetic theory, believing that there was no such entity as a "perfect" poem. Any poem can be modified and improved by a conscious and conscientious craftsman. In a 1922 note in the *Cahiers,* he expresses the belief that a poem is never finished but results rather from an accident (an insistent editor or another impending project, for instance) that makes it a public act. He even goes on to envision a case in which a poet might spend his whole life reworking the same words. "Perfection. It's *work*" (*CII,* 1010–11).

The poet is, for Valéry, an architect or artisan who is constantly tinkering with his verse in order to improve it. In that context, the poems he "rediscovered" in 1912 were around 20 years old, written for the most part before the Genovese crisis, and, above all, they were exemplary of a poetics that he had long since rejected or surpassed ("Fragments des mémoires d'un poème," *ŒI,* 1464).

The word *anciens* in the title of the collection underscores the distance between the dated, derivative poems of his earlier period and the poetics of a mature man. While maintaining the use of classical alexandrines throughout (except in "Le Bois amical" and "Vue"), Valéry shifted the focus from imitation to innovation as both the creator and critic of his own work. The challenge was thus for him to make original works out of dated pieces, indeed to rewrite the poems of his youth with the self-consciousness of a poet in full possession of his powers. The poems included in the *Album* can be appreciated not only for their poetic qualities but also for the way in which they reveal the critical acumen of their author.

"La Fileuse"

"La Fileuse" (The Spinner) occupies a crucial position in the collection as the opening poem. Its musical qualities have made it one of the more widely anthologized pieces from Valéry's early period. The complicated genesis of this initial poem in the *Album* is revealing of Valéry's strategies in the revision of his earlier works. Through a study of the poem's successive versions as well as its intertext, Suzanne Nash makes a convincing case for seeing "La Fileuse" as moving away from symbolist aesthetics toward a renewed emphasis on the natural, sensuous world.[2]

Valéry strives to make the reader see the spinner as she dozes off while seated at her wheel. Rather than freezing her forever in an abstract world all too familiar to his fellow symbolists, he dramatizes an observed scene. Although it is impossible to determine to what extent the poem might have been inspired by a painting, it seems obvious that Courbet's "La Fileuse endormie" is another expression of the theme of the sleeping woman.[3] Courbet's painting is conveniently housed in the Musée de Montpellier where Valéry grew up.

As the woman in Valéry's poem falls asleep, the breeze picks up, the sun goes down and seems to set the garden on fire, while the wool continues to spin through her unconscious fingers. The voice of the observer relates the events throughout the first six stanzas, only to address the spinner herself in the last two lines. The final isolated verse with its imperfect tense seems to suggest that the spinner is no more (an earlier version of the poem explicitly referred to her as dead, "la Morte").

The verse form—terza rima with a final, dangling line of conclusion—is rare and unusual except to readers of Dante. All rhyme endings are feminine (with a silent *e* following the consonant), and the prevalent use of enjambment and insistent alliteration give the poem a particularly rich texture. The interlaced rhyme scheme also suggests that the poet has become a weaver of words, much as the spinner's job consists of twisting fibers into thread. By the similarity in their crafts, the spinner can be considered to be an avatar of the poet himself.

The truncated epigraph from the Gospels, extolling the faithful to accumulate treasures in heaven rather than on earth, would translate, "Consider how the lilies grow in the field; they do not work, they do not spin" (Matthew 6:28). Although the scriptural significance may be limited, it seems obvious that Valéry nevertheless wishes to establish a connection between the lilies and the spinner, both of whom produce beautiful robes without laboring. The white lily, a symbol of virginal purity, stands in opposition to the sensual rose, thus establishing an opposition of Christian and pagan images. The red rose (originally capitalized) is offered up to the spinning wheel in stanza 4 and reappears in stanza 8, where it can also be taken to mean a rose window in a cathedral containing the figure of a saint.

Another possible context might be given to this poem. To the best of my knowledge, no one has pointed out that this spinner may also be related to the mythological spinner of life's thread, Clotho, the youngest of the three Fates. Given that he was deeply involved in *La Jeune Parque* at that time, Valéry certainly had the Fate in mind as he was revising "La Fileuse." In contrary fashion, however, the two characters have opposite trajectories: the spinner fades into unconsciousness as she dozes off at the onset of dusk, whereas the Fate moves from night to day and, correlatively, towards greater and greater self-awareness.

To return to our immediate argument, Clotho is the Fate who spins the thread representing life and human destiny. Furthermore, she is generally depicted wearing blue robes, the dominant color in Valéry's poem, and a crown of stars, perhaps echoed in line 12, "sa grâce étoilée" (starry grace). Pursuing this line of interpretation, the sister in stanza 8 would most likely be Lachesis, the middle Fate, who determines the length of life by the skein of thread. Her color is usually pink, in which case "rose" would suggest more the color than the flower or the cathedral window. The poem obviously deals with cycles—the day, the seasons, etc.—and, by this reference to the mythological Fates, we also reach the cycle of life that leads inevitably to death, as is suggested in the final line. The remnants of Christian lexicon ("le salut vain," "angélique," "une sainte") warn us, however, to exercise caution when seeking to apply any monolithic grid to Valéry's poetry.

"La Fileuse" dramatizes the confrontation of an individual with nature. The first two stanzas depict in simple, everyday terms ("se dodeline," "ronfle") the weary spinner, seated in front of her window, who has drunk her fill of the azure world and dozes off as the garden before her comes alive. The personification will range from the melodious garden, which nods and sways its head ("se dodeline"), to the wool, which is likened to "caressing hair" ("câline chevelure").

In stanzas 3 and 4, we move completely from the spinner to the garden, the latter coming alive just as the former slumbers. The last line of stanza 4 displays Valéry's mastery of metric form, divided as it is into three distinct rhythmic groups of six, four, and two beats: "Dédiant magnifique, au vieux rouet, sa rose" (Dedicating magnificently, to the old wheel, its rose). The spinning activity continues on its own in stanzas 5 and 6, just as the shadow weaves itself into the thread without the spinner's knowing.

Despite the serene setting and soothing sounds, "La Fileuse" depicts a more ominous event, suggesting the repressed suffering of dislocation and rupture. In line 21, "Tout le ciel vert se meurt. Le dernier arbre brûle" (All of the green sky dies. The last tree burns), and line 24, " . . . Tu es éteinte" (You are extinguished [i.e., dead]), both the spinner and the garden suffer a similar fate. They are no more, except, of course, as they were from the outset—scenes and images from the poet's mind crafted and translated into language.

Valéry's irrepressible gift for music can be seen in each of the three lines of the final stanza in which line 1 is dominated by alliteration in *t,* line 2 by *f* and *v,* and line 3 again by *t.* From the earlier stanzas, in which the observer is satisfied with describing a scene, we notice how, by the end of the poem, he addresses the sleeping spinner directly. Although he does not chide the spinner, we sense a subtle, reproachful air of superiority on the part of the speaker, whose authority and power come from an ability to recreate at will the scene of the spinner and the garden. In a related manner, this is also the expression of Valéry's repossession of his past and his will to poetic power. The liminal poem to the *Album* stands as a declaration of his independence from many, if not all, of the nineteenth-century influences that he has since chosen to reject.

A complete study of the next eleven poems in the definitive version of the *Album* would take us beyond the scope of the present overview. Suffice it to say here that nine of the poems are sonnets written with much of the tonality and subject matter associated with nineteenth-century Parnassian or symbolist poetry. They include sonnets to such mythological or historical characters as Helen, Orpheus, Venus, or Caesar. In a more intimist vein, "Le Bois amical" was addressed to Gide, and "Les Vaines danseuses" announces Valéry's preoccupation with dance and the body in movement. The art is one of ethereal, idealized craftsmanship rather than self-reflexivity or self-awareness. The prominent use of plurals reminds us of Baudelaire, while some of the more melodious verses, such as "Féerie" or "Au Bois dormant," contain lilting, musical lines worthy of Verlaine. This remains a highly poeticized world of pure jewels, azure skies, and moonlit woods.

Rather than seeing these *Album* pieces as tired exercises in things past, we should note how Valéry insists more explicitly on the world of the senses and achieves a density, both lexical and syntactical, which we will find pushed to new limits in *Charmes*.

"Baignée"

"Baignée" (The Bath) will reward a diligent reader with numerous surprises and satisfactions. It was written during the time of the crisis of 1892 and already contains in mature terms the elements of consciousness and separation that will appear in the mature poems of *Charmes*. "Baignée" depicts a highly charged moment of sensual stillness that Suzanne Nash has astutely analyzed as containing elements of Mallarmé, especially from *Hérodiade,* included only by Valéry to empty them of their potential presence (Nash, 169–75).

In Valéry's poem, a bather, compared to a "fleshy fruit," emerges from the water of some "young" fountain and is caught, as in a photograph or painting, in one suggestive pose. One can most easily imagine a Renoir painting in color and texture. In a reversal of Mallarméan imagery, her head, though "severed" by the water's surface, remains squarely attached to the body below, her hair forming a sort of helmet around her golden head. Such inclusion of the physical presence through the submerged body prefigures some of the physiological poetry to come, especially *La Jeune Parque*. The linking of the mind (thought) and body (senses) is underscored in stanza 2 with the search for lost jewelry beneath the surface of the water. The rich vowel texture of line 4 with sequential *o* sounds demonstrates Valéry's search for phonic connections that will prove a general characteristic of his poetry. Each of the two tercets evokes one of the bather's arms, the first plunged into the water to try and grab the "shadow of a flower," the second curved towards the sky holding up her golden locks as insects buzz about.

As an image of artistic creation, "Baignée" exemplifies Valéry's interest in moments of transformation and emergence between the fathomless depths and the clear vision, between stasis and movement, between insensate existence and artistic consciousness.

"Narcisse parle"

"Narcisse parle" can be considered the centerpiece of the *Album,* both in its poetic quality and historical importance as a founding myth for Valéry. The myth of Narcissus presided over the whole of Valéry's artistic career, from this early poem written in 1891 to the opening lines of *L'Ange,* which he revised shortly before his death. "Fragments du Narcisse" (1921), contained in *Charmes,* is a masterful piece. Valéry was not alone in his fascination for the Ovidian myth of the adolescent so infatuated with his image reflected in a pool that he couldn't leave its sight. From François Villon to the symbolists, the mythological character had provided a wealth of suggestive poses, not the least of which is the introspective gaze and the self-conscious observation of the poet.

The division of the self into actor and spectator, a vital attribute for a writer, was a commonplace posture in the 1890s, influenced by Arthur Schopenhauer's idealism and Mallarmé's poetics. Gide's own *Traité du Narcisse* appeared in 1892 and was intended to provide a doctrine for the symbolist aesthetic. Given Valéry's intense scrutiny of the inner workings of his mind, given his emphasis on seeing the self seeing the self (Monsieur Teste "se voit se voir"), it is hardly surprising that he instinctively grasped the rich significance of the myth. This reflection that he holds up to his own mind and body provided him with the enigma that he would attempt to elucidate in his writings. As the title of this Narcissus poem suggests, he would seek a voice by which to make his image speak.

Valéry, in a 1941 talk, provided some essential information about the background and evolution of the myth in his writings. He called the Narcissus theme a sort of poetic autobiography (*Œl,* 1560), suggesting through the reflective image the type of intense scrutiny that he imposed on his mind. Consciousness, rigor, and clarity were his guides and companions in the lifelong quest for knowledge and understanding of the mind.

Valéry recalls also how he enjoyed walking through the botanical gardens in Montpellier, and especially around a tomb reputed to be that of a young woman named Narcissa, daughter of the English poet Edward Young. According to local legend, Young had to bury his daughter himself and in secret because she was a Protestant and therefore excluded from the official graveyard; what is sure is that he wrote the *Nights* (1742), which contain haunting echoes of his daughter's demise. The epigraph to "Narcisse parle"—*Narcissae placandis manibus* (to placate the *manes* [spirits of the departed] of Narcissa)—is taken from the inscription carved on Young's daughter's tombstone. The site, the legend, and the name set in motion a series of poetic associations. "Narcissa" soon became "Narcissus" under Valéry's pen.

When Gide came to Montpellier to pay a visit to his uncle in 1891, he met Valéry and the two young men spent a long while meditating over this gravesite. It is difficult to imagine that Gide and Valéry did not discuss their mutual admiration for the mythical figure of Narcissus. Not only did their communion result in "Le Bois amical," a poem of friendship; Valéry also wrote a sonnet that would provide the nucleus of the longer poem, "Narcisse parle," and initiate a lifelong obsession with Narcissus.

Valéry later claimed (falsely) that the present version of 58 alexandrines was written in two days in order to appear in the first issue of *La Conque,* edited by Pierre Louÿs (*ŒI,* 1560). He was nevertheless surprised when his poem appeared in print and even somewhat disconcerted when it received unexpected praise. As I have already mentioned, he chose to send the piece to Mallarmé, whose "Hérodiade" he admired immensely and which bears some resemblance to the Narcissus poem. Mallarmé responded, expressing admiration of the rare tone of the poem.

In 1891, Gide wrote his own *Traité du Narcisse* and dedicated it to his young companion from Montpellier. He intended it to become an artistic manifesto for the burgeoning symbolist movement. When Valéry was preparing the *Album de vers anciens* in 1920, he included his earlier "Narcisse parle" as a perfect example of the kind of poetry he was writing in his youth and probably would have continued to write had he not distanced himself from his art for some 20 years (*ŒI,* 1561).

The poem itself is subdivided into irregular and seemingly arbitrary groups of alexandrines ranging from three to eleven lines. It begins as a monologue, only to become a dialogue between the voices that vie for expression within the character. We must remember that Narcissus speaks, thus adding a further dimension to the traditional myth's insistence on visual image, surface and depth, and desire for unity of the divided self. This added facet displaces the poem's focus from ontological and ethical considerations to an aesthetic search for the voice capable of expressing the multiple facets of the self. This is all the more important in "Narcisse parle" since readers of the poem know the fatal outcome that awaits the mythological hero. He embodies a fate dictated by the gods or poets and thus can retain the reader's interest only through the way in which he enacts his destiny. The countless number of versions of the Narcissus legend attest to its power as a poetic vehicle. If, as Valéry himself claimed, poetry resorts to repetition and variation for its renewal and richness, the interest of his poem lies in its composition and manner.

Narcissus opens his complaint by addressing his brothers and offering his vain tears to the nymph of the fountains, presumably Echo. It was his refusal to respond to Echo's solicitations that had led to Narcissus's punishment of falling in love with his own image. Captured by his own beauty, he languishes (ll. 1, 11) in the pure desire of his reflection in the pool. As the voice of evening casts its spell over the scene, Narcissus sees the "perfidious moon" (l. 8) rise. He acknowledges his inability to love anything other than the magical water that reflects his mirror image (l. 12).

Valéry chose to situate his character in a natural surrounding made up of woods, flowers, and water. Like the Parque, Narcissus is strikingly aware of his body and mind. He contemplates his eyes, arms, hands with bitter awareness of the fate that awaits him (ll. 24–29). If Valéry gives Narcissus a voice, it serves to express the torment of his inability to reconcile his desire of self-possession with his desire of the other. He is caught in a web of introspection that allows neither entry nor escape. As he narrates his own demise in the form of an imminent kiss that will destroy the image reflected on the water's surface, Narcissus begs for the indulgence of a flute player who will sow the "tears of silver" (l. 58) he will shed. Narcissus here is depicted as a victim of his own doing but, more importantly, a victim aware of his fate.

The numerous exclamation points that dot the text express Narcissus's own wrenching realization of his impending death: "Hélas! L'image est vaine et les pleurs éternels!" (l. 18; Alas! The image is vain and the tears eternal!). While the poetry of "Narcisse parle" does not always equal that of many other poems by Valéry, there are some very successful lines or passages, such as in the melodious second stanza or the more aggressive, defiant fifth stanza. The search for alliteration and musical combinations sometimes strains the resources of the language: "L'heure menteuse est molle aux membres sur la mousse / Et d'un sombre délice enfle le vent profond" (ll. 43–44; The lying hour is soft to members on the moss / And in somber delight swells the profound wind). The string of *m* sounds in line 43 becomes ponderous and can hardly be saved by the rich combination of nasal sounds in line 44. Valéry himself later felt it necessary to defend his use of rare or unusual words such as "saphir" (l. 11) or "funérale rose" (l. 33), noting that to banish such terms would lead to an impoverishment of the language (*ŒI*, 1561).

Valéry clearly went to great pains to cultivate the rich texture of "Narcisse parle." As in *La Jeune Parque,* in which words and lines recur at often distant intervals, we can point out the association of calm and hope in lines 5 and 51–52. It would not be too much to suggest that these are echoes, central to the myth of Narcissus and to the poetry of Valéry. The kiss that he projects will break the calm surface of the water, leading to death but also to the hope of renewal, as symbolized by the narcissus flower that he will become or the flute melody that will be heard. Valéry's sensual attention to the natural world distinguishes his from most other treatments of the Narcissus myth. His character makes it clear that his is a world made up of hard jewels and soft plants (cf. stanza 4 or the beginning of stanza 6). Despite its flaws, "Narcisse parle" stands as the centerpiece in the *Album de vers anciens* and inaugurates a long and rich career of writing about this mythological figure.

The subsequent group of poems contains a variety of verse forms, ranging from the sonnets ("Vue," "Valvins") to the ode ("Air de Sémiramis") to the fragment ("Profusion du soir") to the prose poem ("L'Amateur de poèmes"). This disparity of forms and subject matter reflects their more experimental, prospective nature. Some of these poems date from later years after the crisis of 1892 and several of them are dedicated to fellow symbolist poets such as Mallarmé ("Valvins"), Francis Viélé-Griffin ("Eté") or Camille Mauclair ("Air de Sémiramis").

Suzanne Nash has demonstrated throughout her study of the *Album* how the collection can be read as a subversive operation that appears to pay homage to the past while actually undermining its major tenets. Yet, already in "Narcisse parle" we can witness the displacement of interest from the idealistic philosophy so prevalent in late nineteenth-century France in favor of a more naturalistic, pantheistic worldview. This strategy will be pursued throughout these remaining poems as well as in *La Jeune Parque* and *Charmes.*

Chapter Four
La Jeune Parque: Coming of Age

... J'ai là une sorte de poème qui ne veut s'achever, un monstre gonflé des loisirs de mon inuti-
lité pendant la guerre.

(I have here a sort of poem that does not want to end, a monster swollen by the leisure born of
my uselessness during the war.)

Valéry to Maurice Denis, *Œuvres I*, 1624

La Jeune Parque grew out of an unusual set of circumstances at a crucial time in both Valéry's and Europe's literary and political destinies.
After repeated requests by Gide and Gaston Gallimard, Valéry finally
agreed in 1912 to edit a volume of his early poetry, which would become
the *Album de vers anciens* (1920).

Although it was not his intent to break the vow of silence taken in
1892, Valéry nevertheless found himself tempted to put to the test some
of the many theories and ideas he had accumulated over the previous 20
years. He proposed not only to make minor changes to the older verses
but also to add a short poem of some 30 or 40 lines that would be his
farewell to poetry or, as he put it in a typical moment of self-deprecation,
to his "adolescent games" (*ŒI*, 1621). Little would he have predicted
that the drafts and revisions for *La Jeune Parque* would extend to over
800 pages and take over four years to complete. The final version would
run 512 lines, resulting in one of the greatest long poems in all of French
literature. Valéry was obviously proud of this Herculean task since he
noted in 1914 that one would truly appreciate what he kept if one knew
what he had discarded (*CII*, 1000). He would later quip that the poem
grew ten times longer than planned and one hundred times more difficult to read than necessary (*ŒI*, 1621).

As I have already mentioned, *La Jeune Parque* was an immediate success and catapulted Valéry to the forefront of French and European letters. Given the difficulty of the poem, it is hard to imagine it attaining
popular success—yet it did. Valéry wittily observed that it was the
obscurity of the poem that put him in the spotlight (*ŒI*, 39). We must
also note in passing that this long poem contains in embryonic form
much of the poetic matter that would make up the poems of *Charmes*.

It is worth keeping in mind the artistic and political context that prevailed at the time. *La Jeune Parque* was conceived around 1913, that *annus mirabilis* that saw the publication of Marcel Proust's *Du côté de chez Swann,* Guillaume Apollinaire's *Alcools,* Einstein's theory of relativity, James Joyce's *A Portrait of the Artist as a Young Man,* and the Paris premiere of Igor Stravinsky's *Rites of Spring.* The original group of the *Nouvelle Revue Française,* founded in 1909, was also preparing to embark on a literary and business venture that was to become the Editions Gallimard, France's most prestigious publishing house. The outbreak of war in 1914 would alter the course of events, yet it is too easily forgotten that Valéry wrote *La Jeune Parque* against the backdrop of bombs and vicious fighting in the trenches, all the while harboring a deep sense of his own impotence in the face of such cataclysmic events.

While the poem does not seem at first glance to have anything to do with the war, it can be considered as either a refuge or consolation from real events or, more likely, a subtle response to them. Valéry's patriotism leaves no doubt—nor does his poetic ambition. At the very least, we could assert that the discipline that Valéry applied to writing *La Jeune Parque* constituted a sort of moral resistance to the fury raging about him. He wrote in 1917 that, since he was unable to fight for French territory, he could at least work to conserve the French language (*ŒI,* 1630). The backdrop of tension and catastrophe left him little peace of mind and serenity to concentrate exclusively on his poetry (*ŒI,* 1637). Although an overtly historical analysis of *La Jeune Parque* seems out of the question, future interpretations may wish to keep in mind this aspect of the genesis of the poem.

La Jeune Parque is one of the only of his poems that Valéry ever discussed or commented upon at any length. He referred to it in a letter to Gide as a kind of intellectual autobiography (*ŒI,* 1633). In another letter to André Fontinas, he called upon his audience to read an autobiography "dans la forme" (*ŒI,* 1631–32). He presumably meant that, although there can be no direct modeling of the young Fate on the author's person, he poured much of himself into his poem and, perhaps more importantly, received a great deal of self-knowledge in return. The self-awareness that the Fate acquires after a night of struggling with herself bears many resemblances to the night of 4–5 October 1892, when Valéry himself underwent a severe emotional and intellectual crisis. It would not be too much to assert that *La Jeune Parque* signals the end of his personal crisis and his return to the poetic universe that he had shunned for over 20 years. In the pure movements of introspective self-awareness, Valéry attains the total intellectuality and self-consciousness of which he had so long dreamed. He is the spectator of his own creation.

Despite the increased importance of feminist criticism, surprisingly little mention has been made of the obvious fact that a male poet, Valéry, here creates a female voice with marked sexual discourse.[1] Although he declared that the sexual passages were late additions and that the celebrated song to Spring was an afterthought, we cannot but wonder if the sensuality of the poem would not have differed under a woman's pen. The lessons of *La Jeune Parque* were as much an exploration of the poet's psyche as they were the revelation of any particular discovery about the character herself.

We must nevertheless keep in mind Valéry's own belief that the poet does not hold the final word as to the meaning of his poem. Indeed, he provides very few specific clues as to the interpretation of any particular passage. *La Jeune Parque* is also the longest of poems by a poet who, as a worthy successor to Poe, believed that poetic virtue was to be found only in short, condensed works. The unusual length of the poem can be attributed to the complex nature of the subject, which could not be shortened except at the risk of placing even greater demands on the reader. For Valéry, the "subject" of a poem is to be found in the worst verses, not in the parts where the poet finally tells the reader what he really wanted to say. Valéry himself described this subject as "la peinture d'une suite de substitutions psychologiques, et en somme le changement d'une conscience pendant la durée de la nuit" (*Œ I*, 1622; the painting of a series of psychological substitutions and, in a word, the transformation of a consciousness over the course of a night).

The narrative flow of the poem allows us nevertheless to follow the unfolding of a dramatic event—the awakening of a young woman, presumably the youngest of the mythological Fates, to the sensual world. Alone at night on the rocky shore of an island, she thinks that she has just been bitten by a serpent, a personage of erotic portent. The reader follows her growing self-awareness, doubts, and temptation as she struggles with herself and with the lure of the serpent. She hesitates between the call of consciousness and voluptuous nature, finally attaining a whole sense of her own richness that will allow her to reconcile and overcome the divisive forces within her. Through a dramatic monologue (or what might be more aptly called an internal dialogue), the young woman's awakening consciousness is exposed and explored as she considers her fate and responds to the world around her.

By refusing a chronological narration, Valéry depicts the Fate's changing moods and developing consciousness through a series of modulations and nuances. He compared his poem to a recitative from a Gluck opera—one long phrase for contralto (*Œl*, 1629)—thus putting music to the service of poetry. The recitative style, with its emphasis on a solo voice and its simple melodic line situated between ordinary speech and true singing, suited Valéry's purposes particularly well. Rather than a plot-driven opera, *La Jeune Parque* can be understood as an attempt to "translate" into poetic language the musicality of the spoken word. Valéry insisted on the importance of modulation in his poem, thereby underscoring how he shifted from one key to another in the transitional sections of such a long work. More than mere technical prowess, this principle as applied to poetry allowed Valéry to harmonize the poem with the *C.E.M.* (*Corps, Esprit, Monde* = Body, Mind, World), each sound reverberating and echoing on several levels at the same time. This goes a long way towards explaining what Valéry meant when he qualified *La Jeune Parque* as a course in physiology, as an attempt to follow "the physiological sensation of consciousness."[2]

If the sounds and rhythms of *La Jeune Parque* so haunt readers, it could be because they are born of extreme attention to certain natural rhythms such as breathing, walking, or the beating of the heart.[3] The other obvious references in Valéry's quest would be Richard Wagner, Jean Racine, and Mallarmé. Rather than stringing together a narrative sequence of events, the poem thus develops around what Valéry called "knots" (*Œl*, 1636) and which are the rich tableaux that make up the organic structure of the poem. The successive states of consciousness of the young Fate are the focus of each sequence. In light of the emphasis on modulation, Valéry acknowledged that he had had a particularly difficult time with the transitions between the different parts (*Œl*, 1636). Therein lies one of the obvious dangers inherent in such a long undertaking as compared to a sonnet or other shorter, more condensed poetic form.

Valéry sought to reveal the inner workings of his character's consciousness becoming aware of itself; thus he could talk about it as "une rêverie dont le personnage en même temps que l'objet est la *conscience consciente*" (*Œl*, 1636; a dream in which the object is both the character and the character's conscious consciousness). He reiterated that the content of the poem was of little importance in comparison to the form. He expressly wanted the most classical alexandrines with caesuras but with no enjambment and with no weak rhymes (*Œl,* 1636).

The formal rigor could not, however, suppress the musical quality of the language that Valéry painstakingly crafted word by word, verse by verse. The form of any poem is contained in language, and Valéry was acutely aware that he was composing a piece of music, not with pure notes but with imperfect words. The play of approximations, images, and allusions can be explained in large part by the necessity to find suitable terms for thoughts, sensations, and feelings for which no words exist. He would qualify this process as involving an artificial fabrication that followed a natural development (*Œl,* 1633). Although written in a state of anxiety and anguish due to the events of the outside world, *La Jeune Parque* reveals a kind of serenity or, perhaps more precisely, contained fervor.

Title, Epigraph, Dedication

Valéry considered at least a dozen other titles before settling on *La Jeune Parque.* Most of the poem was composed under the working title "Psyché" (*soul* in Greek). This mythological character was the object of Cupid's desire, but their love was long frustrated by the gods. Her character must have appealed to Valéry since it combined sensuality and spirituality, eroticism and intellectualism. With the poem almost finished, he nevertheless had to find a new title when he discovered that his old friend, Pierre Louÿs, was writing a novel of the same name. The epigraph was nevertheless taken from Pierre Corneille's play of that name, *Psyché,* and utilizes the same erotic figure as in Valéry's poem, the serpent. Given that the bulk of the poem was written in 1915–16, the belated choice of the definitive title may be of only limited significance and may explain why there is only one reference to the Fate(s) in the entire poem (l. 358).

Valéry nevertheless remains within his beloved classical world of mythology by referring to the Fates who control human destiny, the movement of the heavenly bodies, and the harmony of the universe. The youngest of the Fates would be Clotho. Her name signifies "to spin" since she spins the thread of life, which will then be sorted and eventually cut by her two sisters, respectively, Lachesis and Atropos. Valéry must have been attracted by her youth as well as by the dilemma that she confronts on the threshold of adult life. Finally, he dedicates the whole

"exercice" to Gide, thereby underscoring its formal properties and avow-
ing once again his belief that a poem is never a finished object, but
rather a tool that can serve different purposes in different hands.

Since Valéry does not break his poem into numbered sections, I have
chosen to follow his irregular grouping of verses, giving the correspond-
ing line numbers. He often composed a fragment or a block of verse
around one word or line of poetry. It is also important to keep in mind
his own claim about how difficult he found the transitions in his poem.
While there are several ways to subdivide the poem, we shall follow the
most obvious organization, which considers the poem as a diptych—the
first half of the poem dealing with the "Harmonieuse MOI" at night,
giving way at line 325 to the "Mystérieuse MOI" in the light of day.
This division, while convenient, cannot take into account the complexities of space and time that Valéry wove into his poem, as well as the
many things that seem to take place between each of the "knots" that
makes up the poem.

Lines 1–49

The setting of the poem, although never fully described, is that of a
rocky shoreline under a starlit sky ("diamants extrêmes," l. 2). The first
three lines of the poem show irregular rhythms so as to suggest the disorder in the young woman's mind as she awakes from a dream. She finds
it difficult to distinguish between the cry of the wind and her own weep-
ing since both sounds seem to emanate from some point beyond her person. Although not clear from the first line, we soon realize that the
questions posed by the Fate are to herself and not to some other presence. She will henceforth carry on a long dialogue with herself in which
she will weigh the seductions of erotic desire against the attraction of
intellectual purity.

Beginning with line 4, the poem moves into a fairly regular scheme of
rhyming couplets made up of classical alexandrines. The Fate brings her
hand to her face to wipe off an anticipated tear. The ebb and flow of the
sea on the shore is particularly well rendered in lines 9–12 with their
dominant sounds of *u, m,* and *r.* The hand that she hardly recognizes, the
bare breast that is like an island under the star-studded sky point to the
physiological world to which the Fate is awakening. Fragmentation
("fonde," "divisé," "brisé" [melt, divided, broken]) and lament ("Une

rumeur de plainte et de resserrement" [l. 12; A murmur of moaning and tightening]) characterize the newfound awareness of her duality that has resulted from the serpent's bite.

She turns her attention to the sky, sole witness to the dramatic events that have transpired. The apostrophe to the stars (ll. 18–36) comes in response to what she terms her "soif de désastres" (l. 17; thirst for disasters), her desire for complete awareness of herself in light of the knowledge of her duality brought on by the serpent. The unattainable purity and supernatural beauty of the stars make them all the more attractive. Like Mallarmé's "azur," they are ever-present reminders of human shortcomings and limitations, thus adding a universal dimension to a private drama. Did the pain that awoke her come from some crime that she committed or from some wrong done against her (l. 27)? Or was it all a dream? As in Monsieur Teste's famous observation about seeing himself seeing himself seeing, the young Fate is divided into actor and spectator of her actions: "Je me voyais me voir . . . " (l. 35; I saw myself seeing myself . . .). The serpent has instilled in her not only sexual desire but also desire for knowledge. Furthermore, she finds herself desiring desire and aspiring to complete awareness of her own consciousness. This multilayered and multifaceted movement is typical of Valéry, resulting in the extreme self-consciousness of a poem where awareness is both the end and the means to that end.

The serpent, used again by Valéry in "Ebauche d'un serpent," suggests at first glance the Tempter in Genesis. It is responsible for awakening in the young Fate, as in Eve, her dormant sensuality and her thirst for knowledge, especially knowledge of herself. A specifically Christian reading of the poem due to the apparition of a serpent seems out of the question in light of Valéry's own agnosticism. The serpent, one of Valéry's favorite images, also suggests a new beginning and a circular form when it lies coiled upon itself. In any case, the external existence of the serpent is never confirmed, and it seems more than possible that the serpent lives within the young woman. The poison of lucidity now flows in her veins (l. 44) as she acknowledges the presence in herself of a "secret sister" (l. 48).

Lines 50–101

In this segment, the Fate bids farewell to the serpent, that "ornement de ruine" (l. 54; ornament of ruin) come from a "race naïve" (l. 50; naive species). She no longer needs him and the seductive words that he pours into sleeping virgins. She has entered into awareness of the boundless

riches of her soul. Like the serpent, she is coiled around herself (l. 51).
She is her own theater (l. 69), and her intellect contains limitless treasures that she must now discover and explore. Given that the Fate has
had her eyes opened by the painful bite of the serpent, she can triumph
by her own lucidity and clairvoyance and no longer needs the viscous
reptile. Among the many orders she gives, the Fate tells the serpent to
seek out other prey in whom to awaken the dual desire of sensuality and
lucidity. The last five lines are set off from the rest and contain a brief
evocation of her self before the serpent. She wonders if her body will be
able to summon up its passion and maintain the intensity of the
"douleur divine" (l. 97; divine pain) without the aid of the serpent.

Lines 102–48

This passage deals with the former harmonious self that the Fate was at
a time when she lived in innocence and purity. The imperfect tense translates this period of naive harmony with the surrounding natural world. The
preponderant use of alternating *v* and *l* sounds in lines 105–06 accents the
rich texture of a highly contrasted passage. In some of Valéry's most majestic and most sensual verse, the Fate luxuriates in the sun's luminous rays,
offering her body like a ripening fruit to the light and warmth from above.
This is Valéry's ode to joy. She has not yet received the bittersweet knowledge that would come with the serpent's bite. The nostalgia of this time of
innocence reinforces the rude awakening to the plenitude of life. It was a
time of pagan pleasure with her bare shoulder and her honey breast turned
to the sun as she crossed fields of flowers, which made up her only dress.
The sight of her shadow, a direct result of the sunshine, reminds the Fate of
her own duality, of her own mortality. The second section beginning with
"Je regrette à demi . . . " (l. 133) confirms her mitigated longing for those
earlier days of innocent pleasure when desires were immediately translated
into deeds (l. 137). In a striking image, "entre la rose et moi" (l. 145;
between the rose and me), the Fate, now lucid of her mortal condition,
acknowledges that every gesture by which she confirms her will to live will
result in a shadow that will remind her of her own destiny.

Lines 148–72

The figure of death, which appeared at the end of the preceding passage, will henceforth become the primary subject of the poem. Still in
the light of day, the Fate develops her thoughts about the cruel knowledge exposed in the previous section. Armed with awareness of the

imminent void that is existence, reminded of the transitory nature of her surroundings by the perfume of the orange trees that vanishes (l. 151), she realizes the vanity of life. Her eye now casts a somber look over a world that has lost the splendor it once held. Her thoughts turn to the Pythia, who longs for inevitable death. The language has become more reflective and less poetic as a result. The passing of a bird, probably a variant on the "miroir aux alouettes" that lures birds to their deaths, reminds her not of momentary freedom but rather of inevitable death.

Lines 173–208

The next passage or "psychological substitution," as Valéry conceived his method of composition, deals with the results of too much lucidity. The seemingly endless succession of days, monotonous and predictable, leads to a fate worse than death—*ennui,* the eighth deadly sin in Baudelaire's cosmogony. The Fate is half-dead (l. 180) in a sluggish world deprived of pleasure and sensation; she is half-immortal (l. 181) because she is condemned to live in that state of ennui for eternity. Time is thus a source of torment and confusion, compared to a diamond (l. 182) that completes her diadem but weighs heavily on her forehead. The serpent has not yet awakened the young Fate to other possibilities.

Time appears distinctly in the final segment of lines 185–89. The Fate's memory is enclosed in tombs of melancholy (l. 185) from which escape occasionally some remnants of her past. Here she feels for a moment the blush of shame associated with some childhood episode, presumably an early sexual experience.

The subsequent section (ll. 190–208), while set off typographically, is an extension of the earlier evocation of time and memory. The Fate remembers in quite unspecific terms an earlier arousal of her sexuality among the leaves and undergrowth of a wood. This encounter awoke in her feelings of confusion at hearing a voice she had never heard before. Although tempted to yield to seduction, she resists, not without some regret. In a marked physiological progression, the blood that causes her to blush (ll. 190–92) will be called upon to consume the pale thought of her past (l. 196). She is left with more questions and doubts than awareness or knowledge.

Lines 209–324

The first part of this section contains an inscription that continues the previous part. The Fate considers her earlier erotic desire as synonymous with a desire for death. Her eyes would trace her *templum*, the open space in the sky for divining the future. Her body is here in a state of trouble and disarray that will spread to her mind and soon overtake her whole being. Her consciousness is her being, although here it does not obey her will. Since the awareness of death has entered into the framework of her awareness, she comes to wish for death as deliverance.

Beginning with line 225, we find the celebrated "Springtime" section, in fact an earlier poem titled "Renaissance," which Valéry altered and inserted at this point. He later declared that all of the erotic sections of his poem were an afterthought (*Œl*, 1630). It is hardly surprising that the Fate undergoes physiological responses to the physical changes that are associated with the coming of Spring: the melting of ice (l. 226), trees swelling with sap and donning leaves ("écailles," l. 230), nature coming alive. In reaction to this overpowering eruption of nature, the Fate's body also responds. Her heart beats faster and her breast heaves (l. 254–55) as she feels the awakening of her sexuality. She indeed sees herself as an "altar of delights" (l. 262), referring back to the exemplary altar of line 210. Her maternal powers are also awakened, only to be suppressed after she remembers that death will finally take away any life that she might deliver: "Chaque baiser présage une neuve agonie" (l. 266; Every kiss forebodes a fresh agony). Her consciousness here seems to have overcome her instinctual response to nature in a series of refusals between lines 265 and 278. She expresses a feeling of pity for all human life and wonders at the mysterious ways of the gods (l. 279).

Her only response is a tear that wells up within her, the progess of which will be followed throughout the entire section beginning at line 280. We must remember that the Fate was first seen on the rocky shore awakened by someone crying—herself? She seems ever further from resolving the dilemma between the light of lucidity and the potential obscurity of a simpler physical existence. Neither path holds the promise of an answer to her interrogations; neither path seems to lead to any worthwhile destination.

We follow the tear from deep internal grottoes throughout her body as the Fate wonders about its provenance and purpose. Why, for whom, and to what end does her body wander in the dark night (l. 303)? Like the swan with which she identifies herself, she is a captive of her own doubts and fears. She finds a semblance of support as she treads on firm earth, but even this solid, secure foundation turns out to be dangerous. The Fate finds herself on a rocky precipice where she contemplates suicide, the "oubli vorace" (l. 322; voracious forgetting) that might be found at the bottom of the ocean. But even that decisive gesture would not bring an answer to her questions. She finally retreats and implores the earth once again to carry her (l. 324). There would appear to be a temporal break between lines 324 and 325, suggesting that she dozes off or temporarily loses consciousness, only to regain it as the sun rises in the next section.

Lines 325–47

The movement beginning with "Mystérieuse MOI . . . " (Mysterious SELF) inaugurates the second half of the Fate's drama. It is also meant to recall the "Harmonieuse MOI . . . " (l. 102) in one of the multitude of connections that span Valéry's poem. The stars (l. 329; "signes") fade away as the rising sun mirrors itself in the east. In a dual movement, the sun traces a vertical line as it rises while its light brings forth the horizon (l. 332). The young woman here awakes from another sleep as the somber night and high sea of the preceding section give way to dawn, sunlight, and calm sea. Despite the more clement conditions outside, her inner divisions and doubts remain "bitterly the same" (l. 327). Her pure arm, a reminder of the hand in line 4, carries forth the dawn (l. 344) just as the dawn makes her arm apparent (l. 343); this dynamic reciprocity across such a distance gives Valéry's poem a dimension beyond simple exposition or illumination. This awakening and awareness serve only to reveal that she is still prey to her former desires, still plagued by memories. The sea, which she had dreamed of making her tomb, now replies with a universal peal of laughter (l. 347).

Lines 348–60

This short evocation of the archipelago of islands that the Fate first apprehends in the light of dawn also reminds us that Valéry once considered "Iles" as a title for his poem. Let us also remember that Valéry, like Rimbaud, was particularly attracted by the promise of renewal and discovery contained in each new dawn. His *Cahiers* are the fruit of many early mornings spent at his desk writing by the light of his lamp. The description of the islands is, however, limited because the Fate knows them all too well. Valéry stated that his intent was to express some of the weariness that the Fate felt at the prospect of yet another day with little hope of renewal or resolution (*ŒI,* 1630). The islands are cast in the future since their clear existence will only reach its full force once day has arrived. The attention to light and the suggestion that they are divinities of the terrestrial rose and the marine salt (l. 348) can only have been written by someone who had an intimate knowledge of the sea.

The islands will soon be swarming with activity as animals and ideas resume their daily activities. In the predawn haze, the Fate compares the virginal islands to other Fates (l. 358) who, like herself, have splendid flowers on the emerged surfaces but whose feet are anchored deep in the cold water (ll. 357–60). This image can obviously be given a psychological interpretation with the subconscious being the submerged part of the organism while we see only an exposed, conscious part of each individual. Such a line of interpretation, while not contrary to the words of the poem, certainly was not Valéry's intention as he was elaborating his poem.

Lines 361–80

In this short section, the young woman provides a much calmer, more lucid account of her temptation to commit suicide. Her disgust and resolve had been complete. If she had obeyed her will, she would be no more. She had been so close to offering up her despairing, nude body to pure death. Her soul in an instant of total sacrifice had listened to the beating of her heart, but this final gesture did not occur. Such anticipation was vain since the Fate took pity on her own being as she saw herself in the mirror crying over what might have been.

Lines 381–424

These first few lines are the ones that Valéry declared to be closest to his ideal of what he was trying to accomplish in *La Jeune Parque* (*Œl,* 1631). The entire section is a further expansion of the dominant theme of death, with the Fate wondering if she ought not to have gone through with her disdainful plans for suicide. By attaining the pure transparency of death, she would at least have presided over her own end. Rather than her actual demise, the real focus is on the Fate's consciousness and her contemplation of the act. At line 397 begins a striking evocation of the smoke from her funeral pyre ascending into the heavens. She calls on the majestic tree, a favorite symbol of Valéry's suggesting an overreaching gesture spanning earth and sky, human and divine. Was she not, at the opening of the poem, linked to the unknown sky (l. 16)?

Realizing the vanity of these lugubrious thoughts, she decides to turn her back on the idea of death and rather explore the world of the living.

Her mission will be the diametric opposite of what it has been up to now. Like Ariadne, she will follow the thread that will lead to the decisive moment in her past when she had to choose between lucid intelligence and obscure instinct. Régine Pietra has justly insisted on the conflation of memory and consciousness at this decisive moment when the intelligence strives for some lucid comprehension of its own past (Pietra, 465–66). The image of the serpent reappears in her mind at the close of the passage, a reminder of her earlier sensual awakening and a call to follow the sinuous paths by which she has reached her present state.

Lines 425–64

The opening reference to yesterday is the first explicit temporal mark in the poem. This flashback takes the Fate back to the serpent episode at the beginning of the poem when she was betrayed by her senses. The drama of the flesh vanished behind the overpowering need for sleep. Her subconscious took over and carried her away. She wonders now in retrospect how she could have allowed herself to be betrayed, how she could have sacrificed her intellect to the exigencies of her body's desire for dreams and caresses. Human consciousness, born of division, holds also the only hope of reconciliation or, at the very least, comprehension. There is, however, a sort of happiness in this descent (l. 455), even if it may at times seem terrifying or just strange. The final four lines in italics are as incoherent as anything that comes out of a dream-state, although this uncontrolled chaos may not be so bad after all: "Le noir n'est pas si noir" (l. 464; The black [dark?] is not so black [?]). Although Valéry did not share Freud's enthusiasm for dreams as doors to the unconscious, he suggests here the treasures that might come from willing descent into the underworld of sleep and abandon.

Lines 465–512

Here the young Fate awakes and sings the praises of the bed that has been the scene of such contradictory, conflictual feelings. Her corporeal wholeness seems to have triumphed over the arid, sterile intellect, although the poem itself is proof that she has cultivated a consciousness that allows her, despite herself, to recognize the limits of the mind. The forceful evocation of nature in this final passage reminds us and the Fate of the vanity that comes with human illusions of control and superiority.

The body and the mind remain inseparable, even if they continue to be antagonistic forces that require each other's presence. They are here rhythmed according to the sun and the sea. The Fate thus sheds her veil and devotes herself to the rising sun in an affirmation of her total being. The natural world, presented here in magnificent terms with the blowing wind and breaking waves, occupies the final 17 lines in one long, sustained passage. With a sense of awe and humility, the "vierge de sang" (l. 511; blood virgin), a virgin with golden breasts, affirms her harmony with the natural universe by offering herself to the rising sun. This awakening is both a renewal of the Fate's being and a powerful affirmation of life in its many facets. In the warmth and light of the sun, a world of possibilities begins anew.

Chapter Five

Charmes: The Many Voices of the Serpent

On a ôté les bottes plombées, et l'on danse.
(We have shed our boots of lead and can dance.)

Valéry, *Lettres à quelques-uns*, 182

The monumental task of writing *La Jeune Parque* came to an end in 1917. The outcome of that grueling exercise proved to Valéry that he could and should continue his poetic activity. The creative well, which had once appeared dried up, was now primed and ready to yield even greater results. This would lead him to write, as in the epigraph above, that the time had come to shed the boots of lead and to dance. Valéry proceeded to compose a series of original poems, written for the most part between 1917 and 1922, attacking a variety of subject matter, using a wide range of verse forms, exhibiting a virtuoso command of poetic language. Many of the these new poems existed in embryonic form in *La Jeune Parque,* this previous work figuring as a reservoir containing more poems than it could possible produce. True to Valéry's basic precept, a poem's form generally dictates its substance, and the hero of his new poetic adventure would be language itself. The result was the publication of *Charmes* in June 1922, certainly one of the outstanding collections of verse in French literature.

It is interesting to keep in mind that the years during which the majority of these poems were written were also the formative years of the surrealist movement. Apollinaire died in 1918 just as the war was drawing to a close and just as the poetic landscape in France was undergoing profound transformations. Paris would soon become the major pole of the Dada and surrealist artists, attracting Tristan Tzara, André Breton, Louis Aragon, and Philippe Soupault as well as painters such as Pablo Picasso, Max Ernst, Yves Tanguy, and Giorgio de Chirico. Valéry had even suggested the title of the avant-garde review *Littérature,* which was directed by Breton and Soupault and destined for fame. His friendship with Breton would prove short-lived, the future pope of surrealism disapproving of Valéry's election to the Académie française, the elder

Valéry considering that Breton's band of poets was indulging itself in facile scandalmongering. Valéry had never been a proponent of radical, unbridled experimentation, and the 21 poems of *Charmes* remain quite classical in their formal conception and craftsmanship. Evolution, not revolution, would have been his motto. The journal publication of many of these poems as well as the notoriety achieved by *La Jeune Parque* gave Valéry such a reputation that a 1921 poll taken by the review *Connaissance* elected him the greatest living French poet.

Each poem in *Charmes* is a marvel of perfection and originality, playing on the gamut of forms and sounds available to the poet, creating musical effects rarely surpassed in French poetry. They are, in the best sense of the term, music for the mind, utilizing as they do the language of pure poetry as far removed as possible from the mundane, quotidian words of the marketplace. Let us remember that Valéry had once defined a poem as being made up essentially of fragments of "pure poetry" set in the matter of discourse (*Œl*, 1457).

These poems also appear on the whole to be less obscure and more accessible than *La Jeune Parque,* more profoundly original and personal than the *Album* poems, more in touch with the sensuality and mystery of the outside world. It was in his response to the commentary of *Charmes* offered by the philosopher Alain that Valéry launched the critical notion of allowing the reader complete freedom of interpretation (*Œl*, 1509). This would suggest at first glance that readers might be free to attribute whatever meaning they choose to his poetry. Valéry, however, would certainly have scorned extravagant interpretations, and he probably meant more to imply that a poem defies immediate understanding. Whatever a poet might have thought he was saying, the reader has only the words of the poem on which to base his own interpretation. In his written thoughts on the "Cimetière marin" or on Alain's commentary on *Charmes,* Valéry reiterates this notion of the autonomy of verse vis-à-vis its creator (*Œl*, 1496–1507, 1507–12). It cannot be consumed like prose but rather requires repeated readings and constant pondering before it becomes an intimate part of the reader's mental and emotional landscape. Poems are intended to rise from their own ashes under the impulse of each new reader's new interpretation (*Œl*, 1510). When Professor Gustave Cohen in 1928 devoted an entire course at the Sorbonne to a commentary of "Le Cimetière marin," he had one famous student— Valéry himself. We know that the poet was pleased to find that the professor's scholarly exegesis corroborated most of his own interpretations of his most celebrated poem.

The title to the collection has a double meaning: "charm" in the modern sense of a pleasing allure or seductive posture, and the Latin root *carmen, carmina* (chant, poem) suggesting a magic spell or incantation. Valéry often resorted to such etymological meanings in his work. A lifelong proponent of work and craft as opposed to inspiration, he was led in 1941 to add the subtitle *Dudecere carmen,* meaning "to make verse," "to write poetry." In order to remind certain critics who were becoming more and more extravagant in their interpretations, he added the following subtitle in 1942: *Charmes*: (c'est-à-dire: *Poèmes*). Valéry wanted to inform his readers that his poems were, above all, poems and not other forms of discourse that can be used for all manner of personal or philosophical investigation. The form of a poem emerges even before the poem itself, inducing the poet to account for the crucial moment when the words of the poem catch up with the form.

Most of the poems in *Charmes,* in addition to their particular thematic interest, demonstrate a constant preoccupation with the very conditions of their creation. The intimate function of the inner workings of the mind remain here of greater interest than the thoughts that such a mind might produce. *Charmes* was born of the encounter of the inner sensitivity of the poet with the rich outer world. The natural world is anything but banished from his poetry: trees, fruits, sun, and sea abound. These pieces are exercises, like *La Jeune Parque,* but with a constant striving to move the reader at least as much as the poet himself was moved. The wealth of critical attention devoted to this volume attests to its ongoing appeal to readers of poetry the world over.

It would be impossible here to begin to examine each poem in the collection in the depth of detail that it deserves. The bibliography provides ample information to allow for further reading or research beyond the limits of the present study. I have therefore chosen to concentrate on several of the most representative poems, keeping in mind those poems that are most widely accessible to students of French literature.[1]

"Aurore"

Charmes opens most appropriately with a poem to daybreak, "Aurore," like a bridge arching back to the world of the Fate, which closed on just such a moment. Dawn is especially prevalent in Rimbaud's poetry, in which it represents the hope and promise of new beginnings. Valéry himself was an early riser, finding in the early morning light not only a propitious moment for consigning his thoughts to his *Cahiers* but also feeling in that moment the passage and transition that he always admired from one state to another. He follows here the fleeting instants between dreams and waking, those moments of semiconsciousness before intelligence takes over full possession of the self: "Je fais des pas admirables / Dans les pas de ma raison" (ll. 9–10; I take admirable steps / In the steps of my reason). The renewal of movement and energy that comes with wa(l)king prefigures another poem devoted expressly to the subject, "Les Pas."

Words and sensations precede ideas, according to Valéry, since ideas are what he calls "Maîtresses de l'âme" (l. 33; Mistresses of the soul) or "Courtisanes par ennui" (l. 34; Courtiers out of boredom). The poet asks these ideas what they were doing while he was asleep. They respond that they were weaving a web, like spiders, a web of thoughts that will constitute the clear consciousness of day (st. 4–5). In order to exercise his intelligence, he must sweep away this web and attempt to discover his own mind, its images and thoughts (st. 6–7).

"Aurore" ends with a situation Valéry uses elsewhere (cf. "Baignée") where a *naïade* emerges from the water, bringing with her the hope of renewal and self-possession contained in the infinite depths of the pool or the self. The 10-line stanzas allow for a rapid, energetic rhythm, yet full expression of each stage of the poet's emergence from sleep and awakening to the richness of his own mind and the poetic world around him. "Aurore" and "Palme," the last poem in *Charmes,* were originally part of the same poem until Valéry decided to place them at the beginning and end of the entire collection. The prevalent use of the first person makes "Aurore" a very personal poem, although Valéry obviously extends his lesson beyond himself: "L'éveil est bon, même dur!" (l. 72; Waking is good, even if harsh). Always attentive to the senses and the sensual world, he evokes in "Aurore" a privileged moment when the body and the mind strive to conjugate their efforts to reach heightened states of awareness. The intimation of worlds greater and more vast haunts Valéry, whose gaze settles on the richness of a visual, sensual universe yet to be exhausted.

"Au Platane"

The fresh optimism of "Aurore" gives way in "Au Platane" (To the Plane-tree) to the more sobering thought that we do not enjoy the freedom of movement and thought that we so need and desire. Contrary to the "Cantique des colonnes" where there is harmonizing of the mind with the outer, material world, this plane tree will oppose the mind's attempts to seduce its matter. The figure of the plane tree, typical of Valéry's beloved Mediterranean, illustrates the poet's lifelong fascination for trees as exemplary of a certain human condition (e.g., "Palme," *La Jeune Parque,* or the magnificent *Dialogue de l'arbre*). This ode is one of the most melodious poems of *Charmes,* alternating as it does in each quatrain the majestic alexandrine with the halting 6-syllable line. Valéry seizes here on the natural beauty of the tree in order to pursue a prolonged meditation on movement, solitude, sensuality, and language. The opening stanzas contain an ironic reflection on the fate of the plane tree, which, on the one hand, strives towards the heavens but, on the other, remains firmly attached to the "black mother" earth (l. 7). Its leaves and branches may blow in the wind, but its roots, compared to a hydra (l. 18), anchor it firmly in place. All trees know the same fate (st. 5–8) of living separated from their kind, condemned to absence and solitude.

The poet compares them to four young women (l. 26), natural equivalents of the classical columns of the "Cantique des colonnes," and goes on to pursue the question of desire and complicity in sexual terms. The virgin responds to Aphrodite's evening call by an awakening of her body and her senses that is reminiscent of *La Jeune Parque.* Beginning with stanza 11, the winter winds appear and twist and whip the tree, causing it to moan as if to respond to the disorderly voice of the wind. The highly sensual joining of the sky and the tree pressing each other in the act of love creates sound and therefore leads to the emergence of language (ll. 63–64).

Behind the mythological references in the penultimate stanza, the poet reveals his desire to sing the plane tree's plight in his poetry, flattering its "polished body" by immortalizing it with words. The proud tree, however, rebuffs the poet's offer with a resounding and surprising "Non." It prefers to remain an isolated object in the world, even if that means being exposed to the hostile elements like all natural things. The tree would seem to prefer its autonomy, even in harsh solitude, rather than allowing itself to be "captured" in language by the poet forever. This defiant urge to remain oneself rather than be absorbed into the metaphorical, anthropomorphic web of language reminds us of the "Dialogue de l'arbre." Like Tityrus expressing his love for the tree as a tree, the plane tree embraces reality, rough though it be, as preferable to allowing oneself to become, like Lucretius, a "tree of words."

"Cantique des Colonnes"

The "Cantique des Colonnes" (Canticle of the columns) was first published in March 1919 in the inaugural issue of Breton and Soupault's surrealist review, *Littérature.* Despite the classical subject of the temple columns, despite the religious overtones of the canticle, despite the constant parallel between female beauty and architectural perfection, Valéry adroitly avoids the obvious dangers of grandiloquence and oratorical showmanship. Nor should the rapid rhythm obtained here by the six-syllable line obscure the profound sense of harmony that Valéry obtains. Poetry, music, dance, and architecture all unite in this hymn to the classical, Mediterranean ideal of perfection. Valéry, in "Paradoxe sur l'architecte" (1891) and the Socratic dialogue *Eupalinos* (1924), numerous times throughout his life expresses his fascination for architecture as a formal art. The poet, like the architect, works with materials that are found, not created. His task is to construct harmonious arrangements of stones or words that will appeal to our aesthetic sense. The speaker who addresses the columns in this poem recognizes them for what they are—man-made objects that have projected into the material world an ideal of perfection that came from the architect's mind. The very visual layout of the 18 stanzas on the page forms a column when observed from a distance. The organizing principle throughout the poem will be the comparison between the classical column and a female figure: for example, the "chapeaux" (hats) in line 2 echo the "chapiteaux" (capitals) that sit atop a classical column. Rarely has Valéry so perfectly expressed his passion for music and architecture, marrying them in a controlled, proportioned work of art.

The meditative, intimate tone is set by the poet's address in lines 1 and 5, "Douces colonnes," in which he softens by his words the hard marble of the columns. The columns are personified and made to sing as if oblivious to their own weight, thus giving full force to the musical quality of their voice. Theirs is, however, not a solemn hymn but more an ode to joy and fulfillment (odes, in ancient Greece, were originally meant to be sung).

Their birth is detailed in stanzas 6–7 as they emerged from the quarry and the sculptor's chisel. Much attention will be paid to their anatomies in subsequent stanzas—eyes, toes, nose, knees. They become alive, vital entities that remain from a time when gods ruled the earth from their heavenly seat. The time of such divinities has passed, leaving the columns to bask in the consummate pleasure of the "honey-colored god," the sun (l. 52). For the poet, these "Filles des nombres d'or" (l. 49; Ladies of the golden mean), embody a mathematical perfection that is reminiscent of Pythagoras's belief that the universe was ordered by certain underlying mathematical principles. The sun's daily caress does not, however, seduce these "incorruptible sisters" (l. 57), who have known other loves and who have managed to march through time without succumbing to the vanity of their charms. This can best be attributed to their self-awareness of their splendor and beauty. This constant search for perfection, whether in poetry, nature, or the arts, leads Valéry here to a divine meditation on the creator and his craft. The result is a perfect harmonizing of form and matter that enchants the ear and excites the intellect.

"L'Abeille," "Les Grenades," and "Les Pas"

Before examining the longer poems of *Charmes,* let us remember that Valéry excelled in the short, concentrated poem of which we can point out three superior examples: "L'Abeille" (The Bee), "Les Grenades" (The Pomegranates), and "Les Pas" (Steps). In addressing the blonde bee in "L'Abeille," the woman deplores her languid state and entreats the insect to sting her into action—better a beneficial albeit painful sting than a slow, suffering loss of desire. This appeal can be situated at two levels, erotic and poetic, since her desire to be awakened can be from a lack of love or from a period of artistic sterility. Let us remember that the Fate, in the sensual Primavera section of *La Jeune Parque,* likewise asks a bee for a "prompt" awakening to the light of intelligence (ll. 250–54). Valéry controls the rhythm of the eight-syllable lines through a skillful utilization of punctuation, inverted word order, and unusual rhyme scheme. The quatrains with their plodding, feminine rhymes give way to notable acceleration in the tercets with their three masculine rhymes. Several commentators have also pointed out the *préciosité* in this sonnet.[2]

"Les Grenades" is another octosyllabic sonnet but with a more regular development around the central theme of the pomegranate. This Mediterranean fruit is depicted with the richness and vibrancy of a Cézanne still life. The whole poem is based on an analogy between the grains of the ripe, bursting pomegranate and the brain cells contained within the human skull. Their explosion under the impulse of the sun or the richness of ideas leads initially to an outward movement. This will be followed by a look inward to that eternal subject of fascination for Valéry—the intricate workings of the mind and its "secrète architecture" (l. 14; secret architecture). He may be suggesting how the mind, like the pomegranate, can expand to yield "rubies" and "gems" when the force of poetic movement is such that it can no longer be contained within its shell. As with a fruit that must die before sowing its seeds to produce other fruits, the poem resists expansion into a definitive form that might bring about its metaphorical death. Such a transformation is nevertheless the condition of future form and life, as Valéry suggests in stanza 5 of "Le Cimetière marin" in which the fruit melts, thereby assuring the life of the body that it nourishes.

"Les Pas" captures a moment of anticipation, a moment in time that prefigures a commencement such as with the dawn of "Aurore." These advancing footsteps have been interpreted as the onset of poetic inspiration or, on a more sensual level, as the arrival of the poet's beloved. Valéry himself, objecting to some of the more fanciful interpretations of his poetry (and despite his own stated belief that readers have the right to attribute their own meaning to a poem), wrote in 1944 that "Les Pas" is a purely "sentimental" poem and not a symbol about inspiration (*CII*, 1054). In four balanced quatrains, each composed of octosyllabic verses that swing like a pendulum, Valéry evokes that most dramatic of moments—the moment *before* the moment he awaits. Contrary to the refusal of the plane tree to join forces with the poet, this poem of steps evokes a rhythm for which the poet must find words that will embody the moment of anticipation. That the poem deals foremost with the theme of waiting for love cannot be denied; what this means beyond the lyrical expression of tenderness is less clear. It seems that the awareness of love, the most mysterious and complex of sentiments, is at the very least analogous to consciousness becoming conscious of itself, a favorite Valérian trope. "Les Pas" therefore would express that poetic moment between acts past and present and before future acts have substituted themselves for the present. The "naked feet" (l. 8) or the puckered-up "lips" that nourish the poet with kisses (st. 3) are perfectly complementary with the "tender" (l. 13) act of poetry. Although the kisses of stanza 3 are intended for his mind ("A l'habitant de mes pensées"), the last stanza provides a perfect conflation of the heart with the steps, justifying Valéry's insistence on the sentimental, sensual thrust of his poem. This focus on a single image in a short, concentrated verse form counterbalances the more sustained poems of *Charmes*.

"Fragments du Narcisse"

Charmes contains four such long pieces: "Fragments du Narcisse," "La Pythie," "Ebauche d'un serpent" and the famous "Cimetière marin," all of which are closer to *La Jeune Parque* not only in their length but in their aspirations. Valéry thought that a poem was built around a few exceptional lines that were gifts of the gods. Within its 316 lines, "Fragments du Narcisse" contains a great number that haunt the reader's memory and have been characterized as combining the perfection of Racine with the density of Mallarmé.[3]

The epigraph from Ovid asks the pertinent question, "Why have I seen a thing?" This applies to the self that Narcissus sees reflected in the water, the self that he wishes to join to the detriment of all other relations. To see himself, to know himself, is to perish. For having preferred himself to Echo, for having refused to embrace life, he is condemned to a supreme solitude and certain death. Yet unlike the Narcissus of the *Album* poem, this one is a more dynamic, dramatic character whose destiny will be rendered all the more bitter because of the haunting words of the poet. His quest for self-knowledge, his contemplation of the inner self, and his desire to unite the irreconcilable division of his being lead Narcissus to the disturbing conclusion that there is nothing behind his image. The impossibility of the full possession of oneself, the challenge of solitude, the inability to reconcile our image and our self, while devastating for Narcissus, will become a poetic wellspring for Valéry. The pure egotism of Monsieur Teste finds a variation in Narcissus, who here becomes aware of the absence of any purpose to the search for self-knowledge, except in the pure act of searching. This tragic awareness is fittingly rendered in the magnificent verses that Valéry instills with depth and vigor.

The poem is divided into three parts written at different times. Certain lines from the earlier "Narcisse parle" are included in this new offering. Narcissus opens his monologue with a memorable if ambiguous line: "Que tu brilles enfin, terme pur de ma course!" (How you shine at last, pure end to my journey!). The scene is immediately dramatic after Narcissus (in anticipation of discovering himself) has accomplished his long journey through a forest just as night descends upon the scene. His quest has led him at last to the pool in which he will discover and contemplate the image of himself reflected in the mirror of the water's surface. He knows that his success will be his demise, and he therefore implores the wood nymphs and the creatures around him not to cause even the slightest ripple in the pool. The descending twilight distracts him momentarily from his infatuation with his image in several lines transposed almost literally from "Narcisse parle" (ll. 35–39). This distraction will be short-lived, however, as Narcissus returns to the love of self and to his cruel solitude (l. 41). He loses himself momentarily in the rapt contemplation of a sunset. The eight lines beginning "O douceur de survivre à la force du jour" (l. 48; O how sweet to have survived the force of day) were proclaimed by Valéry himself as the most difficult to write and as the most perfect in his entire body of poetry (*Œl,* 1673). They came closest to his ideal of pure poetry precisely because they achieved musical harmony while remaining untainted with ideas.

But in this pure water where herds have never drunk (l. 60), Narcissus finds not calm but death. Knowledge of self translates here as knowledge of death. His disarray will result in a less regular, less harmonious rhyme scheme with alternating rhymes and octosyllabic verse in several stanzas. The silence that had thus far prevailed in the forest is broken by the evocation of Echo (ll. 94 *et seq.*), the woman whose love Narcissus had refused and which led to his current plight. The surrounding nature reminds him of his presence and of his impossible union with himself. The sight of a naked fiancé, "Délicieux démon désirable et glacé!" (l. 114; Delicious demon desirable and icy!), only heightens his suffering and *ennui.* The instinctive pleasures of his handsome body are no more, reminded as he is of his own division: "Et que la nuit déjà nous divise, O Narcisse, / Et glisse entre nous deux le fer qui coupe un fruit!" (ll. 126–27; And night already divides us, O Narcissus, / And slips between the two of us the blade that cuts the fruit!). He is a "naked slave" to his desire (l. 135), knowing that if he yields to it, he will perish; if he resists it, he will be forever unsatisfied. Narcissus declares proudly in the last section of Part 1 that no other being, neither nymph nor young woman, could rival his attraction for his own image. The mythological character has become a self-conscious creator of a myth of which he is the actor and spectator—the myth of the inexhaustible self (l. 148).

The second fragment of the Narcissus poem effects a shift in perspective towards the fountain and away from the monologic voice of Narcissus. We are given to see what the fountain mirrors to others. Like a constant presence, the fountain knows all and sees all: "Astres, roses, saisons, les corps et leurs amours!" (l. 159; Stars, roses, seasons, the bodies and their loves!). In exemplary fashion, the central theme of this whole central section is introduced in line 171: "L'amour passe et périt . . . (Love passes and perishes . . .). Valéry explores here in graphic detail the physical passion of the two lovers who, intertwined, form a "dying monster" of love (l. 187). If only this were the supreme expression of human activity, Valéry seems to say. Yet his answer would be that the obsession with sexuality hampers the development of the intellect and never truly satisfies the body or the spirit. The same lovers who abandoned themselves to Eros on the banks of the pool will return later to sigh from nostalgia at what was theirs and is no more.

The romantic theme of love, time, and destiny is familiar to readers of Lamartine's "Le Lac" or Hugo's "Tristesse d'Olympio." Contrary to his predecessors, Valéry does not afford his lovers the consolation of a beautiful natural setting. The sea breeze and the scent of the rose in the air torment memory more than they appease desire (ll. 207–08). The memory of their passion lost forever is a source of infinite suffering. Narcissus resumes his monologue in a lyrical passage made up of alexandrines and octosyllabic verse:

> Mais moi, Narcisse aimé, je ne suis curieux
>   Que de ma seule essence;
> Tout autre n'a pour moi qu'un cœur mystérieux,
>   Tout autre n'est qu'absence. (ll. 231–34)

> But I, beloved Narcissus, am curious
>   Only of my own essence;
> All others are for me but mysterious hearts,
>   All else is but absence.

Given the vain failure of the lovers to unite durably and harmoniously into one, is this not further proof that his love of self is the only valid path? His moment of hope is dashed as soon as he realizes that union with his image is impossible. Love of self is as illusory as love of another. It extends here to his bitter disappointment at the idea that he can never join that other part of himself that he sees reflected in the water. Solitude and separation are his lot.

The third and final section of "Fragments du Narcisse" pushes Narcissus's desire to further reaches and to its disastrous conclusion. In a curious reversal of roles that proves especially effective in dramatic terms, it is his reflection in the pool that now seems to want to seduce him. Despite the impending menace of death, he leans closer to declare his love: "J'aime . . . J'aime! . . . " (l. 274), asking what one can love besides oneself. His body alone is all that separates him from death (l. 276). After a line of periods that divides the section, Narcissus addresses a passionate plea or prayer to the gods: stop the course of time, make the day last longer so that he can contemplate his image even more fully in the light. In a highly sensual passage, he admires his body, the calm torso that is purer than that of any woman (l. 290), likening it to a temple that separates him from divinity (l. 293–94). Narcissus realizes that if he moves, if he breaks the immobility to which the water has condemned him, he will in essence be destroying himself. His final gesture, the kiss he lays on his image, is an attempt at union with himself, which will seal his destiny. The final verse is left fittingly without a responding rhyme, without the reply of Echo. Love has broken Narcissus and his image through this last desperate move, which is a form of self-destruction. Self-love and self-knowledge reveal themselves to be impossible ideals that lead to the annihilation of the body and spirit. The perfect union of the lover with the object of his love can result only in death. Contrary to the energetic reaffirmation of life that we find in *La Jeune Parque* or "Le Cimetière marin," this Narcissus poem ends on a somber, despairing note not unlike two of the other major poems of *Charmes* that we can examine, "La Pythie" and "Ebauche d'un serpent."

"La Pythie"

These poems are contemporary, composed at least in part during the years 1916–1917 when Valéry was finishing *La Jeune Parque* (line 165 of this earlier poem contains a direct reference to the "Pythonisse"). "La Pythie" remains one of the most vigorous and most enigmatic of Valéry's poems. The two female figures, the Fate and the Pythia, bear some resemblances, not the least of which is the way in which they have been bitten by the serpent of self-discovery. Valéry himself, in 1937, places them together as examples of the "physiological sense of consciousness" (*CI,* 289).

We know that "La Pythie" grew out of a challenge by Pierre Louÿs, who thought that Valéry had not yet shown that he could master the octosyllabic verse form perfected by Victor Hugo. The dedication to Louÿs is his reply to the challenge. As elsewhere, the content of the poem evolved out of the form, or more exactly, a line that found its way one day into Valéry's head: "Pâle, profondément mordu" (l. 5; Pale, profoundly bitten). Such "found" or "given" verses stand in opposition to "calculated" or "constructed" verse and invite the poet to craft them into more perfect entities. In this case, the rest of the poem was written around this key line, keeping the rich sounds in *p* and *m* (for instance, ll. 11–12; "Sur le mur, son ombre démente / Où domine un démon majeur") and weaving it into a series of 23 ten-line stanzas with a regular rhyme scheme: *ababccdeed*.

Valéry turned once again to a classical subject. The Pythia was a young virgin taken to be a priestess at the oracle at Delphi. She would sit perched over the vapors emanating from a crack in the earth until she went into a trance and thereby became a medium through which the gods could reveal the future. Coiled around her three-legged stool was the serpent, Pytho, that was slain by Apollo, the god who subsequently established the oracle at Delphi.

The first three stanzas of the poem evoke the Pythia's torment in graphic, physiological terms: her body is twisted in violent spasms, demented, resembling an animal more than a human. The priestess takes over in stanza 3 and deplores her cruel suffering. During her trance, the gods invade her body and, through this violation, she becomes a medium for their message. This will also make her tragically aware of her duality. She has lost "her mystery" (l. 28) as the gods inflict upon her the terrible suffering that is supposed to fecundate her with divine inspiration. Her only crime, she cries out, is having lived (ll. 51–52). By way of reaction, not unlike the Fate, she takes refuge in memories of happier times from the past.

The serenity of stanzas 9–10 contains delicate, sensuous memories of her past state of bliss before everything was interrupted by the oracle. Like Narcissus, she relished in her sensuality and total being without questioning her nature. In a passage reminiscent of *La Jeune Parque,* the Pythia wonders why the serpent would have chosen to sow the seeds of evil in a virgin's body (st. 13). In another sequence reminiscent of *La Jeune Parque* tears well up and flow through her like rivers (st. 18–19) as the prophecy, depicted as a "thick herd of horrors" (l. 203), rushes to be expulsed from her now sullied body into the light of day.

The final two stanzas mark the return of calm, and the deliverance from suffering by the message that the Pythia articulates. The heavens finally open up and allow her to speak with a feeble, new voice. These two sections are couched in terms that are sufficiently ambiguous so as to allow several interpretations as to who is speaking in the last stanza. For P. O. Walzer, we do not know the lesson of her oracle, and it is the poet who takes over the discourse.[4] James Lawler takes the opposite view that it is the prophetess herself who delivers the wisdom that has been acquired (Lawler, 133).[5] It is also dramatically possible to read this discourse as being pronounced by the mirthful pontiff evoked in line 216. Christine Crow takes a more cautious route and affirms that this final stanza underscores the "potential self-referentiality of language," which, as she points out, is one of Valéry's constant preoccupations.[6]

While it is tempting to see this final section as a conclusion to the Pythia's long monologue, it requires some imagination to accept as possible such a sudden return to lucidity after such an exhausting struggle with herself and the gods. If the "august voice" (l. 227) belongs to the Pythia, it has undergone a dramatic recovery after such an ordeal. On the other hand, it stands contradictory to almost all of Valéry's principles to see such a powerful, lucid profession of faith resulting from such raging loss of self. That would be tantamount to recognizing the virtues of uncontrolled inspiration. The poem's message comes from the simple fact that language, from whatever source, has won its combat with demented, hysterical raving. That the Pythia is endowed with that most human of qualities, "Honneur des Hommes, Saint LANGAGE" (l. 221), seems obvious from the poem itself. Whether the final stanza is her discourse remains another matter.

One can nevertheless discover here a poetic principle whereby the intellect, through arduous work, fashions poetry out of the unwrought ravings of an undisciplined soul. Valéry, who frequently recognized that Romantic inspiration might serve as a starting point that could lead to Classical rigor (cf. *CII*, 1185), stands resolutely in favor of the processes of intellectual effort that will yield pure poetry.

"L'Ebauche d'un serpent"

"L'Ebauche d'un serpent," (The Sketch of a Serpent) contemporary to "La Pythie" and *La Jeune Parque,* uses the snake image of self-knowledge in even more explicit fashion. Whereas "La Pythie" refers to classical Greece, Valéry makes use here of the biblical story of Satan's temptation of Eve in Paradise, one of the rare times Valéry turns to Christian mythology or lore. The poem is dedicated to Henri Ghéon, a minor dramatist and poet, close to the founding group of the *Nouvelle Revue Française,* who was involved in the wave of conversions to Catholicism that swept through the literary world in the early years of the twentieth century. The figure of the serpent appears several times in the poems of this period—*La Jeune Parque,* "La Pythie," "L'Ebauche d'un serpent"— and also appears on the colophon designed by Valéry himself, which represents a serpent entwined around a key that is set between the initials *P* and *V.* It is consistently a representation of knowledge in the three major poems in which it appears. In a curious notation from 1944, Valéry dreams of a snake chewing on its own tail until it has its head in its jaws. Is this what is meant by a "theory of knowledge," he wonders (*Paul Valéry vivant*, 276)? Knowledge, especially of self, does not go without pain and torment.

The 31 stanzas, all dizains, are not nearly as regular as those of "La Pythie" in terms of rhyme scheme, caesura, or tone. Indeed, Valéry here plays on the gamut of possibilities available to the serpent—mocking irony, grotesque exaggeration, cajoling lies. The serpent's monologue is punctuated by a striking number of exclamation points and by rhetorical and poetic devices that modulate the tone of his discourse. Valéry himself declared in a letter to the philosopher Alain that he had concentrated his efforts on the difficult task of indicating "changes in tonality." He goes on to admit that, in order to accomplish this goal, he exaggerated on purpose the assonances and alliterations (*Lettres à quelques-uns*, 184). Every strophe contains examples of this sometimes elegant, sometimes heavy-handed striving for effect:

> La splendeur de l'azur aiguise
> Cette guivre qui me déguise. (ll. 15–16)

> The splendor of the azure sharpens
> This serpent that disguises me.

Or these lines with the insistent repetition of *d* sounds and the awkward position of the article *les* at the end of the line, which were singled out by the poet himself as evidence of his burlesque intent (*ŒI*, 1682):

> Dore, langue! dore-lui les
> Plus doux des dits que tu connaisses! (ll. 181–82)

> Sweeten, tongue! sweeten for him the
> Sweetest of words that you know.

As might be expected, the serpent makes prevalent use of *s* and *i* sounds to suggest hissing. The phonetic texture of "L'Ebauche d'un serpent" is among the richest in Valéry's *œuvre*. The serpent, not entirely unlike the poet, measures success by his ability to manipulate language and move his listeners to believe even his lies. Valéry cannot completely condemn the serpent's craft without pointing a like finger at himself.

The serpent, sometimes like the poet, can even fall prey to the seduction of his own words. It is perhaps this extravagant manipulation of language that made this James Joyce's favorite among the poems of Valéry that he knew.

The poem opens with the serpent wrapped around a branch of a tree in the garden of Eden, delivering a resounding attack on God's world. In a clever parody of philosophical argumentation, the serpent addresses the sun beginning in stanza 3, thanking it for its help as an ally in deceiving humanity. The sun creates an illusion of clarity that makes a reality out of fiction. Out of vanity or pride, God created the world and thereby compromised his absolute purity:

> Que l'univers n'est qu'un défaut
> Dans la pureté du Non-être! (ll. 29–30)

> That the universe is but a defect
> In the purity of the Non-being!

The imperfect universe resulted therefore from a mistake, an error in judgment that broke the ideal unity that existed before the creation. It was not pure love, but love of self, that led God to create the world, this act of creation being a double-edged event. God himself acquired knowledge of his existence at that moment; the irreversible division had taken place. The serpent goes on to explain how he stalks his prey, infiltrating pure hearts and spreading evil (st. 11–12).

Stanzas 13 to 27 recount the serpent's favorite exploit—the biblical episode of the temptation of Eve. She is depicted as a beautiful nude (st. 14) and the serpent's ploy will be to weave for her a garment of words (st. 18). Beginning with the prolonged sequence of direct speech in stanza 21, he uses all the tricks and ruses that language affords to convince her of her freedom to eat of the forbidden fruit. The slow awakening of Eve as she begins to be moved by the serpent's discourse is related in sexually-charged terms until the seduction is complete and she has been integrated into the tree of knowledge (st. 27). By yielding to her curiosity, the interminable process of our insatiable desire for knowledge, a constant source of wonder for Valéry, comes alive. Eve and her successors will thereafter know death, despair, and disorder (ll. 299–300) as they attempt to gain complete knowledge of self and world. This nihilistic ending is saved only by the final three lines, which proclaim the pride of human endeavor and the spirit of revolt. The giant tree of knowledge and its serpent have grown to become the equals of God. This victory could also be considered to be that of the poet who has pushed his art to its highest point of perfection.

"Le Cimetière marin"

"Le Cimetière marin" (The Seaside Cemetery) is Valéry's most famous poem, the one piece read by every student of French poetry the world over. It has also been translated into almost every language, including the version of a retired colonel who considered it difficult to understand and proceeded to translate it into French (Walzer, 323)! Valéry noted in 1945, with some obvious pleasure, that he had recently learned about a black farmhand in Louisiana, "fou de poésie" (mad about poetry), who knew it by heart (*CI,* 317). He also added that he did not know it himself by heart.

The poem has been analyzed, dissected, and interpreted as have few other poems in any national literature. Among the myriad comments on the "Cimetière marin" is Valéry's own, written after attending the explication given by Professor Gustave Cohen in his course at the Sorbonne in 1933 ("Au Sujet du *Cimetière marin,*" *ŒI,* 1496–1507). The poet's own comments remain quite vague, however, so as to avoid dictating any single, narrow interpretation.

The poem is certainly his most personal, most lyrical effort, in large part because the setting of the poem is a real site—the cemetery that overlooks his beloved Mediterranean port of Sète. Valéry's tomb even bears the last two lines of the first stanza expressing the calm and serenity of his final resting place above the changing sea. It is perhaps the personal nature of the subject matter, the meditation of the pure self on the surrounding world, the controlled composition of a poet completely conscious of himself and his art that explain the exceptional nature of the poem.

As we have come to expect with Valéry, "Le Cimetière marin" was inspired not by an idea or an image, but by a rhythm that Valéry found one day in his mind. It was the four-plus-six rhythm of the decasyllable, the 10-syllable verse that had been used in the first great work written in medieval French, *La Chanson de Roland.* Interestingly enough, Valéry himself qualifies it as "dantesque" (*ŒI,* 1504), perhaps to reinforce the universal dimension of the death theme that pervades both works. Despite periodic use in poetry, this metrical form had fallen into disfavor since the Renaissance poets had imposed the sonnet as the preferred style for noble verse. In order to retain some of the force and majesty of the more popular alexandrine, Valéry by and large respects the caesura after the fourth or sixth syllable, thus making half of each line in his poem a regular alexandrine hemistich. The 24 stanzas are all made up of six lines with a regular rhyme scheme: *aabccb*. Such was the framework for which Valéry had to discover the substance since, in his process, form preceded sounds, which preceded words. The decasyllabic verse form was, in the poet's own words, an "empty rhythmic figure" (*ŒI*, 1503). It was only once these formal considerations had been resolved that Valéry began to explore the memories and reflections associated with that particular spot above the sunbathed Mediterranean shore that would become the thematic core of his poem. He insists, however, on the fact that the rhythm of the verse led to the choice of a monologue that would be both personal and universal in its form and content (*ŒI*, 1504).

His long piece was apparently begun in 1915 and might today have a very different form had it not been for a fortuitous event that Valéry recounts in his "Au Sujet du *Cimetière marin.*" Jacques Rivière, literary director of the *Nouvelle Revue Française,* paid a visit to Valéry one afternoon in 1920 and found him working on his long poem, revising sections, changing words, and even rearranging whole stanzas. Upon reading the poem, Rivière persuaded Valéry to let him publish it shortly thereafter, which effectively cast the poem in its "definitive" form (*ŒI*, 1500). "Le Cimetière marin" appeared in the June 1920 issue of the *N.R.F.* before becoming a part of *Charmes* two years later.

The epigraph from Pindar was a late addition and can be translated, "O, my dear soul, do not aspire to immortal life, but rather exhaust the range of possibilities." Valéry thereby announces a prolonged and intricate meditation on life and death, immobility and movement, being and knowledge—all themes that are constants in his poetry and thought. The first stanza inaugurates the serene yet dynamic contemplation of the sea from the cemetery above. The surface of the water below, dotted with sails, becomes a tranquil rooftop on which white doves strut. This unusual image created some consternation among early readers of the poem. The noonday sun, like a higher deity, bathes the scene in light and gives existence to the eternal sea. The gods bestow on the spectator a reward in allowing him to contemplate this scene of peace and tranquility. The rounded, rolling nasals and *m* sounds contribute to the atmosphere of intense calm that reigns here. The repeated *p* and *t* sounds punctuate the stanza like the tides of the sea below.

It is important to point out that the poet has not yet identified the speaker in this anonymous preamble, which thereby takes on a general, universal context. This generality is further accentuated by the evocation of pure sensations and observations; the mention of thought ("pensée," l. 5) contains, nevertheless, a germ of division since it stands in contrast to the eternal calm of the gods (l. 6). In other words, human consciousness is already at work in the most imperceptible ways, even against the background of such a stable scene.

This feeling of pure communion with some higher being or reality continues into stanza 2 where the vision of a grander, more absolute universe is suggested by the glistening diamonds that are the sun reflecting off the sea. This placid scene of total identification between spectator and spectacle is echoed in the repetition of the association between purity and work ("pur travail," l. 7; "Ouvrages purs," l. 11). The suggestion that the sun might come to rest in an abyss (l. 10) contains a foreshadowing of divisions yet to come, even though the observer is absorbed for now in the present brightness and harmony of the scene. In an intimation of eternity, time seems to stand still and true knowledge depends even more on bringing our senses in tune with the universal force that *is* around us (l. 12). Could this be the work of an "eternal cause" (l. 11) of divine stature by which individual consciousness and universal consciousness harmonize in a timeless coexistence?

Stanza 3 aligns several images that are the treasures of the sea. In an astute transition, the poet associates this wealth with the contemplation of his own soul. The sea becomes the temple to Minerva, goddess of wisdom and the arts, which conceals riches that cannot be seen by the casual observer. It is like the eye in that respect, which is often referred to as the mirror of a person's soul. This temple, a "mass of calm," serves also to represent a work of architecture, usually associated with perfect construction (cf. "Cantique des colonnes"), that will be reflected by the "edifice in the soul" (l. 17). The tile-covered roof of the sea (l. 18), like the temple, like the soul, thus contains secret treasures of unknown shape and value.

The temple of wisdom becomes the temple of time in stanza 4. The poet, now identified by a first-person subject pronoun, rejoices in that moment that is an eternity when his consciousness is divine. A single sigh can contain all eternity (l. 19). His look out over the timeless sea is also a look into himself. The poet's disdain for the changing universe is underscored by the insistent alliteration in *s* found in the last two lines of stanza 4. These first four stanzas thus form a coherent unit by way of which the poet, who climbs to the heights of the cemetery overlooking the eternal sea below, has managed to gain awareness of his awareness, only to be faced with the thought of mortality and immobility as inextricably linked to life and movement.

The rapt immobility of the first four stanzas gives way in stanza 5 to the poet's human consciousness of movement and change. In a striking metaphor, the sensual fruit "melts" into pure pleasure as its form changes and "dies." Death is directly mentioned here as an acceptable price to pay for the privilege of knowing life. "Je hume ici ma future fumée" (l. 28; I breathe here my future smoke) suggests how the imperfect being lives and thereby is consumed by time and change; his body will be reduced to smoke and ashes. The motif of change continues in stanza 6 with the poet addressing the sky, the absolute, unified being, in order to affirm his human change. The sight of his shadow passing over the sepulchers of the dead has reminded him of the vanity of his wish to join the immobile, immortal forces. In his heightened awareness of self, the poet asks the superior being to look at him (l. 31 and again l. 41) as he moves in the human dimensions of time and space. Consciousness here has become a mirror since, as suggested in stanza 7, the light of the sun exists only by contrast with the mournful world of shadows. The eye, a crucial image up to now, invites the sun to look at itself in the eye of the beholder (l. 41). This goes one step further in the process of separation from the eye imploring the sky to look at the changes that the observer was undergoing in stanza 6.

In stanza 8, the self has become completely self-absorbed, aware of its division and its mortality. He is like the poem that awaits to be written, caught between pure potentiality ("le vide") and fulfilled creation ("l'événement pur," l. 45). The self is like a well whose depth and content are not known and whose bottom is never measured until reached. The space of the soul cannot be known except by the echo obtained from the unknown limits of the self. Complete self-knowledge seems always to be put off until some future time. Like Narcissus, he will only possess himself completely in death.

Stanza 9 inaugurates the long central section of the poem devoted to death. The poet returns to the sea and the sun, although his attention is devoted here to the cemetery and the dead. His eyes are closed (l. 51) for several reasons: because of the bright light reflected from the gulf, out of introspection and knowledge, and perhaps so as not to see death too plainly. A spark of thought for the departed takes on a personal tone since Valéry knew some of the people buried in the cemetery at Sète, including his own family ("mes absents," l. 54).

In stanza 10, the poet declares his admiration for this place of peace and calm, where marble tombs shimmer in the brilliant sunlight yet cover over a world of shades. He appreciates the calm order of the cemetery linked with the sea that, like a loyal dog, sleeps on top of the tombs (l. 60).

The canine metaphor continues in stanza 11 wherein the poet entreats the "chienne splendide" (splendid female dog) to be vigilant and to chase away any of humankind's traditional consolations in the face of death. This stanza, with its pastoral, Christian imagery, clearly underscores the agnosticism of Valéry. It is easy to understand here why Valéry specifies doves, symbols of the Holy Spirit, instead of sea gulls or other more common marine fowl. The rhyme endings in -ombes and -eux recall those in stanza 1, a technique that Valéry uses frequently and which requires the reader to connect verses across great distances. In stanza 12, he affirms that such beliefs are only signs of spiritual laziness (l. 67). The décor inside the cemetery is one of waste and desolation—an insect (ant or cicada?) scratches the dry earth; everything is burnt and undone.

The lucid poet nevertheless realizes that he must accept this consciousness of absence with calm and serenity. In stanza 13, the protagonist admits that the dead themselves are probably well off in their graves. The immobile sun of the first stanza reappears as a reminder of how mortal beings are creatures of change destined to perish; however, the poet possesses the thought of the sun along with the realization of his own mortality. Man is the imperfection in the otherwise perfect diamond (l. 81) since he is able to conceive of perfection and doubt, eternity and time, death and life. The dead have already sided with the forces of immobility, suggesting by contrast that the poet may still resist for some time the path of resignation.

Stanzas 15 and 16, reminiscent of Villon or Baudelaire, contain a macabre, physiological evocation of the decay of the dead, whose bodies go the way of all flesh. They have been transformed into something else, leading the poet to wonder either about what they were or what they have become. The second of these stanzas is not devoid of erotic connotations and follows a rhythm that is surprisingly rapid for people who are not in a hurry to go anywhere. The poet reaffirms the lessons of his meditation by acknowledging that everything must pass and that life is short, whereas death is long.

After the body, it is the soul that will fall prey to death and degradation in stanza 17. All human activity, however noble, however venerable, is ephemeral. The idealized realm of Plato is mocked here as a pleasing illusion without foundation. Valéry takes a jab at our ability to believe such nonsense: "Allez! Tout fuit!" (l. 101; Come now! Everything flees!). Even the hope of immortality will die (l. 102).

This lesson is continued in stanza 18 in mocking horror. All our hopes are but pretty lies or pious ruses (l. 106), leading only to an empty skull and a cosmic laugh (l. 108). Valéry, who decorated his Parisian apartment in 1894 with a reproduction of Ligier Richier's skeleton, obviously has not forgotten the lesson of man's vanity and powers of imagination in the face of death. Immortality of the body is no more likely than immortality of the soul.

Stanzas 19 and 20 return to the subject of human consciousness and thought. The real worm eats not only at the dead who lie peacefully under their slabs of marble, but also at the living. This worm is, of course, thought itself. The *v* sounds in stanza 19 connect the word *ver* (worm) with the word *vie* (life). The gnawing worm, whether love of self or hatred of self (l. 115), finds fertile ground in the poet, follows him even in his sleep, reminds him constantly of his mortal condition. As suggested in the final line of stanza 20, the poet "lives" because he "belongs" to the living worm that, like thought, is inseparable from the body on which it thrives. "What does it matter," he asks, that the worm "sees, desires, thinks and touches" (l. 118). It follows here in abbreviated form the process that leads from perception to sensation, which is, as we now know, the vital trajectory in life and poetry. This realization will prove necessary to his acceptance of life and movement in the final four stanzas. The worm, perhaps an avatar of the serpent images so important to Valéry, appears here as a reminder of the fate to which the poet has been awakened. Consciousness is both a source of torment as well as the only viable response to that affliction.

In stanza 21, Valéry uses the sophisms of the pre-Socratic philosopher, Zeno of Elea, to show how denial of movement leads to denial of life. Valéry's interest in Zeno goes back well before the composition of the "Cimetière marin" since there is a 1902 entry in the *Cahiers* that refers to the sophistry made possible by language (*CI*, 484–85). Zeno, a fifth-century Greek philosopher, asserted that there was nothing beyond the finite, motionless world that we know and that motion, time and space were all illusions. In the first of his paradoxes used here, an arrow follows a trajectory that is a motionless line; by following that line, the arrow cannot truly fly because it would remain stuck in a fragment of time that can be infinitely subdivided, thus preventing it from ever reaching its target. Likewise, fleet-footed Achilles could never catch a rabbit because each step they take would only reduce the distance that separates them without ever completely closing it. Mention of the sun (l. 125) not only serves to remind us of the outside scene that was so important earlier in the poem and will soon reappear, but it also creates the shadow of the tortoise, which gives the false appearance of non-movement. Likewise, we cannot detect the subtle, imperceptible movements of the mind, yet we know that it is active and alive. The very fact that we are conscious of it proves that it is functioning. According to Valéry himself, this use of the absurd reasoning of a philosopher was meant to underscore the cruel separation between *being* and *knowing* that results from being conscious of consciousness (*Œl*, 1506). The sound of the arrow vibrating through the air proves its movement and the fact that it kills me is undeniable, even if it is unexplainable (l. 123–24). Living creatures are caught in the movement and becoming that are life. Our ability to answer all questions and to solve all enigmas often falls short of our aspirations and expectations. This is, however, no reason to abandon the quest. It is perhaps for these reasons that Valéry often pointed out the limits of philosophy and seemingly rational discourse to explain and solve problems that are metaphysical in nature.

Rather than resigning oneself to eternal immobility, especially of the mental or poetic sort, Valéry issues a call to action. This is most eloquently suggested by the way in which the cemetery disappears from his concerns by the end of the poem, condemned by silence. The urgency of this whole matter is reinforced by the numerous exclamation points that dot the final stanzas. The cry of revolt is given in the first line of stanza 22: "Non, non! . . . Debout! Dans l'ère successive!" (No, no! . . . Arise! Into time's succession). The "Non, non" in this stanza echoes back and responds directly to the earlier stanza's repeated call to "Zénon! Cruel Zénon!." Rather than remain in the quagmire of pure thought, Valéry proposes to live in the world of action and duration. This affirmation of life means breaking out of old, static molds and breathing the air of newfound liberty. It is, interestingly enough, the body that breaks the "pensive form" of pure contemplation and immobility (l. 128). The sea, from which all life emerged, appears here no longer as a reflection of immobility but rather as an invitation to renew life. This rebirth through water reminds me of a baptism, although without any religious connotation.

The dynamism and vigor of the poet finds expression in the words that accelerate at an astounding pace in the final stanzas. The "non" of refusal that opened stanza 22 gives way to a "oui" of acceptance in stanza 23. Through a succession of images that rival Rimbaud's "Bateau ivre" for their energy and powers of suggestion, the sea is whipped into tumultuous movement and inhabited by mythical creatures. Like the Hydra, who has the gift of infinite self-regeneration, we are wrapped around ourselves, caught in a continuum that is symbolized here by the image of the mythical creature gnawing at its own tail. The climax of this renewed energy comes in the form of a resounding affirmation of sensation, motion, and life.

The final stanza brings these disparate forces together in a resounding crescendo. The breeze picks up; the waves pound the shore; the wind scatters the pages of his poem. Contemplation can now yield to action. The poet may never rival the supreme being; he may never unravel the metaphysical questions of our place in the universe. He nevertheless accepts here the human condition and declares his eagerness to get on with life in its diversity and richness. The sea that had seemed so fathomless at the beginning of the poem is now implored to become an active element with waves breaking twice in the last two lines. Their "joyous waters" (l. 143) are even called upon to bring down the "tranquil roof" of the beginning of the poem. In a final gesture of closure, Valéry evokes the sails ("focs") on the sea's surface for what they are in reality instead of for the fanciful doves that they were in line one of the poem. This distance from his own poem is underscored by the use of the imperfect "picoraient" (l. 144; to peck). The verbal vigor of the final lines stands in marked contrast to the static beginning.

Like the Hydra gnawing at its tail, we exist in a great circular universe of movement that leads to death, but which contains life. For an intellectual who spent so much of his time and energy thinking, this call to the world of physical action and sensation might seem surprising. It is, however, a brilliant affirmation of the whole being and the complete individual, sound in mind and body, able in thought and emotion to live in a universe whose secrets have not yet all been unlocked. This comes from a poet who once declared that the "good ship of the mind floats and rocks on the ocean of the body" (*CI,* 1125). "Le Cimetière marin" admirably avoids the pitfalls of philosophical, didactic poetry by way of its separation and unification of so many different elements. In his essay, "Au sujet du *Cimetière marin,*" Valéry responds to questions about what he meant in his poem by stating that it was not his intent to say anything ("je n'ai pas *voulu dire*") but rather to do something ("*voulu faire*"); it was the intention to *do* that *willed* what he *said* (*ŒI,* 1503). If, as he claimed, a poem should be a "feast for the intellect," it must be recognized that "Le Cimetière marin," by its profound meditation cast in a brilliant network of musical sounds, rhythms, and images, is an inexhaustible source of poetic stimulation. It is a singular achievement, the crowning glory of a great poet at his best.

"Palme"

"Palme" is the final poem of *Charme* and is dedicated to Jeannie, Valéry's wife. This might explain the more familiar tone of the poem, although the piece deals very little with people and a great deal with poetry. If "Palme" sounds familiar, that is because it was originally intended to be part of "Aurore," the inaugural poem in the collection. They form the two poles of Valéry's work, even mirroring each other in their verse form: nine stanzas of 10 heptasyllabic (seven-syllable) lines and following the same rhyme scheme (*ababccdeed*). The uneven syllabic count is responsible for the swaying rhythm that inhabits many lines since there cannot be a perfect caesura in the middle of an uneven line.

Despite their common features, the tone of the two sister poems could hardly be more different. Whereas "Aurore" was filled with joy and energy and anticipation of dawn and light, "Palme" is a contained, meditative poem with a deliberate, forceful rhythm. As suggested by the repetition and rhyme in lines 8–9, "calme" and "palme" form a patient couple. The angel, after depositing the bread and milk on the domestic table, proceeds to deliver a parable of the palm tree, a parable extolling the virtues of patience and perseverance rather than haste and relinquishment. The palm, like other trees in Valéry's poetry, embodies "being" and, like the plane tree, lives between the lure of the sky and the weight of the earth. Unlike the plane tree, however, the palm is not troubled by consciousness; she ("palme" is feminine in French) is a fulfilled tree because she has learned to live between light and shadow (l. 22). She is a stable fixture in the desert landscape, capable of plunging her roots deep into the sands in search of water to nourish the fronds at her "summit" (ll. 69–70). Her thirst is not always satisfied, just as the poet's work is not always rewarded immediately. Valéry chooses to end his collection with a final reiteration of the worth of craft over pure inspiration. Like palm dates, poetry must ripen and mature; it becomes even more precious when it grows to such a degree of sweet density in such an arid setting. Rather than being subjected to time and desire, the palm tree measures her wealth in the slow maturation that brings out the fruit wherein is accumulated all of the "aroma of love" (l. 50). "Chaque atome de silence / Est la chance d'un fruit mûr! (ll. 73–74; Every atom of silence / Is good fortune for the ripened fruit!), declares the angel. One day, a breeze, a passing dove or a woman leaning against the tree will cause the fruit to fall to earth to the delight of all. The metaphorical intentions as far as poetry is concerned should seem obvious at this point. In the final stanza, the poet returns to himself, wondering if the gestation of such treasures exhausts his powers or if, on the other hand, such exercise does not ultimately increase his gifts. These gifts imply recognition of the need for others who receive the gifts, confirming in turn the existence and worth of the giver. Valéry confirms this principle quite clearly in the *Cahiers* where he states that one needs Others in order to be Oneself (*CII*, 325, 333). "Palme" thus closes *Charmes* on a note of accomplishment achieved through organic growth and patient maturation, leaving readers with the distinct impression that each poem has yielded some of its wealth without depleting its immense store of treasures, human and poetic.

Chapter Six

Prose Works: A Kaleidoscope of Forms

Il ne suffit pas d'expliquer le *texte*; il faut aussi expliquer la *thèse*.
(It is not enough to explain the *text*; one must also explain the *thesis*.)

Valéry, Cahiers I, 298

Although Valéry in a dramatic moment turned his back on poetry after the crisis of 1892, he continued nevertheless to write, especially short prose pieces as well as his daily entries in the *Cahiers*. We have already noted his scorn for prose writing, at least of the fictional variety. He also has Monsieur Teste rail against the simplicity and stupidity of the novel and drama (*ŒII*, 38). Despite this refusal of the genre, Valéry originally envisaged *La Soirée avec Monsieur Teste* to be the opening chapter in a prose project that can best be called a novel. Long after he had renounced this project, he declared that it was meant to be "the novel of a brain" (*ŒII*, 1386).

This dismissal of prose fiction stems in large part from his view that the novel is essentially an arbitrary undertaking, portraying characters in whatever way the novelist decides will make them most revealing of life and will give them the closest resemblance to real persons. In a letter written in 1943, he nuanced his position by stating that novelists have, of course, the right to free and arbitrary creations. His criticism stems primarily from the fact that they do not want to admit it (*ŒI*, 1835).

Novels, in his opinion, do not result from any inner necessity, as is the case with poetry, which enlists all the resources of the body and the mind. Fiction encourages passivity by taking the reader away from himself, whereas poetry puts him in greater contact with himself. A novel must lead somewhere, towards an end, thus resembling the goal of walking as opposed to the dance of poetry.

These criticisms of the novel, as well as Valéry's views on time and memory, will come out clearly in his 1923 "Hommage à Marcel Proust" (*ŒI*, 769–74). His veiled compliments betray a clear disdain for the novelist's undertaking despite certain glimmers of success; for example, he does recognize Proust's merit in writing a reputedly difficult work that does not yield to the general reader's search for easy, digestible prose. In what can only be described as a backhanded compliment, Valéry goes on to add that this training might even help readers prepare their skills for approaching the likes of a Montaigne, Descartes, or Bossuet. Whatever one might think of the novel, it is undeniable that Valéry understood quite well what was at stake in the debate and that he objected to novelistic practices with a great deal of acuity and lucidity. Certain of his criticisms, especially about the contrived and useless nature of plot and character, would become tenets of the French "new novel" that began more than a full decade after his death.

The genre that has attracted so many writers and readers because it is, in Gide's words, "lawless," left Valéry skeptical for the very reasons that explain its success—mimesis, verisimilitude, psychology, slice of life, portraiture, depth, description, identification. Valéry was led to criticize all of these aspects of the novelistic genre that has been so dominant for over two centuries. Valéry's critical pieces as well as his original, creative works scarcely resemble fictional narratives as we today understand the term. In this way, he remained loyal to symbolist doctrine and to his own ironic dismissal of any work that would begin by telling its readers how the marquise had begun her evening. In order to appreciate Valéry's state of mind at the time of *Monsieur Teste,* it might be helpful to refer to this excerpt from his 1923 Preface:

> I was afflicted by the sharp pain of precision. I pushed to the limits the senseless desire to understand and I cultivated within me the sensitive points in my faculty of attention.
>
> I therefore did what I could to obtain any increase in the duration of certain thoughts. All that was easy left me indifferent and was anathema to me. The exertion of effort seemed to me a desirable goal in itself and I showed no appreciation for even the successful results that came only as a result of our native ability. That is to say that the results in general—and that meant, by extension, the *works*—held less importance for me than the energy of the worker—substance of his wishes and desires. This only goes to prove that theology can be found almost anywhere. (*ŒII,* 11)

Although Valéry typically expresses these kinds of demands for the more noble art of poetry, it is interesting here to see how he extends the same principles to other areas of artistic endeavor. Over the next half-century, he produced an impressive quantity of articles, Socratic dialogues, and reflections and meditations on a vast array of topics. Whereas poetry took him long hours of work, he wrote elegant prose with relative ease and speed, despite frequent doubts about his ability and its worth. I have therefore chosen to present a cluster of the most characteristic and innovative prose works, whether short stories, novellas, essays, or dialogues.

Monsieur Teste (1896)

Monsieur Teste is a masterpiece of style and wit written with an extraordinary economy of means in order to obtain a maximum effect: every word counts and every pithy phrase strikes home. As a prose work, it escapes the pitfalls of the novel by the way in which everything is calculated to establish a dialogue with the reader. Valéry clearly remains loyal to Poe's aesthetic by calculating and composing every element in his depiction of the unusual Monsieur Teste. There are no major concessions to the reader's urge to be amused or diverted from his everyday preoccupations. The very banality of Monsieur Teste as the central character proves Valéry's intent not to create a hero in the traditional sense of the term. One could, indeed, meet someone of Monsieur Teste's ilk, at least externally, and hardly notice him.

Despite its compactness and overt difficulty, the tale has survived to our day with surprising force. André Breton apparently knew extended passages of La Soirée by heart, and the surrealists' short-lived honeymoon with Valéry was due in large part to the way in which they identified Teste and Valéry. Roland Barthes summed up the text in a felicitous formula: " . . . it is really a text that demonstrates the intoxicating nature of consciousness, or, more precisely, consciousness considered as an intoxicated state" (Magazine Littéraire, 29). The limitations placed on the character of Monsieur Teste are by no means a sign of Valéry's inability to conceive and execute his work. They result from a conscious effort on his part to portray a character at the limits of human existence, a character who is his own limit. By avoiding the trappings of traditional philosophical, psychological, or moral literature, Valéry has also written one of the most conscious "modern" texts.

Begun in August 1894 when Valéry was not yet 23 years old, La Soirée avec Monsieur Teste was published in 1896 in the Centaure, one of the ephemeral literary reviews that flourished around the turn of the century. It remains the centerpiece of an array of texts that Valéry added over the years. The 1946 edition of *Monsieur Teste* includes 10 pieces of varying length and focus, to which we might add a fascinating, if dense, prose poem called *Agathe* as well as parts of the *Cahiers*. While the second text, the *Lettre de Madame Emilie Teste* is a delightful, witty, and funny portrait of Monsieur Teste by his wife, many of the other texts remain of only marginal value in comparison to the *Soirée* (unless, of course, that was precisely Valéry's purpose). In what reads like an uncharacteristic aside in the *Lettre d'un ami* (1924), there is a particularly scathing attack on the false pretense and vicious attitudes of members of the intelligentsia (*ŒII*, 54).

These other texts, as well as the numerous mentions of Teste in the *Cahiers,* make him a central figure throughout Valéry's intellectual life, a sort of alter ego to whom he turned in his moments of greatest doubt. Valéry elaborated on his project at greater length in this letter from 1936:

> I was 23 years old when I wrote *An Evening with Monsieur Teste.* It was my intent to give as precise as possible a literary portrait of an imaginary intellectual character as precise as possible. In fact, I proceeded to combine together a certain number of vivid observations of myself in order to give some idea of the possible existence of a character who was quite impossible. (*ŒII,* 1381)

Monsieur Teste is a hero of a peculiar sort, fascinating yet hardly viable. Like his creator, Teste lives in a highly intellectualized world where he holds all the keys to accomplish whatever he might choose. Yet contrary to Valéry, contrary to Leonardo da Vinci, he chooses to accomplish nothing.

Teste refuses to attempt anything that might restrict his pure self, anything that might limit his world of immense possibility. He is obsessed by the question that recurs several times throughout the text, "Que peut un homme?" (What can a man do?). His answers, like his entire attitude, remain negative. He is more interested in understanding the functioning of the universal mind than in any of the possible applications of that knowledge. Teste no doubt expressed Valéry's own refusal, at least at this period in his life, to seek personal recognition and prestige from the fruits of his thoughts. He is much more interested in the knowledge that he could do something with his insights if he so decided. He invariably decides to remain silent and not to act.

Valéry himself wanted to explore at least one path of extreme existence via the divagations of this curious character, this "intellectual animal," as he qualified him in 1910 (*ŒII*, 1383). The lesson of Teste would lead, however, to the abolition of all thought and all writing. Fortunately for the future of French literature, Valéry did not idolize Monsieur Teste forever and chose to break his self-imposed silence by writing and publishing *La Jeune Parque* some 20 years later.

It is not difficult to see why Valéry was easily confused with Teste, who was invented, according to the author, " . . . during an ecstatic period of my will and in the midst of strange excesses of self-awareness" (*ŒII*, 11). Like his hero, Valéry wanted to explore the workings of the intellect without running the risk of diminishing or compromising his intellectual power. This cerebral dimension to his undertaking is further stressed by the homophony between his name, Teste, and the word *tête* (head). Teste is a construct of his mind, a hypothesis whose existence beyond the written page is impossible to imagine, yet whose suggestive powers are extremely strong. Valéry himself admitted that Teste could not last in the real world for more than a few minutes (*ŒII*, 13). He is a character entirely turned in upon himself and unable to survive in the outside world where real persons or fictional characters carry on their daily commerce.

This idealized character is a "monster" of intelligence (Valéry uses the term several times in his Preface) who has learned to train his mind and increase its powers to a point beyond ordinary human limits. Indeed, there is very little about Teste that is human or humanistic. He is a character of pure potentiality or, to use Valéry's term, possibility (*ŒII*, 14). Enclosed as he is in a virtual world of limitless potential, he chooses not to act. In a sense, Monsieur Teste resembles what Valéry meant by the extreme form of the "pure self" that remains a hypothetical ideal of complete self-knowledge that could result only in some short-lived form of individual.

Various models have been suggested for the character of Teste. Mallarmé and Degas (to whom Valéry wanted to dedicate *La Soirée* but who refused) are mentioned most often. Valéry himself denied any explicit model for this unique character (*ŒII*, 1383–84). If Monsieur Teste resembles anyone, it is his creator, although there should be no direct, facile conflation of the two. What is certain is that Valéry, in the span of a couple of years, had created the two central figures in his personal mythology—Teste and Leonardo da Vinci, who together would preside over much of the next 50 years of his literary career.

The famous first sentence of *La Soirée avec Monsieur Teste*, "La bêtise n'est pas mon fort," was rendered into English on at least two occasions during Valéry's lifetime. The first translation was done by the American "amazon" of French letters, Natalie Clifford Barney, who wrote "Foolishness is really not my forte," while the second translation by Ronald Davis reads, "I cannot abide stupidity" (*ŒII*, 1376–77). Valéry wrote a laudative introduction to this second translation that now serves as the preface to most editions of the Teste cycle.

La Soirée opens like a conventional autobiography in which a narrator tells about himself and about his encounter with a remarkable individual. The theme of the doppelganger so widely used in literature here finds a less psychological usage than is commonly the case. Monsieur Teste will be the object of numerous analyses and commentaries, all of which explain only one facet of a hopelessly complex character. Valéry very adroitly plants the seeds of curiosity and doubt in the mind of his reader by providing just enough information about his character to whet our appetite without ever completely satisfying it. Monsieur Teste becomes a sort of Everyman of the intellect, combining all influences and forces to make himself as universal as possible.

After the formal introduction by the narrator, the tale soon takes on a direction that cannot be classified in our critical language. Perhaps the best appellation would be simply "text," as is suggested by its alliteration with the name of the main character. At the time that the narrator meets him, Monsieur Teste is leading a banal, uneventful existence. We learn that he is fortyish and lives off the income from his modest investments. His lifestyle is mediocre and mundane—regular meals at the same restaurant on the rue Vivienne, occasional visits to the bordello or the opera, no social contacts or external ties. We discover later that he is married, although it seems more important to others than to him. His quick speech is accompanied by the lack of gestures and by an impassive demeanor, " . . . he had succeeded in killing the marionette" (*ŒII*, 17), suggesting to what extent he has taken total possession of his life with total disregard for what others might think or do.

The narrator is, however, immediately struck by Teste's phenomenal memory. He has trained his memory like a machine to the point that he has lived without books or notes for the past 20 years. In his 1941 play, *Mon Faust,* Valéry will imagine the Teste-like character of Faust writing his memoirs in such a way as to make all other books and knowledge superfluous or redundant. In a sense, Monsieur Teste has already read the words that will end all other words. He discards useless thoughts and accumulates only those ideas that will serve some purpose tomorrow. The narrator thinks that he has unlocked the very secrets to the work-

ings of the mind. Valéry himself will often return to the notion that repetition of what has already been said, thought, or done is a sign of sterility or decline. Teste is in such control of his mental faculties that he
seems to realize the shortcomings of his thoughts even as they are being
materialized. His mind has the ability to foresee affective, emotional situations such as pain, love, or fear (*ŒII*, 19–20), thus allowing him to
defend himself against their assault. There are several veiled references to
Teste's sufferings, past and present. As we shall see, the dialogues will
also contain a similar reflection on the ills that remind our brains that
they are also connected to our bodies and the world around.

One evening, the narrator and Monsieur Teste go to the opera (*ŒII*,
20–21). Rather than being attracted by the spectacle on stage, Teste
spends his time observing the audience. He and the narrator note the
almost mechanical way in which the spectators become passively
absorbed in the stage play. This initial phase of observation will be theo-
rized in *L'Introduction à la méthode de Léonard de Vinci*, which Valéry was
elaborating during the same period. Their intense awareness of the audience is perhaps more an expression of Valéry's own interest in the effect
of his text than it is of his fictional characters' admiration of their fellow
theatergoers. As Monsieur Teste comments, "We are beautiful and extraordinary only for others. *They* are devoured by the others" (*ŒII*, 20).

This monster of egotism makes it clear that he has decided to live
without depending on others for intelligence or understanding. The
audience takes on the appearance and shape of a uniform mass instead of
a collection of individual consciousnesses. Monsieur Teste's and the narrator's scorn for the spectacle of cultural and aesthetic consumption was
widely shared by many of Valéry's generation, who felt that a successful,
popular work could not have great artistic merit. The spectators are
apparently enthralled by some "sublime" moment on stage, which, for
Teste and the narrator, can only confirm their lack of discernment.
Leaving the opera, the narrator wonders at the type of theater that
would be inspired by Teste's meditations, to which Teste responds, "No
one meditates" (*ŒII*, 21–22). Teste's genius will be kept for himself. He
has no intention of displaying his powers vis-à-vis the outside world. At
this stage in his life and career, Valéry-Teste likewise showed little interest in public glory and acclaim.

After the curtain goes down, the two men return to Teste's "abstract-
ly" furnished room where he talks about money and the stock market.
They thus go from the enclosed space of the theater to the enclosure of
Teste's room, which, like his mind, is sheltered from any outside influ-

ence. Since our knowledge of Monsieur Teste up to this point is exclusively filtered by the narrator, we should perhaps remember that his fascination for this singular creature has not been substantiated by any evidence or proof that Teste has thought or achieved anything worthy of admiration. Valéry has given us here a demonstration of the abolition of thought, a negative example that contains the very seed of its own destruction. Teste then takes his medicine and gradually falls into a slumber, continuing all the while his reflections. He wonders again and again, "Que peut un homme?" (What can one do?) (*Œ II*, 25).

Although an intellectual monster, Teste also suffers and feels. His suffering makes him somewhat more human, even if it loses some of its poignancy due to the fact that he has already foreseen the whole course of his suffering—including his own death. Madame Teste will give a very harsh portrait of her husband, who can be "as hard as an angel" (*Œ II*, 27). This more personal, less compromising portrait of Teste counterbalances the fascination that the narrator shows for this monster of the intellect.

As Teste falls asleep, his hyperconsciousness is expressed in the crucial lines near the end of *La Soirée,* which capture the evanescent state of sleep and consciousness that will be so crucial to *La Jeune Parque*: "Je suis étant, et me voyant; me voyant me voir, et ainsi de suite . . . " (*Œ II*, 25; I am being, and seeing myself; seeing myself seeing myself, and so forth . . .).

Valéry would return to the dream-state with a fascinating, if extremely abstract, text, *Agathe,* written in 1898 (*Œ II*, 1388–93). The tale's alternate title, *Manuscrit trouvé dans une cervelle* (Manuscript found in a brain), speaks eloquently for Valéry's preoccupations. In the case of Teste, he has so acutely observed himself in the act of observing himself that he has gained what seems to be complete control over his consciousness. Like art, material comfort, and human endeavor, he has understood them all so well that he has chosen not to act on anything. This may be his implicit answer to the recurring question, "Que peut un homme?"

Valéry's character is therefore a sort of working hypothesis who has refined himself out of existence. Vis-à-vis the real world, Teste leads to a void. Valéry himself undoubtedly relished the anonymity and secrecy that surround his impossible hero. Contrary to Leonardo, Teste's genius does not unlock doors that will bring about brilliant new creations and discoveries. Since he is always one step ahead of himself and the world, he is caught in a loop that makes all action impossible. From a strictly human point of view, we cannot know the mental landscape of Monsieur Teste any more than we can know the inner workings of a black hole. His mind has turned inside itself so intensely that nothing can escape and no signal or symptom of productive life can be evidenced. As his wife will put it speaking of her husband's eyes, "The very object that they scrutinize may be the same object that his mind wants to annihilate" (*Œll*, 26). Monsieur Teste nevertheless corresponds to certain refusals that Valéry himself was deciding at that time, most notably his decision to turn his back on poetry. Valéry's intellectual demands, especially those he applied to himself, were quite authentic. His quest for the pure self and for understanding of the inner workings of the mind were not the search for some facile formula to write greater poetry or think greater thoughts. The Faustian quest was more a literary hypothesis than a real option for him. Inversely, Valéry's poetry and his thoughts must be considered as ways by which he hoped to gain greater knowledge and understanding of his own mind.

The lure of pure introspection and the search for complete knowledge of the self will preside over important periods of the next 25 years of Valéry's life. Teste will recur later throughout his career as an expression of this fascination with solitude and silence.

Introduction à la méthode de Léonard de Vinci (1895)

Contemporary to Teste but diametrically opposed to him in the sense that he is an active creator and inventor, Leonardo da Vinci first appeared in the *Introduction à la méthode de Léonard de Vinci,* written in 1894 at the behest of Madame Juliette Adam for the *Nouvelle Revue* (published in 1895). Valéry returned to the celebrated Renaissance man on other occasions. *Note et digression* (originally there was an *s* after "digression") was published in 1919 as a preface to a new edition of the earlier essay on Leonardo, and *Léonard et les philosophes* appeared in 1929 in the form of an open letter to Leo Ferrero.

I shall concentrate on the first two essays, which go hand in hand despite certain notable differences, especially in tone, between the younger, more provocative Valéry and the wiser, more measured voice of a middle-aged man. In fact, before executing the essay commissioned by Madame Adam, Valéry had already adopted Leonardo's motto, *hostinato rigore* (obstinate rigor), in an almost natural attraction for the Italian inventor, artist, and thinker. Leonardo represented the highest alliance between the artistic and the scientific modes of thinking, which, as we know, was one of Valéry's constant concerns. Leonardo also kept note-books not unlike the *Cahiers* that Valéry was beginning to fill with draw-ings, observations, and aphorisms. Above all, Valéry saw in Leonardo an example of genius, not only the potential for brilliance, such as with Monsieur Teste, but a superior intelligence that had been applied to tan-gible ends. Who better to study than Leonardo da Vinci in an attempt to unravel the complex mental processes that were Valéry's obsession?

Neither essay provides the biographical background nor lists the numerous accomplishments of Leonardo da Vinci. It was not Valéry's aim to provide an introduction to the person in the usual sense of the term. In all events, Valéry scorned the study of biography as a means to understand the work of an illustrious person. The author, no more than the criminal, is the cause of his deed; he is rather the effect, making it thus impossible to find the "deeper" meaning of a work through a patient accumulation of facts about the life of its author (*ŒI*, 1230–31).

The crucial word in the title is *méthode,* a term that Valéry opposed to *système,* the idea of a system being too mechanical, too universal. Like Montaigne, he is more interested in discovering *how* a mind works rather than in cataloging the contents of that mind. The process interests him more than the product. In that way, Valéry takes a specific example from which he derives a universal law. Leonardo is really a pretext for the exploration of his own intelligence. This affirmation of the self through another is a curious way of demonstrating how individual consciousness is the necessary condition of all knowledge. Valéry nevertheless keeps in mind that his subject did not remain a virtual genius. Leonardo went on to create in a wide range of fields using that superior method that he had devised. As with his own poetry, Valéry shows himself to be especially interested in that moment when creation occurs, in that passage from concept to realization, from idea to work.

The *Introduction* contains a strong injunction to abandon all preten-sions of glory and superiority in the creation of ideas (*ŒI*, 1157). It will be necessary to banish all vague terms such as *life, genius,* or *inspiration* in order to understand how one forges a method of knowing. Most impor-tant, the goal of the method is not only to master a system, but also to be aware of thoughts as they are being formed. The starting point for the universal mind is contemplation or observation, Valéry reminds us in his essay as well as throughout the *Cahiers.* Our vision is unfortunately the result of hasty conclusions based on stock images: a cubic shape, whitish, upright, and adorned with windows will immediately be a house, THE house, for most people (*ŒI*, 1165). This occurs when we see with our minds rather than our eyes. Tampering with the arrangement disorients our ability to judge, whereas a masterpiece should be a constant reminder of how little we actually see.

The observing subject relies on sense impressions and experience. The vision must be prepared to change as external reality changes. Phenomena and objects are never simple to understand, nor can they be seized outside of a given context. Our mind puts things in order or searches for continuity beyond what it actually observes. We can imagine the trajectory of a straight line once it has gone out of sight, for example, by continuing the line's path in our mind. Only an agile, universal mind can truly hope to come to understand what it observes.

Our observations are subsequently transformed into mental images, thus subjected to metaphor, abstraction, and language (*ŒI*, 1174). Leonardo da Vinci exists in any mind that carries out those operations that tend towards greater understanding, whether it be of a smile, a machine, or the human body. Attentive to the finest detail and sensitive beyond ordinary, Leonardo was able to translate all of these observations into images thanks to his prolific *imagination* (*ŒI*, 1177). Is the "flying man" the result of an artistic or a scientific mind? Both, Valéry would undoubtedly say, since the complexity of a given construction cannot be fully understood by a limited mental vision. Valéry, here as elsewhere, speaks eloquently against our modern bent towards greater and greater specialization and in favor of universality. Most important discoveries, he points out, result from the ability to confront and compare ideas across disciplines (*ŒI*, 1180).

The final part of the essay and the end of the method is the ability to create or to construct (*ŒI*, 1181 *et seq.*). This means taking a mental image and bringing it into existence by the elimination of all the variants that our mind might imagine. The creator must take the countless abstract alternatives that the mind conjures up and turn the possible into the real. Herein lies the major difference between Teste and Leonardo, or between Valéry the thinker and Valéry the poet. To create means to bring into time and space that concept that was heretofore only an abstract possibility. He places great emphasis on the "ornamental" part of a work of art in an extended passage (*ŒI*, 1184 *et seq.*). Rather than judging a creation by its intrinsic, isolated value, the ornamental gives a sense of the complex ordering and combining power that give value to each part. This emphasis on context and interrelationship is typical of Valéry's own art, especially in regard to his poetry.

One particular type of construction nevertheless stands out for Valéry—architecture. It is the supreme form of creation that relies on both artistic and scientific endeavor, that relies most heavily on combination and context between its many parts. Despite the overriding importance given to analysis and understanding, Valéry nevertheless does not give them absolute authority. Intuition can also prove a powerful means to discovery.

Leonardo remains a striking example of brilliant ideas that are only being verified four centuries later. Valéry sees in him the example of a mind that has arrived at an original method as opposed to following a pre-established system. His many discoveries in all areas testify to the validity of a vigorous intellect that sees the world with fresh eyes. Like Leonardo during the Italian Renaissance, like Mallarmé during his own lifetime, Valéry was ready to turn his back on all gods and idols, on quick success and glory, as a necessary condition to discovering his own voice and thought.

Note et digression

The 1919 essay, *Note et digression,* returns to the example of Leonardo da Vinci with even greater force and clarity than the *Introduction*. Conceived at the time of Valéry's return to poetry—*La Jeune Parque* had recently been published and certain poems of *Charmes* were already written—it contains extended passages on love, death, and the "moi pur" (pure self). Valéry nevertheless makes it clear once again that his goal is not to provide a portrait of the *real* Leonardo, but rather to refer to his subject as an ideal of universal knowledge. The focus of the essay is therefore on Valéry more than on Leonardo.

Note et digression begins with a retrospective glance at the *Introduction* in an attempt to explain how he rejected the historical, biographical approach to Leonardo in favor of a more ambitious one—to discover the very thought processes that Leonardo used. In one of his famous aphorisms, Valéry quips, "L'enthousiasme n'est pas un état d'âme d'écrivain" (*ŒI,* 1205; Enthusiasm is not a writer's proper disposition). His goal was to explore the workings of the human engaged in creating. Valéry therefore rejects the study of personality, a vague entity, in favor of Leonardo's "obstinate rigor." Individual consciousness shall be the only guide and judge in determining what from the past or the present is worth retaining (*ŒI,* 1210).

Valéry goes on to treat two subjects of special concern for Leonardo and for himself, love and death. Both of these topics obviously benefit from the many entries in the *Cahiers* in which Valéry fleshed out his views (cf. chapter 8). He quotes from Leonardo's notebooks certain observations on the grotesqueness of physical love with its intertwined, twisted bodies. This perplexed attitude remains despite Leonardo's well-known interest in human anatomy. The Italian artist himself considered sexual intercourse to be a "cosa mentale." Death is seen as a disaster for the soul because it loses its residence in that "divine thing," the body (*Œl, 1213*).

Leonardo had, according to Valéry, a "naturalistic" approach to the thorny problem of the relationship between the body and the soul, affirming their interdependency. These thoughts, however, have led Valéry astray from his real subject—himself. He observes that one does not need to furnish a special effort to find the self since one can never truly lose it. Valéry then begins his examination of the self by postulating the duality of consciousness, one part of the self always observing the other. He also shows himself to be resolutely opposed to the notion of "depth" since a single light enclosed in a palace full of mirrors will reflect to infinity (*Œl, 1216*). The self not only reflects the surrounding universe but also is conscious of itself in the process of reflecting. The spirit therefore strives for a greater universality and a greater presence that will allow it to feel itself as spirit. We would like to imagine our consciousness as being above the processes of fluctuation and variation; however, life constantly casts illness, dreams, or desires at it. The natural reaction is to seek refuge in an absolute world of protected values.

The pure self will be that unique part of the individual that is eternally present yet above the vicissitudes of the outside world. This "moi pur" demonstrates a seemingly inexhaustible capacity for thinking, while also resisting the move to limit itself to any one thought. It is that abstract part of us that escapes falling prey to lesser functions and events, that resists the lure of relativity and transitivity. Our ability to know is limited only by our awareness of our being—and perhaps our body (*Œl, 1233*). Rather than filling the mind with all of the sum of knowledge available today—assuming that this would be possible—Valéry stresses the importance of mastering the *form* by which knowledge manifests itself. It is a posture of detachment, yet one that suggests an active view of all that goes on.

How to tread the fine line between the sterility of total detachment and the absorption in the chaotic universe resides at the heart of Valéry's thinking in those years, whether in this major text or in his poetry. "Le Cimetière marin," from the epigraph to the concluding stanza, provides a resounding expression of this dilemma.

Eupalinos ou l'architecte (1921)

Eupalinos carries on in the line of Teste and Leonardo, combining the former's absorption in thought with the latter's capacity for action. Valéry here turns his attention to the example of the architect, estimable in his view as one who combines the highest aesthetic sense with the goals of a practical art. From his adolescent readings in the works of Owen Jones and Viollet-le-Duc to his own writings from even the earliest formative years, architecture had always fascinated Valéry. One of his first texts is titled "Paradoxe sur l'architecte" (1891) and already he recognizes architecture to be an Orphic art, analogous to music in its search for other-worldly forms (*ŒII*, 1403–06).

Among the many other writings in which architecture is discussed, we can mention the *Introduction à la méthode de Léonard de Vinci* (*ŒI*, 1153–99), "Air de Sémiramis" (*ŒI*, 91–94), as well as certain poems in *Charmes* such as "Les Grenades" (*ŒI*, 146) or "Le Cantique des colonnes" (*ŒI*, 116–18). The architect embodies the consummate artist for Valéry, searching for perfect forms, divine harmonies, and pure proportions.

The personal background to *Eupalinos* deserves some mention, if only as proof of the extent to which Valéry managed to dissociate his private life from his writing. As he notes in a 1940 passage from the *Cahiers,* this dialogue as well as *L'Ame et la danse* were written in a "ravaged" emotional state due to his stormy relationship with Catherine Pozzi throughout a good part of the 1920s (*CII,* 535). After recognizing that such difficulties of the heart can provide powerful intellectual stimulation, he also adds with some satisfaction that no one would have ever noticed all that was going on in his private life just by reading his works. Valéry managed here as elsewhere to dissociate the events of his life from his thinking and writing, the former never directly providing the raw material for the latter. But since he is only human, Valéry nevertheless inserted a Greek epigraph that clearly dedicates the text to "Karine."

Eupalinos was commissioned by the review *Architectures,* whose editors knew of Valéry's passionate admiration of their art. They imposed one constraint, however, that the poet grew to appreciate as he advanced— the final piece must contain exactly 115,800 characters. Valéry adopted the form of the Socratic dialogue, which allowed him to expose a complex debate without speaking in his own name. Socrates and Phaedrus are shades who meet in the underworld. Phaedrus relates the exemplary case of Eupalinos de Mégare. The historical Eupalinos was, it appears, more of an engineer than an architect, although the dialogue has no more to do with his person than did the Leonardo texts with the Italian artist.

Valéry's choice of characters and setting must not be considered determinate since, despite his lifelong interest in the classical world, he never set foot in Greece and had only an imperfect knowledge of the language and culture. Eupalinos never even appears in the dialogue. His views are presented by Phaedrus. Embodying Valéry's ideal, he epitomizes the perfect marriage of universal knowledge and extreme consciousness in the exercise of his art.

Eupalinos's guiding principle is that "There are no details in the execution (of a work of art)" (*ŒII*, 84). Art, whether architecture, poetry, or music, cannot be left to uncontrolled forces. It is the result of the skill of the artisan who commands every detail. This guiding principle, which came to Valéry from Edgar Allan Poe and Mallarmé, finds here a fresh expression of its timeless wisdom. Socrates ironically points out that this is true in every discipline except philosophy, which builds and demolishes worlds that do not even exist! Eupalinos himself never betrayed this principle, overseeing all of his workers down to the finest detail, displaying his deep appreciation of what Phaedrus calls "the mysterious virtue of imperceptible modulations" (*ŒII*, 86). In another echo of one of Poe's doctrines, Eupalinos also never loses sight of his audience in an attempt to induce in them a sense of the beautiful.

From the vantage point of the dead, Socrates and Phaedrus wonder as to whether beauty is an ephemeral value or whether it transcends death. For Phaedrus, it has the gift of elevating the individual above nature. In Eupalinos's view, the creator must separate himself from his creation rather than submitting to its power. The aesthetics of separation also play an important role in "Le Cimetière marin," which was first published in 1920. In the course of the act of creating, the artist also creates himself (*ŒII*, 92).

Eupalinos then furnishes the example of a temple at Corinth that he designed. It lives for him and embodies perfection because, as he reveals, it is built along the mathematical image of a woman that he loved (*ŒII*, 92). This insight helps Phaedrus to understand the intricate workings of the creative process. It is also quite likely that there is in this monument a veiled reference to Valéry's own love affair with Catherine Pozzi.

By way of explanation, Eupalinos proceeds to make a crucial distinction that reinforces the analogy between architecture and music. There are three types of edifices: those which are mute, those which speak, and those which sing (*Œll*, 92 *et seq.*). The first type deserve only scorn. The second type, such as a well-constructed market, court, or even prison, can be admired since they fulfill their mission and reflect some civic or popular value.

In a lyrical passage, Eupalinos evokes the beauty of a port as it meets the sea and the fascinating potential that he feels in admiring a vessel ready to set sail on the high seas (*Œll*, 95). His focus is set entirely on the instant of creation when the lucid mind joins the universal consciousness, when the virtual becomes real. Beauty is not only a need; it is also and above all a desire, a sort of will to power that summons up the mental and spiritual faculties of the artist. What will be results from what was. The artist affirms his liberty in that fraction of time when the object becomes itself. The whole being, body and soul, is engaged in the process, and it is only through a concerted effort of the whole being that perfection can be attained (*Œll*, 100).

Socrates is still curious to understand what Eupalinos meant by those architectural forms that sing. He postulates an analogy between architecture and music in terms of space and time. Rather than deforming our sense of space and time, as is the case with a painting, architecture and music both present a total, enveloping experience. They enclose the being while allowing themselves to be enclosed. The individual is both inside and outside the work, resulting in a complete apprehension of the self and the object.

This awareness, which is crucial to Valéry, results from a direct experience of the harmony between the total self and the created object. Of greater importance than the product is the *ability* to create that product by summoning at will the entire gamut of riches at his disposal. The soul is thus raised to new heights of purity by the limitless expansion that makes it live an infinity of lives (*Œll*, 105).

Neither painting, nor poetry display this ability, whereas music and architecture stand in this world "like monuments from another world" (*Œll*, 105). They are constructs of the mind that strike our sensitivity directly. As Phaedrus puts it, " . . . a statue makes one think of a statue, whereas music does not make one think of music and a construction does not make one think of a construction" (*Œll*, 106). This is because they are geometric figures. Pure sound must be created since nature contains only noise (*Œll*, 107). The creation of pure forms does not result from accidents, as the surrealists believed, but rather from conscious volition and skilled attention on the part of the artist. The artist's awareness of his art is not a vague feeling but rather a lucid procedure dependent on language, the "Saint Langage" of the Pythia. The totality and interdependent sum of our productions make up the wealth and richness of our intellectual, spiritual, and artistic lives, Socrates would argue. In his own case, he regrets not having had the opportunity to become the architect that he potentially was: "There was in me an architect that circumstances never got around to training" (*ŒII*, 114). The individual is born with infinite potential and, during the course of a lifetime, makes choices that reduce those potentials until he reaches death with one fixed identity. Socrates himself is the individual that the judges and the vial of hemlock made of him.

In another lyrical passage, Socrates recounts the sensation of walking along the shore where land and sea meet, where one world is transformed into another, when he spies a curious object at his feet (*ŒII*, 116). Could it be the product of some artisan somewhere in another land, or a fishbone that had been slowly worn by the sand and tide, or a fragment of some marble replica of Apollo? Socrates makes the point that an artist could have produced this object in short order, whereas it took nature countless years to reach the same end (*ŒII*, 119). A work of art would then be one that is crafted out of time, against time.

After contemplating the object for some moments, Socrates throws it back into the sea. His thoughts nevertheless continue to revolve around it, wondering as to its true nature and unable to find any answers to this enigma. By comparison with an object that presented no recognizable form, he begins to wonder about the seemingly familiar objects that surround us all the time. He concludes that the totality of a complex object is at least as great as the sum of any of its parts; for example, a tree cannot be less complex than its leaves, trunk, or roots (*ŒII*, 122).

Socrates then exposes his idea that human beings do not need all of nature, but only a part of it (*ŒII*, 125). This is because we do not focus our entire attention on all of the complexities and implications of a given act, but rather on that aspect which serves our immediate purposes. He gives the example of driving a nail, which is a utilitarian gesture satisfying a specific need. No one stops to philosophize on the many questions that could be inspired by this commonplace act. According to Phaedrus, Socrates represents the hesitation between constructing and knowing (*ŒII*, 126). We can only act because we refuse to know certain aspects of a situation. Our partial knowledge is what allows us to get on with life.

Valéry elsewhere makes similar observations about language. It works mainly because it is vague and can be interpreted. Valéry here criticizes vain speculation by taking Pascal's famous formula and putting it in Socrates' discourse: "Et les humains, de mille manières, ne s'efforcent-ils pas de remplir ou de rompre le silence éternel de ces espaces infinis qui les effraye?" (*Œll*, 126; And don't human beings seek one of a thousand ways to fill up or to break the eternal silence of the infinite spaces that terrify them?). Only philosophers waste their breath on such futilities.

Contrary to those objects that exist in nature, such as a rock or a tree, products of human design result from an act that creates disorder. In nature, there is a direct equivalence between the parts and the whole. Socrates goes on to explain that man discerns three things in the greater scheme—his body, his soul, and the rest of the world (*Œll*, 129). This triangle of vital forces will often be studied in the *Cahiers* under the acronym *C.E.M.* (*Corps, Esprit, Monde*). What is created to be useful is for the body; what is beautiful is for the soul; however, what is created for the rest of the world expresses a search for solidity or duration. This is because its existence can only result from disturbing a previous order and altering a given state. Architecture stands as the highest expression of this process of transformation since it gives substance and lasting value to a form that everyone can admire. It requires the greatest combination of freedom and rigor, containing nature and being contained by nature. The real world, according to Socrates, is too complicated to be understood completely by human thought (*Œll*, 133).

Phaedrus then describes a Phoenician shipbuilder, Tridon le Sidonien, who was constantly seeking better ways to build ships. This exemplary personage combined both theory and practice. He observed the sea and nature in order to be able to build better vessels. He had to analyze the multifaceted sea in order to understand its complex operations. Knowing and doing here combine to bring to fruition a concept. Not only does Tridon design ships, he also sails on them, thus risking his very life aboard his creations. Socrates regrets the artist that he might have been (*Œll*, 140). He avows his burning desire to have been a builder (*Œll*, 143), thereby rivaling the Demiurge in his ability to create shapes from nature.

In a closing exchange between the two shades, Socrates makes it clear once again that he is conscious of the transitory nature of life, especially from the perspective of the dead. Rather than attempting to create immortal forms, he accepts the need for change and the imperative of living in the realm of pure possibility.

L'Ame et la danse (1921)

This second dialogue, contemporary to *Eupalinos,* is a masterpiece of charm, delicacy, and wit, in keeping with the subject of dance as well as respecting the desire to maintain the poetic nature of language even in a work of prose. Valéry himself declared this dialogue to be a sort of ballet sustained alternately by Image and Idea (*ŒII,* 1408), rich in linguistic leaps and pirouettes, which lend themselves so well to the subject at hand.

L'Ame et la danse was originally a commissioned piece and appeared in a special 1 December 1921 issue of *La Revue Musicale* (interestingly enough, alongside a sonnet by Degas, whose paintings of dancers remain famous to our day). Valéry admits having hesitated before finally writing the dialogue, largely out of his conviction that Mallarmé had already written everything that needed to be said on the subject of dance from a literary point of view (*ŒII,* 1408). He presumably is referring to the two essays in *Divagations* (1897). Valéry's own fascination for *danse* led him to write such other pieces in the 1930s as "Philosophie de la danse" or *Degas Danse Dessin.* We also know that he discussed with the composer Claude Debussy the possibility of collaborating on a ballet (*ŒII,* 1409–10). This project, elaborated in 1900 over lunch *chez* Pierre Louÿs, never materialized.

Dance represents for Valéry the poetry of action carried out by living beings (*ŒI,* 1402), much in the same way that a poem is an act without any utilitarian purpose. Like all other art forms, including poetry, it is an act: "When one starts to recite verse, it's the first steps in a verbal dance" (*ŒI,* 1400). Dance represents the art of movement and the affirmation of our physical existence without which the intellect could not survive. In "Philosophie de la danse," Valéry clearly situates dance both as an unusual form of Time and as a variation on our commonly-held sense of space (*ŒI,* 1396). Rather than moving through an outside world, the dancer derives his/her force from an inner life in which the body thinks for itself. Valéry noted that, from the initial discussion of digestion to the dancer's final syncopation, his abiding concern in the dialogue was physiological (*ŒII,* 1408). As a physical activity, dance relies on the body's movements; we are reminded of the constant emphasis on physiological functions in his poetry, especially *La Jeune Parque.*

The characters of *L'Ame et la danse* are the same ones present in *Eupalinos* except that we here find Socrates and Phaedrus joined by Eryximachus, a physician. The dialogue takes place towards the end of a banquet in fifth-century B.C. Athens when dancers appear and become the focal point of the three men's discussions on life, art and thought. The dialogue is engaged by the men's mutual curiosity as to what the others are thinking or saying. Eryximachus asks Socrates what he was about to say, to which Socrates answers, "Nothing, yet" (*Œ II,* 148). This exchange provides a handy way to begin the dialogue. Socrates is caught up in observing the people around him eat and drink. He points out, perceptively, that their nourishment can benefit both good and evil, love and hate, virtue and vice (*Œ II,* 149).

In feeding life, we are also nourishing the forces that run contrary to life. We live according to cycles, as suggested early on by the references to digestion and later to more grave discussions about intellectual functions. For Socrates, life is comparable to "a woman who dances, and who would divinely cease to be a woman if the leap that she made were to carry her to the heavens" (*Œ II,* 151). Like a dancer, we move from one point to the other on the stage of life, much like the movement of a pendulum. In extremely elegant, sometimes even affected, prose, Phaedrus exposes his view that dance is like a constantly changing dream (*Œ II,* 154), whereas Eryximachus, the man of science, admires the elegant dancers more for their physical ability to move their bodies in such intricate ways (*Œ II,* 157).

One of the dancers, Athikté, particularly embodies the high art that the three men appreciate. Even the grace of her walking movement reminds them that we often take such an everyday gesture for granted. As we have seen in our presentation of his poetic theory, Valéry also saw in the distinction between walking and dance an analogy for the difference between prose and poetry. Athikté's artistic movement reminds the spectators of the need for self-awareness in even the most banal circumstances. Socrates, in particular, will explore the question of the existence of her most minute gesture in time, wondering about the continuity of her movement at any given moment.

There may be here an echo of Zeno's paradoxes about time and movement that appeared in "Le Cimetière marin" and throughout the *Cahiers.* The three spectators share a profound communion of souls in their admiration for Athikté, who seems to be experiencing a total, moving experience. At the same time, the prose of Valéry seems to want to espouse the movements that it is describing, combining the force of Hercules and the agility of a swallow (*Œ II,* 161).

As they attempt to seize the contours of Athikté's dance, Socrates, the perennial thinker, wonders about the nature of what he is witnessing.

Does the dancer represent a moving body that reveals all, as Eryximachus would have it; or does she represent something else, like love, as Phaedrus maintains? Socrates advances that she cannot represent both something and nothing. For him, she is the "pure act of metamorphosis" (*ŒII*, 165). In the midst of his indecision, he nevertheless envies the position of that insect dear to Valéry, the bee, which has the ability to hover over a given spot despite its heavy load.

Carrying on the malady motif, Socrates returns to the opening question as to the nature of humankind's afflictions and possible cures. For him, the real guilt lies with our penchant to see life too clearly, which leads to boredom and *tedium vitae*: "l'ennui de vivre" (*ŒII*, 167). This state of despair and weariness comes from too clairvoyant a perception of life, from seeing things too much as they are. The movement of dance adds color and spice to life and to art. Without such escape, life would be unbearable for the living. While Valéry was resolutely anti-Pascalian, we cannot help but be reminded of one of the seventeenth-century thinker's most famous *pensées,* "Notre nature est dans le mouvement; le repos entier est la mort." (Our nature is in movement; total rest is death).

Speaking via Socrates, Valéry nevertheless goes on to criticize our gestures and movements, which are dictated by base needs or determined by uncontrolled luck. Athikté fascinates her audience because she is so engrossed in the essence of her dance that she embodies a pure and powerful totality. Like some strange animal that lives and thrives in a flame, she radiates the energy of that very flame while seeming to feed on its fire (*ŒII*, 170). She moves within the music like an elemental being who contains and is contained by that mysterious force that moves life. The flame image suggests a momentary flicker, constantly changing yet fixed to its source, somewhere between solid and gaseous states. Like life and death, it can be both a beneficial and destructive element. The flame reminds Socrates of the dance because of the way in which the body moves in and out of itself, incessantly metamorphosing into another shape, giving the lie to what *is* in favor of what is not yet. The soul of the dancer is constantly becoming. It never stops, except perhaps to return to ordinary motion.

As Athikté reaches a paroxysm, she attains that rare state of self-possession that cannot last except as a fragment in time, much like the shape of a flame that is never itself for very long. Artistic endeavor can thus lead to those rare moments of intensity where purity emerges from the ordinary and virtue achieves the temporary state of perfect form. The audience is touched by the rare perfection of such a performance. As Athikté spins and twirls, she gives the impression of penetrating into another world where she defies and momentarily escapes the confines of her physical existence.

This moment of absolute rapture and exalted energy cannot be sustained indefinitely. The dancer must return to a normal state of equilibrium. When she recovers enough to talk to her admirers, she can only reveal that she feels neither dead nor alive (*Œll, 176*). Her sojourn within the realm of pure movement had removed her from the world of materiality—if only for a brief instant. This consummate physical experience was pleasurable and rewarding, although the dancer is left in such a state of exhaustion that she cannot reveal in words the exact nature of her exaltation.

Dialogue de l'Arbre (1943)

This dialogue between Tityrus, the shepherd from Virgil's *Bucolics,* and Lucretius, the first-century B.C. Roman poet and philosopher, is the latest of the group and also the shortest. Its length (about one-fourth that of *Eupalinos*) can certainly be attributed to the fact that it was designed to be presented orally at one public ceremony. Valéry himself read the piece on 25 October 1943 before the Institut de France in his capacity as a delegate of the Académie française.

The impetus for the choice of this particular subject, in addition to Valéry's long-standing interest and affection for trees, was the translation he carried out between 1942 and 1944 of the *Bucolics.* The preface, "Variations sur les *Bucoliques,*" contains many interesting remarks about the art of translation, the place of Latin poetry in the French tradition, and the relationship between the poet and political power.

There are numerous echoes of Virgil's poem in this tightly-knit dialogue, beginning with the opening scene, which places Tityrus under the shade of the beech tree playing his flute as he watches over his flock. We must also remember a poem such as "Au Platane" in *Charmes,* or a clever little piece written for André Gide's wife, Madeleine, titled "Pour votre hêtre 'suprême'" (hêtre [beech tree] or être [to be], depending on whether or not the aspirate *h* is pronounced). As in the previous dialogues, it is the questions that constantly rekindle the debate. In keeping with the other pieces, the *Dialogue de l'Arbre* opens on a query by Lucretius, "What are you doing there, Tityrus?" (*Œll, 177*), which duplicates almost verbatim Phaedrus's question to Socrates at the beginning of *Eupalinos* (*ŒII,* 79). This is effective dialectical practice, even if it is obvious that neither Socrates nor Tityrus is actually *doing* anything.

The lively exchange that ensues will oppose Tityrus, the more rustic yet more creative spirit, and Lucretius, the philosopher who will attempt to analyze and reason wherever possible. For Tityrus, the beech tree is above all a tree, a figure of desire that stretches its limbs towards the heavens. Lucretius, the thinker, cannot accept the mystery of such a naive appearance and responds that he "thinks" the tree and therefore possesses it in his own way (*ŒII,* 177). The harmonious cohabitation of Tityrus with the tree cannot but remind us of Athikté in *L'Ame et la danse,* whose movements, like the branches of the beech tree, seem to reach for the heavens in an attempt to escape their physical weight.

Just as Tityrus's soul, living in the instant, feels harmony with the tree, so Lucretius will point out that he is "metamorphosis," rendering the same judgment as Socrates had expressed about the dancer—a "pure act of metamorphosis." While Tityrus expresses his love for the tree as tree in a highly lyrical passage (*ŒII,* 178), Lucretius cannot help reflecting on the roots, the part of the tree hidden deep beneath the surface. He thereby expresses the urge to *know* as opposed to the willingness to *be.* Knowledge seeks to unveil and uncover what is hidden, whereas being accepts the immediate and palpable reality.

Their apparent difference becomes evident in the second half of the dialogue through the opposition between reality, defended by Tityrus, and truth, the guiding principle of Lucretius. Partisans of reality have only to see and touch the tree to confirm its existence, whereas it is much more difficult to demonstrate the truth of the tree. Lucretius answers that he harbors in his soul the ability to contemplate internally the "Idea of the Plant" (*ŒII,* 185), as if to suggest that its inner network of roots holds the deepest grain of truth.

It is necessary, from this perspective, to wonder as to the origins of phenomena such as trees or dreams and yet remain unable to explain from where they come and who or what conceives and crafts them. If the tree is created like a work of some unseen force, then it is vain for Lucretius to spend time and energy attempting to unravel such an enigma. For Tityrus, and for Valéry, our knowledge will always remain imperfect (*ŒII,* 188). For him, reality stands superior to truth since it can be known.

Lucretius wonders if truth is not "the natural frontier of intelligence" (*ŒII,* 188), leading Tityrus to suggest a reconciliation between these two positions. Once truth is found, even by the use of much artifice, it still remains necessary to return to the creation and appreciate its reality. Tityrus thereby confirms that reality is richer than truth since it overarches and subsumes the idea of the thing *and* the thing itself. Truth, coming from some obscure region of the human mind and tainted with so much doubt, cannot ever be a reliable measure of worth.

"AU COMMENCEMENT ETAIT LA FABLE" (In the beginning was the fable), declares Tityrus, the shepherd-poet, echoing a similar reflection of Valéry himself collected in *Mélange* (*Œ I*, 394). Our understanding of the most intimate workings of a tree or a poem will not automatically allow one to reproduce that tree or poem. The mind forges ideas and invents stories that we can know and understand, but which remain unique and mysterious. They cannot be duplicated. In that way, the artist claims a certain superiority over the philosopher or thinker, who can analyze and reason but who cannot necessarily create.

Lucretius attempts to explain and analyze his own feeling that he is himself a plant at times, a plant that thinks, that presumably can envision itself in all its characteristics, that can be both a plant and the idea of a plant (*Œ II*, 192). The fable, that primitive form of the idea, haunts Lucretius, who wants to discover the idea of a plant as much as the plant itself. For Tityrus, this notion is difficult to accept, at least insofar as he understands the meaning of the words used to convey Lucretius's idea. In addition to confirming the power of art to represent intelligent functions, Valéry also seems to suggest that the words of the writer have the power to charm and the power to mystify. They do not, however, always serve to tell the truth.

As Lucretius describes how, as a tree, he exposes his thousands of leaves of inspiration to the breeze and to the sun, he also reveals how he has become, according to Tityrus's expression, "a tree of words" (*Œ II*, 193). This tree, growing within him, creates a state of exaltation while Tityrus, ever mindful of the reality in which he lives, closes the dialogue in order to go tend to his flock. The artist, having received the fable by an incomprehensible process, now must confront that vague idea with the reality of the world in which he lives.

L'Idée fixe ou deux hommes à la mer (1932)

This, the longest and perhaps most unusual of Valéry's dialogues, was completed in 1931 and published in 1932. It was destined specifically to be read by members of the medical profession. According to the preface addressed to his close friend and literature connoisseur, Doctor Henri

Mondor, the dialogue was also written in great haste (*ŒII,* 195). This would explain, at least in part, why *L'Idée fixe* breaks with the classical, Socratic situation of composed debate around a consistent topic and branches out into myriad subjects in what might seem haphazard fashion.

The dialogue presents two characters, a writer and a doctor, who meet along a rocky coastline and strike up a lively conversation. It has a modern frame of reference complete with mentions of sunbathing, modern medicine, and Albert Einstein. The setting lends itself to a supple, free-form discussion of ideas. This dialogue also strikes the reader as being more spontaneously oral than the others, with frequent digressions and leaps between subjects as would be the case in an ordinary, everyday conversation. The wit and humor of the two interlocutors also cannot go unnoticed.

This is not, of course, an idle chat between passersby. Valéry wants to suggest not only the ramblings of the mind left to its own devices but also the way in which the course of events can ultimately be influenced more by random chance than by intellectual rigor. In his preface, he observes how the rapid rhythm of the dialogue is at least as important as the content of the exchange, thus privileging form to substance in a work of prose as he did in his poetry. While admitting the need to write more like one speaks, Valéry, in a revealing note of irony, adds that this direction was especially valid at the time when people spoke well (*ŒII,* 196). This would presumably suggest the refined, dignified style of the eighteenth century, and many critics have pointed out the dialogue's flavor and tone that remind one of Diderot, especially in *Jacques le Fataliste.* As MOI quips, "Man is made for talking" (*ŒII,* 214). The animated exchange of ideas also might give us some idea of why Valéry himself was considered a brilliant conversationalist by those who frequented literary gatherings and salons, where he was regularly in attendance.

Before the actual dialogue begins, the narrator/interlocutor (identified simply as MOI in a later edition; a reference to Edmond T. would make him an avatar of Monsieur Teste) provides a brief introduction to his present state of suffering. The theme of affliction and healing, already exploited in *L'Ame et la danse,* recurs here in its more intellectual form—the MOI suffers from the torture and torment of thought. This poisons his existence. The only remedy for such a pain is either work or movement (*ŒII,* 197), so he sets out to walk down to the shoreline in order to escape even momentarily from the thoughts that haunt him.

As Socrates had already pointed out to Eryximachus, another doctor, we seek in what *is* a remedy to what is not, and in what is *not,* a remedy to what is (*Œll*, 150). The theme of the absurdity of a random existence is underscored by his insistence on the rocky path, which is "hazardous," and the further mention that the big cement cubes that he must hurdle are like dice (*Œll*, 200).

Their dialogue proper ensues, beginning with a variation on the question that we have found at the beginning of the other dialogues: the MOI, instead of asking his doctor acquaintance what he is doing there, wonders if he is painting, if he is fishing, or if he is painting *and* fishing (*Œll*, 201). The doctor proceeds to explain that he suffers from "activity sickness." Like the sorcerer's apprentice, he cannot turn off the drive to think, do, discover, act, and wonder. In a remark that has lost none of its relevance, he points out that there is a relationship between research and discovery not unlike the one between drugs and addicts.

In the exchange, which gives its name to the dialogue, the narrator develops for the doctor his conviction that there can be no such thing as an *idée fixe* (*Œll*, 204–05). For him, and we can imagine for Valéry, an idea cannot exist in isolation nor in a fixed, stable state. In fact, an idea is defined by its transitivity, by its ability to change. Its material support is the mind, yet its material existence is null. An idea, a word, or a phrase exists only by its capacity to change into an act.

In a passage loaded with monetary and mathematical images, suggesting the dynamics of exchange, the MOI exposes the theory that there are two types of ideas: those that have a high probability of returning to their original state with little change (these are widely-held ideas that demand no real attention), and those unstable, constantly changing "idea-events" (*Œll*, 206–08). They have no equivalent and cannot last long, quickly moving on in search of their own liberty. He gives the analogous example of a dancer who pirouettes for a brief moment or of sexual intercourse in all of its intense brevity (*Œll*, 208). The motto of this new republic's order would be "Intensity, brevity and rarity" (*Œll*, 211).

Continuing the negative logic of his exposé, the MOI affirms that, just as there can be no idée fixe, neither can there be any depth below the observable surface: "The deepest part of a man is his skin" (*Œll*, 215). There are many aspects and many regions, whether of the mind or the body, that we cannot know perfectly. Valéry thereby strikes a blow at our penchant for metaphysical speculation in lieu of natural evidence. Philosophical discourse, as he would put it later in *Mon Faust,* consists of combining a dozen or so vague and undefined words in a hundred different ways and believing that one has explained everything (*Œll*, 366–67). Indeed, the very existence of an idea is dependent upon the words by which it is expressed. The dialogue therefore contains numerous mentions of the relative instability and indetermination of language, which makes it a questionable vehicle for expressing ideas.

Rather than obeying some grand scheme, life would seem to be a great accident, but one which then made up rules and laws to explain and justify itself after the fact (*ŒII*, 231). Valéry proceeds to introduce via the MOI a new notion for which he had to forge a new term, *implexe* (*ŒII*, 234). By this, he means neither the psychological concepts of the subconscious or the unconscious, whose very mention by the doctor makes the MOI threaten to throw him into the sea. It is not an action or a force at all, but rather what he calls a "capacity." The *implexe* would be our latent ability, whether physical or mental, that remains in a virtual state of possibility instead of being transformed into a finalized act.

Our mental complexion can be considered to be made up of a vast number of connections, which, like a gigantic web, are all linked at different levels until some parts are removed in order to be used. Adult human beings, contrary to animals and children, have their lives absorbed by many useless gestures, that is, those which satisfy no immediate need (*ŒII*, 218–19). Although no direct mention is made here of Gide's notion of *l'acte gratuit*, one finds a strikingly similar investigation into causality, determinism, and freedom in the acts by which we define ourselves.

Throughout their rambling discussion, the characters return several times to the notion of liberty and automatism. According to both men, we live in the most imaginative century but also the least individual (*ŒII*, 257). The very title of the dialogue suggests our obedience to obsessions rather than our free ability to invent and create. There would seem to be more things under heaven and earth than are dreamt of in our philosophy, as Hamlet would have put it. There are more things that we don't know than things of which we are sure. Modern science, for all its pretense to answer life's truly important questions, has, in fact, failed to provide fundamental insights despite its increasingly impressive accumulation of data and observations.

The MOI wonders why, with all our scientific knowledge, we have never managed to describe in systematic fashion the gamut of human functions (*ŒII*, 245). The aging Valéry, who had devoted his entire life to the study of the intricate functions of his mind, may be wondering the same thing. In like manner, they wonder why historians concentrate only on "official events" such as treaties and dates, while they ignore such cataclysmic but unexplainable events as the spread of syphilis or similar diseases (*Œll*, 210).

Valéry then turns to two emblematic characters, one fictional, one real—Robinson Crusoe and Albert Einstein. They are both independent individuals who think not according to pre-established norms but as original, free minds. Robinson Crusoe, one of Valéry's favorite person-ages, exemplifies thought that has escaped the social and ideological mold that hinders original ideas and views.

Einstein, whom Valéry knew personally, defies narrow specialization in his quest for fundamental laws that will govern other systems and theories. Despite his scientific rigor, Einstein also recognized that there were some hypotheses that he could not prove and that he could only postulate on faith. His thought processes, as he seeks a bridge between theory and practice, can be likened to the work of an architect, one of Valéry's constant models of high intellectual functioning (*Œll*, 264). Confronted with the disarray of modern thought, Valéry has transposed into *L'Idée fixe* many of the concerns that he shared with others of his epoch.

Mon Faust (1944)

This is Valéry's only serious attempt at playwriting unless, of course, we count the two plays that he wrote at the age of 15, *Le Rêve de Morgan* and *Les Esclaves*. He referred to this project of a "IIIème Faust" as early as the 1920s, thereby inscribing his work in the succession of Goethe's two famous pieces of the late eighteenth and early nineteenth centuries. The general title is *Mon Faust (Ebauches)*, uniting under this name two unfin-ished plays both written in 1940, *Lust* and *Le Solitaire*. By leaving them unfinished, as pointed out by the parenthetical references to "Sketches," Valéry also joins Goethe, whose *Second Faust* remained uncompleted at his death in 1832.

Closer to his conception of the theater as a liturgical drama ("Mes Théâtres," *ŒI*, 1836–38) would be the melodramas that he wrote in 1931 and 1934, respectively, *Amphion* and *Sémiramis,* both of which were accompanied by a musical score composed by Arthur Honegger.

According to the introduction to *Mon Faust,* addressed to his readers "of good faith and ill will" (*Œll*, 276–77), Valéry one day "found" two voices discoursing in his head and proceeded to sketch out their exchange. He does not specify whether these two voices were Lust, Faust, Mephistopheles or the Disciple, although one might conjecture that it was the first two since the greatest dramatic tension arises from their scenes together. The form, while resembling that of a play, reminds one more of the Socratic dialogues. This might explain why, in the second volume of the Pléiade edition, they are included with the other dialogues that were never intended for the stage.

Although *Mon Faust* has been produced as a play,[1] it seems obvious to even the casual reader that it has few of the trappings of traditional theater—little development in character or action, no real stage directions, more attention to intellectual jousting than to the classical tenets of pleasing and edifying the audience. It is also worth remembering that this last major work by Valéry was conceived and written against the backdrop of the Second World War. Despite the bleak images of decline and chaos that appear throughout both plays, they do not seem to mirror directly the troubled state of Europe in 1940 any more than did *La Jeune Parque* in 1912–17.

Lust, La Demoiselle de cristal (*Comédie*) consists of three acts; notes for the unwritten fourth act can be found in the Pléiade (*ŒII,* 1413–15) and primarily concern Faust's love for Lust. Contrary to the well-known tale of Doctor Faustus, who receives extraordinary powers and eternal life from Mephistopheles in exchange for his soul, we find a modern character engulfed in a crisis of thought and values. The devil himself has lost his power to manipulate and seduce people who no longer fear him, who no longer think in terms of Good and Evil (*ŒII,* 296). In a curious reversal of situations, Faust even offers his services to Mephistopheles, who now might need him in order to regain his former prestige!

Faust has a grand project, a book of such unique qualities that it will make all other books useless. He plans to dictate his memoirs to his young secretary, Lust. The finished volume will contain such a complete picture of the inner workings of his superior mind that readers will no longer need to read any other books (*ŒII,* 297). His ultimate objective, not unlike Teste's in many ways, is to gain complete control over his intelligence in order to be able to escape the cycle of life and to die peacefully.

Faust also embodies Valéry's own interrogations into the validity of renewed life—Faust is, after all, "condemned" to a cycle of eternal return and recommencement, which Valéry is suggesting, especially at the end of *Le Solitaire,* might be more of a punishment than a privilege. Faust's desire to write a book to end all books prefigures his desire to push his consciousness and intelligence to a point of no return, thus escaping the need to begin again. We can see his later death wish as a way to break the cycle of birth, death, and rebirth. He wishes to escape the feeling that all events in his life have already been lived and that nothing is really new or unexpected.

Mon Faust is, in this context, something of a personal work for Valéry, who was approaching the end of his life yet who kept writing up to his death in 1945. One of his last entries in the *Cahiers* states his belief that tomorrow holds nothing new for him and that whatever time he has left to live will only be his to waste (*CII*, 388).

In the second act, a Disciple comes to seek wisdom at the feet of the famous genius, Faust. Like the Parque or like the poet/lover in "L'Abeille," he wants to be bitten or stung into a higher state of conscious intelligence. Faust, in condescending fashion, can give him only one mocking piece of advice, "Beware of love" (*ŒII*, 313). As Faust returns to dictating his memoirs, he has a prolonged moment of abandon in the garden when he seems to be letting himself go in harmony with the real world around him (*ŒII*, 321–22). Breathing, seeing, and touching suffice, as he momentarily feels attuned to the present. Lust then instinctively places her hand on Faust's shoulder, and Faust just as instinctively addresses her with the familiar "tu." Their brief encounter, however, will go no further. Faust returns to his dictation.

In a parody of Eve's temptation and of his own "Ebauche d'un serpent," Valéry has Lust pick not an apple but a peach and share it with Faust. The act ends with a comic scene in which the devil, in the guise of a serpent, falls out of a tree, wondering why no one ever offers him even an apple, peach, or pear. This old friend of trees has yet to find the tree of (ac)knowledge(ment) (*ŒII*, 331)!

Act 3 takes place in Doctor Faustus's library, the walls of which are covered with books. The Disciple has fallen asleep with his face buried in one of them. Looking over him are three devils: Bélial, who sullies; Astaroth, who gnaws; and Goungoune, the incubus-succubus, who controls erotic dreams. This fanciful setting exploits not only scenic effects but also the rapid, acerbic language of a Shakespearian clown or a Beckettian nightmare. Mephistopheles bursts onto the scene and calls to order his monsters, commanding Goungoune to stir up carnal desire between the Disciple and Lust (the very name signifies "desire" in German). The latter has ventured into the library in search of a book in order to keep her from having to think. Valéry takes a good stab here at facile uses of literature and at the pretense of literary fame.

In one of the numerous intertextual parodies, Valéry has the Disciple twist Pascal's famous thought about the eternal silence of great spaces in a humorous subversion: "Le silence éternel de ces volumes innombrables m'effraie" (ŒII, 365; The eternal silence of these innumerable volumes frightens me). In a spoof of the traditional pact with the devil, the Disciple tells Mephistopheles that he wants to be "grand"—like Faust (ŒII, 363). His temptation to dominate the mind by his own mental powers will be short-lived, however, in the face of so much knowledge to acquire.

In the final scene, the Disciple's wish to realize his physical power of seduction will also fail as Lust refuses his advances. Is this Valéry's way of casting one final, skeptical glance on the emotional, instinctive side of human nature? In a crucial passage in the *Cahiers,* he notes that the final act, *Lust,* is so difficult to write because he will have to have the courage to conduct a complete analysis of himself and have the courage to be himself. He goes on to observe that he is the only model for his play and that Lust and Faust are *him*—and only him. His experience has shown him that he cannot find that love he seeks in the other and that he cannot expect the other "to take love where it has never been" (*CII,* 556).

This inconclusive conclusion makes it difficult to judge Valéry's dramatic effort, although we can point out from a dramaturgical point of view that the main topic of act 1, Faust's memoirs, seems to have disappeared entirely from the play. It is perhaps fitting that Valéry left this first play unfinished, for its central idea is how to finish thought and life in order not to have to begin the same cycle over again.

The second play's complete title is *Le Solitaire ou les malédictions de l'univers* (*Féerie dramatique*) (The Solitary or the Curse of the Universe [Dramatic Extravaganza]). This dramatic spectacle has in common with *Lust* only the two characters, Faust and Mephistopheles, who are here transported to the summit of a stark, icy mountain. Mephistopheles immediately disappears over the precipice, leaving Faust in a barren, hostile setting that he likens to a "void" (ŒII, 381).

In what would provide a striking scene on stage, the Solitaire rises up out of the ice and emits a cry before beginning to speak in broken, abstruse verse. This singular individual now lives alone atop the mountain, scorning all thought and all human activity. Works of the mind stem from pride, despair, or boredom and are hardly better than intellectual prostitution and pandering. In a resounding condemnation of all mental production, the Solitaire adds, "Anything that can be said is worthless" (ŒII, 388). When Faust tries to spy on the Solitaire's raving poetry, he is thrown into the precipice and regains consciousness down below, only to discover that he is surrounded by fairies.

The conversation between the dazed Faust and the fairies occupies the remainder of the play and is all in verse, sometimes quite elegant. The fairies offer to give Faust a new life of renewed powers and other opportunities to complete his mission among human beings. Has he been touched by the nihilistic lesson of the Solitaire? Is his despair at life and abandonment of desire to prolong his existence a "natural" conclusion in the course of events, even for Faust? Has he reached the final thought, which will allow him to abolish all thought and all existence? Whatever the reason, he refuses to accept the offer for a new life and willingly accepts death. His "NON" will be his last word (*Œ II,* 403), after he has exhausted all possibilities afforded him, after he has exhausted his own will and power to continue to live.

This resounding "no" echoes back to the double refusal at the end of the "Cimetière marin," except that the earlier poem contains a refusal of falsity that is followed by an acceptance that one must "attempt" to live. In a sense, Valéry spares Faust a fate that he wishes to avoid himself— that of being condemned to begin once again a life with full knowledge of where it leads (*CII,* 1345). Only then can he escape the vicious cycle of eternal repetition and incessant recognition of oneself. In other words, once Faust or Valéry has possessed himself totally, can he then dispossess himself of his very being forever?

Chapter Seven
Critique of the Modern World

La vie est quelque chose qui se passe entre 8000 m d'altitude et 8000 m de profondeur.
(Life is something that takes place between 8000 meters in altitude and 8000 meters in depth.)
Valéry, *Cahiers II*, 721

Valéry's almost monomaniacal exploration of the human mind and individual consciousness did not keep him from displaying a lifelong interest in collective ways of life. Indeed, his keen observations of humankind in the public sphere must be considered as a vital component of his knowledge and understanding of the self. Under the heading of history and politics, he wrote and lectured on a number of topics ranging from international relations to social and economic problems to the uncertainties of modern life. The major sources available for grasping Valéry's views on the modern world include *Essais quasi-politiques* from the multivolume *Variété* series (in *Œuvres* I), *Regards sur le monde actuel* (in *Œuvres* II), and the section titled *Histoire-Politique* (in *Cahiers* II). The 1993 volume (no. 7) of the "Série Paul Valéry" of the *Revue des lettres modernes* is titled *Valéry et le "monde actuel."* It contains several papers from the 1986 conference in Montpellier devoted to Valéry's views of politics, society, and education.

While the majority of his pronouncements date from the 1920s and 1930s, when he was often solicited as a public speaker, the earliest pieces go back to the 1890s. Among his first political and historical essays were articles devoted to the Sino-Japanese War of 1895 and the Spanish-American War of 1898. His 1897 essay "Une Conquête méthodique" (reprinted in 1915) contained a cogent analysis of the military and economic organization that Germany was perfecting and which would be unleashed on Europe in 1914. He particularly stressed the disciplined, methodical effort of a rising nation to mobilize military and economic forces toward one common goal.

Although often portrayed as a cerebral man devoted above all to pure thought and lofty speculation, Valéry had many "real world" concerns and views. We should also remember that his secretarial work for Monsieur Lebey at the Agence Havas put him in daily contact for over 20 years with the world of finance and trade, which figures in many of his thoughts. He had also served at the War Ministry for three years (1897–1900) and subsequently met with political and military leaders, from Ferdinand Foch and Philippe Pétain to Benito Mussolini and Charles de Gaulle. His own position in the Dreyfus Affair, which divided turn-of-the-century France, can best be characterized as calculated neutrality since he was an "anti-Dreyfusard," contrary to most intellectuals of the day. The events of two world wars left him with few illusions about man's capacity for organized destruction. In his analysis of political and social problems, from French and European identity to the modern forces of technology and communications, Valéry displays the same critical acumen and insight that characterize his entire body of creative work.

His political positions were most often Eurocentric and aimed less at the polemics of persuasion than at the lucidity of understanding. Contrary to the writers of the generation of Jean-Paul Sartre, who advocated "engagement" by intellectuals in the affairs of the world, Valéry generally refused direct personal involvement in political issues with the notable exception of his outspoken defense of collaborationist writers after World War II. It is, however, too hasty to catalog Valéry in any political or social camp since his major concern was to reach as clear an understanding of the problem as possible, whatever that problem might be. Does he not declare quite bluntly that the affairs of the world interest him only insofar as they are related to the intellect (*ŒI*, 994)? He often wonders how the mind has fared, indeed, how it has survived, in such a climate of crisis. Finally, his prescience cannot go unnoticed since the reader of these pages will find analyses of an array of subjects, ranging from the increasingly prominent role of the United States and Asia on the world scene, to social problems from the abuse of sleeping pills, to the breakdown of modern cities, and to the crisis of values in a fragmented, chaotic world that seems to have escaped the control of its inhabitants.

A constant in Valéry's discourse on the modern world is the scorn and skepticism with which he views history. It is, according to one of the aphoristic formulae of the *Cahiers,* the most naive form of literature (*CII*, 1489). By this, he means that history, like political and economic theory, are as much fiction as fact and that they serve the interests of a small number of individuals who can thereby manipulate the great masses of the population. These "literary fabrications" are based on simplified, controlled images that do not challenge our powers of analysis and critical thinking.

He especially chastises the French for their willingness to accept an idea simply because it has the appearance of being clear and logical (*CII*, 1469). To reduce our understanding of history to a set of great events or clichés of figures in a wax museum is to give the value of truth to a date and factual data simply because these items are irrefutable. For Valéry, however, it is only of secondary importance to know that Louis XIV died in 1715. Such facts mask the more important but more imperceptible factors that made up life at a given moment in the past. Is it not, he asks, more *important* to try to evaluate the role of the invention of quinine, which then allowed the era of colonial expansion, than to study the terms of a treaty signed at the same time (*ŒI*, 1131)? Selective focus on certain issues from the past distorts our perception of whole periods of history.

In his 1932 speech to students at the Lycée Janson-de-Sailly, Valéry enumerates how little of what has transpired in the space of 45 years could have been foreseen in 1887 when he was a student himself. If history does not allow us to look at the past and make deductions about the future, then it is a worthless act of speculation. The problem becomes even more thorny when we realize that such is no longer the case in our modern world, contrary to previous periods when there was a sense of continuity linking the past to the present and even future. Not only has it become difficult to find answers to age-old questions, even the questions have changed drastically (*ŒI*, 1063). In an oft-repeated formula, he affirms that we enter history "backwards" since history is the science of things that are not repeated (*ŒI*, 1135). Our measure of the validity of any study of the past should be its relevance to the present in which we live.

Neither do political systems escape Valéry's criticism. Politics is defined as the will to conquer and conserve power, even to the exclusion of freedom (*ŒII*, 1094). In one particularly scathing note, he qualifies politics as the most ignoble and harmful product of human society since it attempts to make an entire population conform to a model preconceived by the mind (*CII*, 1522). Democracy is at the mercy of advertising (*CII*, 1542). The state or nation has become so closely identified with its leaders that it has taken on a life of its own. Politics can best be compared to a widely-shared myth or fiction that subjects or citizens agree to believe and for which they are prepared to live or die. Europe, by its lack of political unity, has weakened itself and thrown away its preeminent place in the world through wars, transfer of technology, and petty disagreements based on narrow national interests rather than larger ideals.

The political system survives thanks only to the general indifference of the greater number. Valéry continues this analysis with two definitions of politics—the art of keeping people from minding their real business, and the art of forcing people to make decisions about things they don't understand (*Œll, 947*). Societies thus organize the inequalities and disorder on which they are built. If a government is strong, it crushes its subjects or citizens; if it is weak, its people perish (*Œll, 967*). Modern man is a slave of his supposed progress since every technological advance turns against its inventor (*Œll, 968*). Political leaders necessarily obscure issues about which they have no clear, constructive answers since they would immediately lose their power if they started to deal with the realities of their nations.

Many of Valéry's essays contain extended discussions of France, its people, language, history, geography, and mentality. He can be both critical and indulgent, deprecatory and generous, cynical and forgiving towards his home country. He concludes one of his longest and most insightful essays on the subject, "Images de la France," with the observation that France is a work (presumably, of art) and a form. This is a compliment in Valéry's system insofar as, like a poem or a building, the French nation grew out of careful and attentive efforts to build her. Among its salient features are a favorable climate, a wealth of natural resources, and a sense of identity within a diverse population. In numerous passages, Valéry insists on what he considers the prominent trait in the making of France—the ability to assimilate and mix together people of diverse ethnic backgrounds (*Œll, 996*). As in the grafting process by which stronger trees and plants result from crossbreeding, the nation's culture and spirit have been formed by the breadth of peoples who have taken up residence within its borders.

It is also interesting to note that Valéry, in the *entre-deux-guerres* world where colonies were part of the international landscape, made an eloquent plea for true exchange between France and its dependencies. In a short preface titled "Introduction à un dialogue sur l'art," he takes the position that France has as much to learn from a colony like Morocco as it has to teach, thus recognizing the relativity of values and the need for true exchange. Inequalities within the human family produce dangerous political situations that, he predicts, could even prove fatal for Europe (*Œll, 1038*). As a poet, he also considers among the national treasures the French language with its soft consonants and richly nuanced vowels. The wide diversity of accents in France that Valéry noted in his day could be attributed to the very diversity in the country's population. As a keen observer of transformation and change, he also understood that a modern nation such as France could not stop the course of its evolution without running the risk of stagnation and fossilization. In a characteristically brilliant paradox, Valéry concludes that the defining trait of the French is their belief that they are universal. How singular, indeed, to have made a specialty out of embodying the most general of qualities (*ŒII*, 1058).

Valéry's attention to the state of the world turned quite frequently and with perhaps greatest ease to the larger question of Europe and its position in the twentieth century. His perspective was decidedly European, especially important at a time when Europe was experiencing some of its darkest hours. He frequently pays homage to the determining role of the Mediterranean in the formation of European culture, even calling it a machine to produce civilization by associating intellect, culture, and trade (*ŒII*, 1086). We have already underscored the importance of his origins in the cradle of classicism. It came as no surprise that Valéry was named the chief administrator of the Centre Universitaire Méditérranéen in Nice before and after World War II. The initial charter for this unique institution clearly designates as its mission the study of the Mediterranean in all of its aspects—function, physical characteristics, ethnic makeup, culture, history, etc. (*ŒII*, 1128–44).

After the horrors of the First World War, Valéry stopped to meditate on his idea of Europe in the famous essay, "La Crise de l'esprit," which begins with the resounding acknowledgment that our civilizations now have shown that they are mortal (*ŒI*, 988). Are we not as much the product of random forces as of collective will? Valéry then goes on to question the future of Europe. Will it become what it is in reality—a small tip of the Asian continent (*ŒI*, 995)? Beyond the favorable natural conditions that have been generously bestowed upon the European countries, Valéry speculates that it must be the quality of its inhabitants that has allowed it to achieve such a position of preeminence in the world (*ŒI*, 996). Valéry especially points out as one of its strengths the ability to carry on true two-way exchanges with the rest of the world, absorbing inward and spreading outward through its relations, whether artistic, economic, or moral (*ŒI*, 995). The intellectual disciplines that characterized Europe from the invention of geometry by the Greeks to the advances of modern science are now faced with a challenge. Have the Europeans, in fact, given up to the rest of the world the knowledge and techniques that made them the most powerful continent on earth? This redistribution of intellectual and spiritual resources led Valéry, among others, to fear the decline and decadence of Europe, which could no longer automatically suppose its superior standing among the community of nations. Could Europe prove yet to be the author of its own demise, as Valéry predicted? Although he never came to the Americas, he professes a great deal of admiration and hope for these hybrid nations and for their ability to safeguard the best of what Europe has to offer (*ŒII*, 989–90).

Besides his more specific views on France and Europe, Valéry devotes a good deal of thought to what might be termed the state of civilization and the course of events past, present, and future. His analysis of the world on the eve of the Second World War contains many pertinent observations that remain true to our day. He notes the disappearance of unsettled territory, the spread of technology beyond Europe, our great reliance on nonrenewable sources of energy, and the spectacular increase in communications (*ŒII*, 988). Valéry was particularly sensitive to the profound transformations that were taking place in the world and to the climate of crisis that had come to characterize modern life. He was especially distressed to note how our obsession with speed has reduced our ability to take time to cultivate and enjoy the fruits of our labors. We have lost focus in a world that encourages dissipation rather than concentration. The crisis in intellectual values results from a "capitalism of ideas" in which the mind has upset the equilibrium of the world by the rapid introduction and diffusion of so much new, uncontrolled knowledge. His burning question, "Can the human intellect now be used to save the world it has created . . . and to save itself?" has lost none of its relevance a half century later (*ŒI*, 1065).

With the advent of advertising and mass production (even by 1930s standards), Valéry deplored our increasing loss of identity and freedom. We have become interchangeable with the goods we produce, prey to the very machines that we invent but no longer control. The interdependence and uniformity of modern societies have created a whole set of desires and needs that too often mask the profound nature of life. Valéry, in a premonitory remark, even goes so far as to wonder if our technological prowess might not one day bring about physiological changes in our very organisms. The increased demand for specialization has resulted in a narrowing of each individual's field of vision and understanding. For Valéry, the Renaissance ideal of breadth of knowledge still held sway over the modern need for "experts" who cannot compare ideas across disciplines. All knowledge today must come from a comparative approach (*ŒI*, 1072) and a vigilant effort to rethink itself if we wish to protect independence of mind and spirit as well as freedom of thought and inquiry.

Against this backdrop of instability and chaos and as an image of disorder, Valéry stresses the importance of education as a potential remedy to some of the ills that we have created. His confidence in the education system to bring about fruitful change is, however, limited by the fact that our policies are not based on any clearly formulated goals. In view of the lack of any common direction or even vague principles, the only real object of years of education is to obtain a degree. "Diplomas are the mortal enemies of culture," he declares without qualification (Œl, 1075). The old cleavages between tradition and progress have provided sterile debates that skirt the real issues of why and to what end our educational systems should work. The rigorous battery of national exams in France has led to an adulterated mastery of most subjects determined by the exigencies of an exam but with little thought to the long-range goals of that knowledge. Our institutions of higher learning, controlled by mandarins and doctors of all sorts, can be considered excellent places for the preservation of knowledge but mediocre or even poor places for creating new knowledge (Œl, 1056).

As many students of French know, spelling and verb conjugation are often the yardstick for evaluating knowledge on exams where little or no attention is paid to less quantifiable but more important subjects such as the musicality of a phrase or poem (Œl, 1079). Rather than condoning a mechanical transfer of knowledge from teacher to pupil, Valéry clearly advocates awakening and cultivating the desire and thirst for knowledge at an early age. Whether classical languages, French, or mathematics, the result of much that goes on in our education system seems designed to disgust students from ever wanting to learn. As was his own case, Valéry recommends that students be allowed to stumble along the way as they search for their own path, since only that knowledge will ultimately prove valuable.

Chapter Eight
Cahiers: Notes from the Mind

Les autres font des livres. Moi, je fais mon esprit.
(Others work on books. I work on my mind.)

Valéry, Œuvres I, 30

Many readers and critics today would not hesitate to consider Valéry's *Cahiers* to be his crowning achievement, his masterpiece, at least insofar as they contain a clear and extensive expression of his thoughts over a period of some 50 years. Although he doubtless would refuse such terminology, his voluminous notebooks correspond closest to the demanding exploration of his own mind that made up his life's work. The sheer range of thoughts and observations contained in these 26,600 pages (for the C.N.R.S. edition) differ from a more conventional diary or journal in that we learn relatively little about Valéry's daily activities and routine. Occasional mention of a dinner or a conversation with Mallarmé, Gide, or Bergson is included only because it sheds light on the topic at hand.

From 1894 until his death in 1945, Valéry rose well before dawn, made coffee, and rolled cigarettes while consigning to paper for three or four hours his early morning thoughts on subjects ranging from literature and science to language and dreams, from philosophy and psychology to sexuality and religion. They contain the most compelling evidence for Valéry's high stature among modern thinkers and writers.

Since they were not composed with a view to publication, the *Cahiers* are in general loosely organized, and it is not unusual to find mathematical formulae, freehand sketches, and margin notes on the same page. Valéry's thoughts grew and developed organically rather than according to some preconceived system. There can, however, be found certain constants which, like Ariadne's thread, link seemingly disparate parts together. This eclectic structure does not truly appear in the thematic organization of the Pléiade edition which imposes a semblance of coherency that the original *Cahiers* do not provide. They allow, however, a modern reader to appreciate the diversity and unity of Valéry's thoughts. Reflections on language, for instance, underlie most of the other major themes, such as literature, philosophy, or science. Valéry's "mental gymnastics" resemble more his own dialogue with himself through which he could hope to gain a clearer understanding of his own thought processes. Did the 1937 notebook not have on its cover a sentence around which he painted a snake, symbol of human consciousness, and which warns, "What I write here is written only to myself" (*CI*, 11)?

The *Cahiers* are, in a very real sense, the best introduction to the method of Paul Valéry. Although Valéry at times expressed impatience with Montaigne's *Essais,* the two works can be considered related—perhaps even first cousins—by their seeming lack of organization and by their skeptical examination of such a wide range of topics. Like his illustrious predecessor, Valéry talks best about himself when addressing other subjects and hoped to provide by this demanding exercise a greater insight to the mind that created them.

The state and status of the *Cahiers* is a confusing issue in itself, which I cannot develop here in full detail. While it is true, as I have mentioned above, that the various entries in the notebooks were not written with the express intent of being published, it is also true that Valéry himself envisioned eventual publication of selected parts. Numerous fragments of the notebooks found their way into other writings, such as *Tel Quel, Mélange,* or *Variété.* And one entire section, the *Cahier B 1910,* was published several times throughout the 1920s as it appeared in Valéry's original version.

Indeed, the reputation of the *Cahiers* was such that many scholars hesitated to make analyses and draw conclusions about Valéry's work until their publication by the Conseil National de la Recherche Scientifique in 1956–61. Conversely, their publication provided a great impetus to Valéry scholarship around the world. The C.N.R.S. edition is a facsimile reproduction of the *Cahiers* that extends to 29 volumes of over 26,000 pages in all. They allow for an authentic reading of Valéry's original notations in chronological order with certain inherent difficulties, such as the disorder and disjointed nature of such an enterprise.

With the inclusion of additional parts that were omitted in the C.N.R.S. publication, the Bibliothèque de la Pléiade published in 1973–74 a two-volume edition of the *Cahiers* prepared by Judith Robinson-Valéry. Both for its ease of use and for its wide availability, this is the version that I have chosen to use in the present study (represented as *CI* and *CII*). It is a thematic arrangement of passages from the notebooks, which are grouped around over thirty headings; for instance, the philosophy section in the Pléiade runs over 300 pages and contains only those entries dealing with philosophy beginning in 1898 and going up to 1945.

While the advantages and disadvantages of a thematic presentation should seem obvious, it is important to keep in mind that it was not an arbitrary editorial choice. Valéry himself envisioned such a regrouping of his writings as early as 1908 and continued to work on it at various times until his death in 1945. Short of hiring three "intelligent and infinitely flexible slaves or eunuchs" to help him in his task (*CI*, xv), Valéry enjoyed the services of secretaries at various times, as well as recruiting Catherine Pozzi, his intellectual peer and mistress for eight years during the 1920s, to help in classifying the notebooks.

We should finally mention that Gallimard has published three volumes of the complete *Cahiers (1894–1914)* under the supervision of Nicole Celeyrette-Pietri and Judith Robinson-Valéry (1987, 1988, 1990). The publication of so many successive editions stands as proof of the vitality and versatility of these unique documents as they provide an equally unique view of one who was a precursor of so many currents in modern thought.[1]

Cahiers (CI, 5–16)

This rather short section expresses Valéry's self-reflecting awareness of the limits and ambitions of his own writing in his notebooks. The process of writing with the raw material of thought itself cannot result in anything definitive (6). Rather like Penelope, who knits and then undoes her day's labors so as never to finish the work at hand, his main goal will be to work with ideas that he might wish to adopt rather than to produce well-polished products of his mind. Instead of accomplishing a work in the present, he reserves the possibility of pushing that work's finality to some point in the future. This is very much a collection of "work in progress" as it evolves in the mind of the writer. It is the possibility of thought instead of thought itself that he seeks (7).

This unfinished, fragmentary quality to his thought led Valéry to quip one day that he in fact needed a German to finish his ideas for him (69). He is himself the primary recipient of these thoughts, which are like playing scales for a pianist (13). Like physical activity and exertion, they are a natural and necessary function of his organism (15).

Ego (CI, 19–231)

Although Valéry is not prone to confessions or self-portraits, he devotes a great deal of attention to himself, especially to his mind, as a primary object of his study. We might be surprised by the self-deprecating tone of many of these passages, such as these few comments gleaned from 1909–10 alone: "I am nothing. I am worth nothing. I can do nothing" (48); "There is an imbecile inside me and I must take advantage of his mistakes" (49); "Anguish, my true profession" (50).

Such disparaging remarks betray a Valéry who might have appeared brilliant in social or intellectual circles but whose real nature was neither self-assured nor self-confident. It is also the expression of his belief that nothing is definitive and stable but that our lives and our selves must be constantly moving towards another state of their own being.

He quips that he is very sociable but quite solitary (92) and, in a 1928 entry, even imagines an epitaph that would read, "Here I lie—killed by others" (159). His gregarious, debonair manner could easily have been mistaken for worldly pleasure in the social functions of which he was a regular feature in the 1930s. What we call life and society contain hard lessons in stupidity and are futile accumulations of silliness (34). They are useless in the supreme task of perfecting his mind.

In 1941, as he is thinking about Faust, Valéry expresses a need to cultivate his difference from others out of fear that imitation or repetition will catch up with him (192–93). This is also expressed in Teste's killing of the marionette. It is important for his social self to be his own judge instead of implicitly delegating that responsibility to others through shared desires and needs that are the common lot of common man. Such will be his complaint about modern advertising and capitalism of ideas that consider all persons equally easy to influence.

In all areas, but especially in the intellectual sphere, Valéry challenges the individual to reinvent himself constantly in new forms. His desire to be unique and original is more than a search for novelty, one of the criticisms he leveled at Breton and the surrealists. It is rather a call to arms in the ongoing struggle for intellectual independence and self-discovery. After all, new territory, whether of the mind or the map, can really only be discovered once.

In his "Politics of Thought," Valéry expresses the desire to obtain rather than to possess, since one can only really appreciate that which one has obtained oneself (28). Conversely, this self-determination and self-possession are his best protection against being seized and possessed by others. Like his self-conscious heroes or heroines, Valéry is not only conscious of his consciousness; he also suffers from the knowledge that he suffers (54). Under such circumstances, it is hardly surprising that he rarely lets himself go and that he quite instinctively remains disengaged from his surroundings.

Even by the turn of the century, Valéry had already come to reject all ideas that are not his own, that had not been forged by his own mind (26). Numerous times he discusses his inability or reluctance to read, not only novels but any other works that keep him from forging his system. The goal of these fundamental struggles with himself will be the repossession of his being by himself.

Valéry is also acutely aware that his goal of complete self-possession can lead dangerously close to self-destruction. This is what he called his "caligulisme," after the Roman emperor who aspired to give his subjects one head (a Testian figure) and who was assassinated at the age of 41 (226). One of the last entries in the *Cahiers* section expresses this will to be in a revealing formula: "When I write in these notebooks, *I write myself.* But I do not write everything" (16).

Valéry frequently expresses his desire for detachment through the emblematic figure of Robinson Crusoe. The solitary man on an island contains the purest expression of his desire to be the creator of himself without any debt to anyone or anything else (126). As in the Crusoe texts contained in *Histoires brisées,* the challenge facing him is what to do with himself once he has assured his material survival and even carved out large periods of free time with little or no constraints (*ŒII,* 411–20).

Recognizing his propensity to self-centeredness, Valéry equates his ego to Robinson in that only those inventions and discoveries that come directly from himself have any value (158). This explains why he was not a brilliant student in school, where his teachers wanted him above all to learn lessons rather than to think. In a humorous aphorism, he quips that his modesty is great, so great in fact that it reaches as high as the navel of his pride (79).

The best, indeed the only accomplishments worthy of interest come from himself and from no one else. Valéry's resistance to accept outside influences also led him to scorn proselytism since it deprives others of the opportunity to discover their own paths. His distrust of politics is based in large part on this "golden rule" (132).

In the same vein, he also criticizes Gide, whose preponderant influence over the younger generations of their day seemed excessive to Valéry (148). His desire to escape being defined by others explains his wish to shape his own self, sometimes pushing his refusal to the point of making it difficult to seize an idea or concept. Reading Valéry can often give the impression of overcoming great difficulties placed along the reader's path. What is difficult is always new (89), making his writings resist being made vulnerable to facile comprehension.

Ego scriptor (CI, 235–319)

This section deals with Valéry as a writer, his views on literature and the arts, as well as the relationship between the writer and the self. He makes it quite clear throughout that literature has never been the goal of his intellectual quest but that he has always considered it one way to activate and exercise the mind. The aim of an honest work would be to make the reader think (241), whereas much literature, like much thought, has come to mean a sacrifice of the intellect more than a development (247).

Instead of literature being an end in itself, such as is the case with many of the symbolist poets, it represents for Valéry a means to increasing the poet's powers of expression and construction. He states quite clearly in a note from 1922 that he feels as if he has lived through a revolution. The art in a given "work of art" can be found in the very construction and fabrication that went into the work (253). To make a poem is a poem. He goes on to affirm the indissociable nature of form and content.

This aesthetic reaches its highest point of perfection in "Le Cimetière marin." This form is made up of words, making the poem a "linguistic speculation" (241) of some scientific value and interest. In anticipation of a very modern conception of poetry, Valéry sees it not as an expression of the poet's self but rather as a construction of a verbal nature. In the end, poetry is a general "combining" of words (254). As I have mentioned in the chapter on Valéry's poetic theory, this conception of poetry as a "combining game," to use Genette's expression, represents a breakthrough in thought when compared with the traditional art of expression through verse.

Valéry's obsession with purity, whether of the self or of poetry, stems from a desire to separate the constituent elements into their formal parts before utilizing them in the construction of a work. The language of poetry has little to do with the true self of the poet who writes and publishes those words. It would be an error, says Valéry, to seek to reach the inner self of a poet through his writings (253). Literature should serve primarily to allow the poet to improve his capacity to think and to expand his intellect, not to attempt to produce in impure words a duplicate of the writer's world. That would be to fall into the novelist's trap.

The process by which a work comes into existence for Valéry will be compared several times to the art of translation—first from his own thoughts and sensations into his own language, and then into ordinary language comprehensible by potential readers (264–65). The fact that his work eventually finds its way into the public's hands results most often from a chance set of circumstances, since Valéry himself makes it quite clear that by the time of publication he has lost interest in the piece. He writes for the future of his thoughts and not for their past (244).

Gladiator (CI, 323–77)

The unity of this section is provided by the implied comparison between mental and physical activity as represented by the figure of Gladiator, a thoroughbred racehorse. Valéry even goes so far as to envision a form of mental equitation (370) that would aim at training the mind as one practices dressage with a horse. Thoughts must be "mastered" in order to achieve true consciousness of one's potential strengths and weaknesses. He even entertains the possibility of superhuman qualities defined as the effect on a human of human knowledge (326–27).

The physical dimension of such prowess results from intense exercise and training of the sort that allowed Leonardo da Vinci to see every detail of a scene and then transform it into a work of art (336–37). Art may be essentially a question of training. Literature may derive its greatest appeal as a higher form of exercise performed by the "intellectual animal" (340). The true goal of such training, rather than the production of great works of art, is the increased knowledge and fuller possession of the self (331). This can best be accomplished by a union of the anatomist and the athlete (347), who will then be able to practice "sports of the mind" (362). Such sports will allow the individual to build his system of thought and to perfect as nearly as possible the higher art of thought just as one strives for perfection in dance or gymnastics (361).

The ultimate goal of perfection means a full knowledge and understanding of oneself and others (362). This regimen is not designed to provide recipes for the fabrication of artistic masterpieces, which, as we already know, is not Valéry's goal. They are rather the exercise of the means which, for Valéry, constitute an end in themselves.

Langage (CI, 381–476)

The question of language is a constant preoccupation in Valéry's quest for a system or method of knowing and understanding. Most of his remarks about the language we use have some bearing on his ideas about almost every other subject he addresses. Language is a double-edged weapon for Valéry since it is the means by which we know everything else that we know or think we know. Among the many aspects included in his study of language, he accords much thought to the question of definitions, beginning with his search for a suitable definition of "language" itself.

In a passage from 1916–17, Valéry stresses the communicative function of language by defining it as "someone who speaks to someone about something" (403). The difficulty with finding a definition for any given word stems in large part from the variable contexts of words. When we speak, we make our intentions known without using words in their preordained sense. This transitive character of language makes it almost impossible to devise acceptable dictionary definitions for words (391). Work on the dictionary was, of course, one of Valéry's duties as a member of the Académie française.

We inherit meanings from our formative years by playing with language and we then reuse words in the ways we learned them with some leeway for individual variation. A dictionary generally answers the question of meaning by going from the word to the idea. The opposite direction from the idea to the word does not exist because we do not know the true origin of words (436).

It is a common assumption that words mean something that we can formulate, as in a definition. While the designating function of words may have some interest, their true value comes from the more difficult role they play as connectors and instruments of transformation. The combining function of language is one of the cornerstones of Valéry's thought and also, as we know, one area in which he is a precursor of modern linguistic and poetic theory.

Since we use words that are inherited from an impure, imperfect system, the question obviously arises as to the origins of language. Valéry here imagines a tale about a theoretician who studies gestural language and discovers remnants of our most primitive, preverbal communication (419). Although Valéry the poet is especially attracted by the sound quality of words, he does not hesitate to state that sign language is an adequate device for communication in most situations (411).

The earliest appearance of language most likely came about by agreeing upon a correlation between a sound pattern and some object or event. But language has evolved through "universal suffrage" whereby certain words get "elected" and others not. He adds that sometimes writers carry out little *coups d'état* in the course of composing their works (416).

Every century introduces and abandons certain words as part of a natural process (434). Common language is impure by this very formative process that uses and abuses words. It is the ease with which language explores myriad possible combinations that constitutes both its strength and weakness (429). Under such circumstances, Valéry's early dream of founding a language that would be an instrument of "discovery and observation" comes up short of its goal (386). Words that are widely used have unstable meanings and cannot clearly define and represent. Their form and substance have not resulted from the will of any individual but rather from the passivity of the greater mass of people. Communication is made possible by the imprecise nature of the words used to relate messages, making it common for two individuals to carry on a conversation to their mutual satisfaction using words that do not mean the same thing for both persons. The supposed understanding and clarity of such an exchange really betrays a mutually agreed-upon obscurity (417). It will remain clear only as long as both parties agree not to pursue their investigation of the matter.

The question of the relationship between language and thought underlies Valéry's inquiry into almost every other subject. His denial of the validity of philosophical argumentation or of most other forms of speculative discourse is based on the premise that much of the debate revolves around words, which have no fixed meanings. Language lends itself more readily to poetry than to analysis due to its imperfect nature (384). It organizes thought in a strictly historical sense (385), making us tributary to words that have been manipulated and deformed over the course of time.

While it is valiant to attempt to think without words, it is also true that language is what connects thoughts to reality (404). True thought will only emerge when the individual has reappropriated words about which he is sure and which are not simple artifacts passed down to him from ages gone by. Valéry's lifelong goal was to devise his own personal language based not on the reality of others but on the reality of his own thought itself and relying on an inner necessity as distinguished from some outside force (425). We cannot imagine mental activity without language, which gives form to everything we recognize in the world in which we live. But it is more of a convention than the result of any intrinsic quality of language itself.

Philosophie (CI, 479–771)

This is the longest section in the Pléiade classification and goes hand in hand with Valéry's ruminations on language and with his ideas on a system. Part of its length comes from an insistent repetition of many of his views. Coming as it does from an avowed nonphilosopher, it constitutes an all-out critique of philosophical methods that Valéry taxes as specious and fallacious, based as they are on unanswerable questions and aiming as they do at fruitless answers.

There is also some benefit to be derived from reading these comments along with the section from *Variété* titled "Etudes philosophiques" and grouped in *Œuvres I* (787–967). It is his goal not to accumulate and compound the difficulties and obscurities of centuries of philosophizing but rather to attempt to discern and explain where they went wrong. From the earliest entries onward, Valéry makes it clear that philosophy fails because it persists in using words whose meanings have never been adequately defined. He does not hesitate to affirm that all metaphysics comes from a poor use of words (481) and that the main purpose of philosophy is to explain a dozen or so words that everyone uses all the time and with relative ease (566, 589). All of the philosophical debate over *reality* stems from an imprecise value that has been attributed to the term itself (656). Other notions such as liberty, free will, and metaphysics, to name but a few, fall prey to the same recrimination. No one really doubts the "reality of the outside world," says Valéry in a passage from 1944, until people start to erect a myth around the words and forget that these words are only instruments of exchange that retain their fiduciary value only as long as all parties are satisfied with the terms of the exchange (765).

As he points out about language, words have unstable meanings whose communicative power is derived from a tacit agreement not to question their true meaning. Likewise, philosophy, especially metaphysics, pretends to have universal and objective value when, in fact, it cannot agree on the meaning of a common verb such as "to be." Such considerations are useless in Valéry's eyes since the most important problem is the one that stands a chance of being solved (492).

The only philosopher to remain in his good graces almost without exception is Descartes because he undertook the elaboration of an entire method that was systematically subjected to a rigorous, analytical verification. The principle of methodical doubt, as well as the geometrical study of the mind, attracted Valéry, who objected to belief without proof and was attracted by the idea of a method by which to verify assertions.

Otherwise, Benedict de Spinoza, Gottfried Leibniz, and even Immanuel Kant are dismissed with varying degrees of scorn for having posed questions and proposed answers that are founded in vague, incomprehensible language. Modern philosophers such as Bergson or Nietzsche are equally guilty of having made claims to universality when, in fact, their explanations have no objective grounding in reality. Valéry often evokes the Zeno of "Le Cimetière marin" as an example of how a sophist manipulates words out of context in order to deform reality.

The confusion between ideas and things makes all philosophy an ineffective tool for describing and defining the world. Until thinkers have solved the problem of language as a means to express their positions and ideas, we can only listen with skeptical ears. The exploration of the self would seem to provide the only promising terrain for such investigation, although the results will most certainly extend beyond the ill-defined boundaries of traditional philosophy.

Système (CI, 775–865)

The goal of founding a "system" that underlies all thought processes occupied Valéry's whole existence, especially after the crisis of 1892. The passages contained in this section have a direct relation with other headings such as *Ego, Langage,* or *Philosophie.* Valéry's earliest thoughts on the subject call for the use of mathematical science to analyze the transformations of the mind (775).

Almost 50 years later, in 1942–43, he still holds true to his belief in the value of an analytical theory of thought as a necessary first step in understanding how the human mind works (857). It is important to seek a pure, that is, nonlinguistic, model for thought, which supposes the discovery or creation of a new language for this process. Most previous attempts have failed because they have looked at an isolated phenomenon and drawn sweeping conclusions from simple observations.

Valéry proposes a method like that used in the development of music out of noise—separate the pure, constituent elements, determine their individual properties and attributes, then combine them again with the other elements to make up a whole (800). His method to attain knowledge reposes also on the principle that true knowledge will only be acquired when we are able to take into account all of the connections that make up a complex process.

Mathematical and scientific models provide him with the most promising system of representation that he has been able to find. Knowledge supposes a measurable difference or distance between two entities, and that knowledge makes up a sort of geometric *locus*. This relationship is referred to in Valéry's shorthand as $n + s$, meaning "nombres plus subtils."

Rather than searching for yet another illusory tool of explanation, Valéry insists on the representative quality he is seeking to construct in this system of functional images (807). The system aims therefore at the discovery of a form capable of accepting and representing human consciousness instead of trying to analyze it. The scientific model, with its ability to treat numerous variables and to measure phases of transformation, offers the most helpful system (812).

Psychology and physics can combine in a fruitful relationship. The principle of "self-variance" (854) is important in apprehending the many operations of the mind since many thoughts coexist and interact at the same time in one single brain. "Thought = Change" (854), he notes, wondering at every turn how it will be possible to discover laws to govern such a chaotic, unpredictable system. Valéry makes it quite clear that since his goal is not to attempt to explain everything, there will remain gaps that he will not try to fill in with vague words like "will" (806).

It is the "form" of such a system that interests him and that can be useful. All of his "philosophy" is taken up with the question of how to define certain words: "to know," "to be able," "to explain" (813). The conjunction of the scientific model and the representational approach lead Valéry to explore what he called "mental mechanics" (855). Although the comparison of the brain with a machine—what we call cybernetics—has obvious limits due to the multiplicity of functions and transformations that the human brain can carry out, it may still prove to be an appropriate representation.

It would be very interesting to know what Valéry might have thought of the computer as it relates to thought and the brain. This symbolic reproduction of specific mental functions explains nothing. It provides, however, an operative model for depicting the "physics of the mind" that he envisioned. He also recognized that he was quite far from having truly discovered the solutions to some of the problems that he raised, yet remained convinced to the end of his life that he was at least asking the right questions.

Psychologie (CI, 869–1115)

As a lifelong observer of the functioning of the human mind, it might seem only natural that Valéry would devote a substantial amount of time and thought to the subject of psychology in his *Cahiers*. Of greater interest than what is contained in these pages is perhaps what is absent—any serious discussion of modern psychoanalytic theories.

Although Valéry lived through the invention of psychoanalysis with Freud's numerous publications in the early twentieth century, they are only mentioned occasionally and in passing, most often to be criticized. In a letter written in 1935, he calls himself "the least Freudian" of men (*ŒI*, 1789). His deep-rooted distrust of subconscious, irrational forces, coupled with his lack of interest for most events of the past such as childhood episodes that figure so prominently in psychoanalytic schema, made Valéry discard such schools as less than able to shed light on the workings of the human mind.

This might seem all the more surprising given their shared interest in dreams, Eros, thought, and consciousness, yet Valéry could not accord such a prominent role to the same emotional forces that, since 1892, he had been attempting to understand and control. In many ways, his thoughts on psychology are an extension of his whole body of thought with numerous connections to language, consciousness, and dreams.

Valéry makes it clear that the main area of interest for him is the mind as action (1047) since that is the only way to study and dissect its movements and phases. Ideas and thoughts do not exist in isolated fashion. He compares the mind to a spider web in that the spider does not choose to spin the strands (that is done instinctively) but must "think" about the location and construction of the finished web (876).

Our thoughts then are a mixture of past experiences and present situations to which we must respond. Senses play a big role in many of our functions, such as laughter (929–31, 951–53), which is a nervous, reflexive reaction that erupts from an unexpected, unanticipated event. Perhaps the importance of his mention of laughter could be attributed to the interest raised by two other writers on the subject, Baudelaire and Bergson. Although he does not characterize laughter as "demonic," nor does he explore its "mechanistic" qualities, Valéry must have been aware of the interest in such a phenomenon.

Valéry insists on the importance of time and duration in mental processes. Actions and reactions are a function of the speed and number of operations being executed at any given moment (1024). The relevant unit is called a "phase," meaning the number and frequency of possible transformations that take place in a given organism (891). The modification from one state to another with a subsequent return is part of an infinite series of *trans*lations or *trans*formations, to utilize Valéry's vocabulary.

The enormous complexity of human "possibilities," a key word in Valéry's vocabulary, makes him despair at the hope of arriving at any satisfactory understanding of the processes at work in the mind. The human psyche is infinitely more complicated and unstable than in other living creatures, making the mind the only instrument available that has the potential to unlock some, if not all, of its own secrets. The psyche as agent of action is of vital importance in elaborating a system, as Valéry's aspired to do (1085). The sequence of transformations involved in every thought-act are often likened to an algebraic formula, $n + s$, in order to suggest the multiple variables and functions that can come into play at any one moment.

Among the many correlative areas of mental activity grouped together under the heading of "psychology," special mention might be given to Valéry's ideas on communication. Although rather sparse, they are summed up in at least one brilliant passage (978). Valéry begins by reminding us that we communicate with ourselves by the same means as we do with others. Our consciousness, in order to develop, needs to distinguish this alterity, or otherness.

Any communication supposes, then, a common ground between the self and the other, whether through thought or words. "To think is to communicate to the other that is oneself. To speak is to address the other as oneself" (978). In a system of almost limitless variables, the most constant factor in this algebra of human consciousness would then be the self. This process is as continuous as life itself since Valéry insists that there are only partial accomplishments (933) in psychology where nothing is ever complete and no absolute invariables exist.

Soma et C.E.M. (CI, 1119–49)

Soma, currently used as a term in biology, comes from the Greek word for body; *C.E.M.* stands for *Corps, Esprit, Monde* (Body, Mind, World) in Valéry's own shorthand. This relatively short section deals with the body, especially as it relates to the mind and the surrounding world. Contrary to the image that we sometimes have of Valéry as a cerebral poet, he never lost sight of the physical dimension that is of vital importance in attaining the limits of all forms of knowledge (1120, 1124). We can refer to *La Jeune Parque* for perhaps the most compelling use of physiology in Valéry's poetry.

Roland Barthes commented, "There is a body in Valéry that we do not know well" (*Magazine littéraire,* 26). Despite the fact that we do not fully understand its function (1119), the body is the instrument of reference in any undertaking. Valéry's admiration of Leonardo da Vinci stems in part from the important place that the Renaissance man accorded his physical being (1133). "The ship of the Mind floats and fluctuates on the ocean of the Body" (1134), suggesting by that how the mind cannot exist without the body and even how much the products of the mind owe the body for their elaboration.

The hand is a more commendable object of study than the brain, says Valéry, noting especially its universality (1127). His "system" therefore relies on the *C.E.M.,* the body, mind and world, which he calls the three cardinal points of knowledge (1142). Without the body, our senses do not function, and the mind and the world around us are of no use or importance. "The mind is the moment when the body responds to the world" (1125), a phrase that sums up as well as any other the fundamental directions in the method of Valéry.

Sensibilité (CI, 1153–1207)

This short but interesting section deals with sensibility, a term that Valéry acknowledges to be "ambiguous" since it can mean our ability to feel, the production of sensations, a mode of reaction, reactivity, a mode of transmission. It can also mean an irrational link (1206). The importance and mystery of the senses do not escape Valéry, who recognizes their value as the primary sources of knowledge and awareness between the mind, body, and world.

Contrary to the sensualists, who consider all knowledge to come from the five senses, Valéry believes that our senses are only the beginning of the cognitive process (1166). Every sensation, rather than being a direct reception of some stimulus from the outside world, involves an internal transformation or variation (1157). In other words, our perception through the sense organs is only the beginning of a process that involves variations and reactions within the mind.

In the example of a tree, which he uses several times, Valéry separates the sense function into a series of values—the eye captures a green object of a certain shape and size, which the brain then transforms into the idea of a tree. From the zero state of perception to the moment when the mind recognizes the foreign object as a tree, a certain duration in time takes place. "Time is what we perceive in the place of things" (1166), he affirms, meaning that all mental activity hinges on the speed with which we process perceptions and information. That "variation" or "gap" defines our thought process, which is, as we know from *La Jeune Parque,* a series of substitutions that leads to consciousness.

Our "ideas" are nothing without the "values" that we attach to them— for instance, a number between zero and infinity. The energy necessary to transform a sense perception into an idea will determine the value of that idea; the more immediate the transformation, such as in a ready "association of ideas," the less energy required and therefore the lower fiduciary value that can be given the final product (1182). One can only imagine what Valéry might have thought of modern electronics and microchips, the value of which is determined largely by the speed with which they can narrow the gap in the time it takes to process information.

Our sense of sound, based as it is on resonance and vibration, is particularly rich since it has the *possibility* of very wide variations of great value, such as in music (1169). It is hard to imagine what pure visual or auditive knowledge would be, especially since philosophers think mainly in terms of language and therefore limit their ability to envision the range of human understanding (1171).

Senses do not only receive, they also demand (1168). What we "receive" from the senses is not the outside world, but rather the ability to create for ourselves an outside world by substituting our virtual knowledge for the stimuli that are captured by our organs (1193).

What we call knowledge is what is situated within the parameters of our sensibility. What escapes our sensibility is not even available for consideration (1193). Our knowledge is limited by our ability to register and assimilate, that is, to make order from the sensations that solicit our consciousness. Our mind puts order momentarily into the range of sense perceptions that arrive in random, chaotic fashion. This ordering function suggests, however, that the mind discards or ignores those factors that are unfamiliar or incompatible with its patterns. We cannot "think" everything that we "sense," leaving Valéry to believe that our sensibility will always escape the control of our intelligence.

Mémoire (*CI*, 1211–59)

Valéry's conception of memory is best understood in terms of his ideas on sense perceptions and time. "Memory is the future of the past," he declares (1256). Rather than mechanically recalling past events, memory serves the present by recognizing similar, but not identical, forms that connect the past to the present. It is the past become *act* (1252). Walking, for instance, is an action that we learn at some point and then forget that we know. It has become memory in its most adaptable form (1219).

Language works along the same lines since we have at our disposal the words and phrases learned over the course of a lifetime, yet we are unable to remember how or where we heard them for the first time. Without the ability to forget, we would be little better than parakeets (1212).

What interests Valéry above all in this process is the way in which we synthesize and treat the information of the past, forgetting it yet keeping it constantly at hand. Without this fuzzy memory, we could not form ideas nor forge an identity for ourselves (1230). This transitive act of reappropriation of the external world and recognition of some part of that recorded past memory in the present constitutes the fundamental mechanism of our thought process. "All of our thoughts are memories recombined," Valéry states, since the ability to recall everything from the past would probably prohibit us from thinking (1255–56). With the stock of memories available in the brain, it is possible for one of the elements to be excited by some present stimulus that can awaken the whole chain of past events, Valéry observed in 1905 (1214).

The first volume of Proust's *A la recherche du temps perdu* would not appear before 1913, and Valéry, in a tribute to Proust published in 1923, stressed the combining factor in all acts of memory, even on the scale of Proust's immense monument to past time (*ŒI*, 772). The ease with which Valéry dismisses even the most extensive of novelistic explorations of the remembering consciousness should not obscure the fact that Valéry's 1920 evocation of a hammering sound that brings back vivid memories of 40 years ago follows quite closely the same process as Marcel's involuntary memory brought on by the madeleine in Proust's novel (1230). Like dreams, however, memories can also be distorted by their telling, since they undergo the reorganizing effect of being cast in story form (125).

What Valéry calls the "anachronic memory" amounts to the nonlinear redistribution of elements of the past that makes it possible to generate ideas and thoughts in the present using language that is reinvented at the same time (1245, 1257). This ultra-rapid process, he reminds us, is also a very physiological reaction of the nervous system in which synapses are activated or excited by a present sensation.

In this regard, Valéry adds that memory is never lost, only the path of memory (1239). To remember something is to attach a present stimulus (visual, auditive, etc.) to something from the past that bears some resemblance to that phenomenon and allows us to actualize a moment from the past (1255). This accent on the present, even when discussing memory, will characterize Valéry's understanding of time.

Temps (CI, 1263–1370)

Time is an ill-defined category, Valéry notes in 1924 (1319), only to point out five years later that it is but a word (1334). In 1943, he responds to that comment by observing that such a question is absurd since we must then wonder, "What is a word??!" (1368). That places time on the linguistic plane and makes it a notion in search of a meaning, like so many other dimensions in the world of Valéry. Did not Saint Augustine, he writes, know what a thing was as long as he didn't think too much about it, and then cease to understand it once he started to think about it (1334)?

At times, Valéry wishes to discard the term and invent a whole other lexicon to deal with the issue. This leads to a review of all of the previous representations of time from Einstein to Kant to Bergson to—Valéry himself (1342). His "time-sensation-halt-gap-lag-wait" theory leads to the view of time as possibility, and, in a variation on another formula, he distinguishes between short and long time by the quantity and length of our perception of time.

By way of an example, Valéry attempts to contrast the multiple sorts of time that may exist. A man running after a train perceives the time remaining quite short, yet the fatigue of having already expended energy makes him feel like the time he has been running was long (1336). He is, in fact, running after time or the idea of time, which is what conditions his efforts. His *state* of fatigue will make him consider the relative *idea* of the time left to run. He might then decide to run faster or to give up the race.

For Valéry, this is an example of an unequal equivalence between two representations of time whereby the impression of time past influences our expectation of time future (1337). Long time creates a marked sensation of pressure and unbalanced energy since we expect a response that does not arrive as anticipated or desired (1346). Valéry's dream would have been nothing less than to discover a set of laws for time just as Michael Faraday and James C. Maxwell had done for electromagnetism and space (1315).

Most of his comments on time concern our consciousness of time. Of particular importance to him is the present, which he defines as early as 1901 as "the only thing continuous" (1263). Later, in 1918, it is linked to action based on need or desire (1306). Finally, in 1944, it is a function that returns to its previous state and restores and confirms the self (1369).

All of these definitions raise the question of the connection between present time and human consciousness, of the forces that mark change and continuity from one present to another. "Time is an equation between permanence and change" (1278), Valéry points out in an attempt to discover some measurable difference between one time and another. We base our perception of time on our ability to foresee the future, even if only the next second. Our perception of duration is a function of the sensibility that we have to determine the gap between a part of ourselves and the whole around us. He is especially interested in surprise effects that arrive faster than our ability to anticipate and react, thus distorting our perception of time.

Valéry also devotes a good deal of thought to the question of rhythm that is so important in poetry. By the mental substitution according to a pattern that has evolved over some period of time, albeit a few seconds, the mind develops an anticipation of what the future-present cycle will hold. The interval between each occurrence of a stimulus directly conditions our perception of time since we measure and compare the outside action with our corporeal reality. Time can best be represented as the gap between our anticipation of an event and the realization of that event.

Rêve (CII, 5–200)

As we have noted previously, Valéry has little sympathy with Freudian attempts to interpret dreams and thereby gain insight into the workings of the human subconscious. It is easy to imagine what the exploration of the subconscious might have inspired in someone who declared that what is deepest in man is his skin (*Œll*, 215)! Valéry's formal objection is quite simple and, in some ways, echoes the reasons for which he distrusts and dislikes novels. The error in the Freudian analysis of dreams stems from the fact that their interpretations are based not on dreams themselves but rather on the account given of dreams. Once language is called upon to describe a dream, it can only alter its essential character (162). This is all the more complicated since one of the characteristics of a dream is that it is indescribable. Nevertheless, analysts attempt to translate it into ordered, reasoned language (177).

In any case, Valéry was more interested in the formal properties of dreams than in their substance, hidden or other (174). His fundamental objection will help to explain why he sees only limited value in the study of dreams as such. Since it is impossible to have an authentic account of a dream, we must rely on the narration of a dream for any conscious understanding of its significance. These narrations, always given by a subject who is awake, summarize and reorganize the impossible raw material that was the dream itself in order to make it understandable through language to someone with a conscious set of references (90, 112, 122, 190).

To interpret a dream is to interpret what is already an interpretation (60). A verbal rendition of a dream is always false since it relies on language, and words are incapable of depicting exactly what goes on in sleep and dreams. This stems in large part from the difference between dream and waking states, which is the main area of interest for Valéry. In fact, the study of the dream-state serves only one main purpose, which is a better understanding of our waking consciousness (106).

Dreams are different from our awake state in that everything is important in a dream (92), everything is an act (22), everything is "dreamed" (63). Nothing can be taken away from a dream (88) without destroying it, whereas we know that Valéry considered one of the primary characteristics of consciousness to be the ability to ignore certain aspects of the outside world (91). In the tale that one might tell of an event that transpired in a waking state of consciousness, many elements would certainly be deleted without making the story unintelligible. That imprecise, fuzzy quality is what makes language an adequate tool of literature and everyday communication.

In a dream, however, we are naked and without defense in a world where elements combine in a way that is unlike our normal state of consciousness (10). The rigorous mixing of elements from daily life with some detail that is either unlikely or impossible makes it hard for Valéry to imagine that we will ever define laws for analyzing dreams. The several dreams that Valéry recounts all contain a mixture of the familiar and the unusual. A fountain pen that has run out of ink creates "emptiness" in the form of an extinguished cigarette (114); the bathtub overflows in a bathroom that is at one moment protected by tiles, at another vulnerable to seepage through wooden floors and ceilings (35); editors substitute bills of different value in payment for articles they plan to publish (99). Each of these dreams contains some truth in fact into which a fanciful element is interjected.

The fundamental laws of substitution are rendered impossible by the fact that everything in the dream is necessary and seems to respond to an inherent necessity—within the dream itself. Valéry points out, for instance, that we do not read, count, or draw in a dream, yet we effortlessly know the content of a book or the solution to a math problem, and a drawing appears without ever having actually been drawn (183).

All of these examples demonstrate how the dream world imposes a state of being without ever following the process by which acts are carried out. Dreams take place in a distorted time that seems to condense complicated events to mere flashes. As we know from *La Jeune Parque* and other poems, Valéry is especially interested in the periods of transition from one state to another that constitute the metamorphosis of our self. The stages of awakening between sleep and consciousness thus provide a glimpse into the emerging consciousness. In a striking formula, Valéry insists on how he has always been interested in the human system that is undone and dissolved by sleep and reconstructs itself as it awakes (187).

Conscience (*CII*, 203–49)

The manifestations and ramifications of human consciousness would have to figure alongside language as one of Valéry's constant preoccupations. Indeed, the earliest notebooks dating from 1894 contain several fundamental remarks that he will develop and refine over the next 50 years.

The first question, contained on page 15 of the first notebook, asks, "What are the conditions for there to be consciousness?" It is answered immediately: "To be conscious is to compare at every moment what we are thinking or doing with what we could be thinking or doing" (203).

The degree of consciousness thus depends on the quantity of independent variables that can be excited at any one time (210, 225).

It is this plurality that enables consciousness to form, since only when there are multiple possibilities can one begin to distinguish true from false, real from imaginary, and so on (218, 232). This to-and-fro movement over a period of time might resemble a wavelength turned back upon itself as in the case of a radio, which can both emit and receive signals. Consciousness describes the process that takes these random, accidental perceptions and recognizes them as something that can be transformed into nonaccidental patterns or forms (238).

This operation becomes possible because, as Valéry insists, human beings embody a duality that allows them to communicate with themselves (224, 240). This *dédoublement* is a fundamental feature of the human psyche and carries out such complementary functions as "seeing/being seen," "speaking/hearing," or "receiving/producing" (224). One need only refer to the opening of *La Jeune Parque* to discover the poetic implications of such a principle.

A writer's consciousness is directed particularly towards language and aims at associating some idea or perception with a group of sounds (230–31). Anyone who articulates a message first receives his own message. Likewise, we are the emitters of any messages that we receive. The constitution of the self depends upon our ability to distinguish between these two functions (235). Consciousness reveals thought as thought, or, in Valéry's adaptation of Descarte's famous formula, "I think MYSELF: therefore, I am" (204), the confirmation of oneself as oneself being concomitant to thought. A conscious thought or act can be recognized for its qualities since it has become detached from the body that produced it. It has been transformed from an absence into a presence (226).

Valéry does not deny the secret, unknowable side of our thoughts and actions that resides on a subconscious level. Since that realm is unknowable by definition, its main interest lies in what it can help us to understand about the conscious world. Our modern interest in the unconscious nevertheless leaves Valéry quite skeptical (231), just as he saw only limited value in the study of dreams as a way of gaining insight into the conscious world.

Attention (CII, 253–73)

This short section can be considered an annex to the previous rubric dealing with consciousness. Compared to consciousness, which supposes a self-reflexive process, attention refers more to a sustained focus of mental faculties on a given object. The simple fact of paying attention will provide one with observed data about a certain object without necessarily leading to the type of thought process that implies understanding.

Contrary to the consciousness of thought, attention refers to an external object of contemplation and observation. The phase of attention generally has a limited but continuous duration (254) and will enable the individual to grasp the multiple factors that combine together in any phenomenon. Such forces as fatigue or distraction can limit attention. Of the various organs, it is the eyes that seem to interest Valéry most since they have the ability to take in a wide field of objects or to focus on a very minute detail.

Le Moi et la personnalité (CII, 277–333)

Valéry attempts to distinguish between the self and the personality, the former referring to the unalterable whole, whereas the latter is reserved for the less stable particular. The "pure self," in Valéry's terms, is that core of a ring or circle that cannot change and cannot be changed, whether by dementia or by age.

Its invulnerability also makes it less operational since it derives its stability from the fact that it has no discernible attributes and does not interact with the surrounding world (317). This absolute quantity is often represented by zero in Valéry's attempt to devise mathematical representations of the human psyche. Our personality is the sum of our habits and our past encounters and experiences. It is presumably a more knowable commodity (280–81).

In any case, Valéry is most insistent on the fact that an individual is a "SPACE *of possibilities*" (277) and that the biographical rendition of a man's life provides only a sampling of his total being (288, 305). We are the result of the actions and reactions that both reveal us to others and define us in the process. Valéry insists quite clearly in this context that we *need* others in order to become ourselves (325, 333). We are never ourselves totally, however, since we cannot be at any given moment all that has gone into making us what we are over the course of a lifetime (316). The figure of Narcissus appears several times in connection with this whole question since he epitomizes the creation of an identity that is capable of recognizing an image of itself.

Affectivité (*CII*, 337–89)

This study of our affects, or emotional makeup, doubtless bears traces of the crisis of 1892 in which Valéry suffered both psychological and artistic scars. This section also bridges the gap between the study of personality (see above) and love, especially physical, that will be dealt with in *Eros.*

In one of the more personal subjects treated in the *Cahiers,* Valéry here reveals the conflicts and struggles that pitted his emotions against his intellect. The examination of human passions and sentiments interests him, especially insofar as he strives to *understand* them (340) and thereby bring them under control. He shows a great curiosity for feelings and emotions while at the same time being extremely wary of their destructive powers. They are, in their most dangerous manifestations, forces of disorder or asymmetry that result not from pure sources but rather from unknown and unknowable causes. It is the role of the intellect to attempt to keep the resulting effects of some emotion from becoming disproportionately strong to the degree that they end up by overpowering the causes (354). The greatest cause of anger is to realize that our mind can do nothing to control that very anger (366).

There is a possible benefit, however, when the counterreaction of the intellect becomes powerful enough to look at the situation from a fresh point of view that it might otherwise not have considered (357). Valéry therefore does not attempt to deny the existence and force of emotions. At times, he even acknowledges that his attempts to eradicate their negative potential may have deprived him of a possible source of knowledge about himself and the human psyche (360, 363).

Despite penetrating remarks on a wide range of sentiments such as pain (364), happiness (366), or anger (369), his analysis nevertheless leads him to relegate such lesser forces to a lower standing while maintaining respect and admiration for such higher functions as thought and consciousness. Our potential for suffering makes us always vulnerable to minor incidents and changes, to the point that Valéry has yet again transformed Descartes's formula to read, "I suffer, therefore I am" (377). Despite his curiosity for the emotional, affective side of the human psyche, Valéry could hardly consider it worthy of the same attention as mental, intellectual processes.

Eros (*CII*, 393–561)

This most intimate of subjects reveals a Valéry both fascinated and repulsed by the physical and psychological manifestations of love. The struggle between the body and the mind takes on greater proportions as a man and woman come together and experience "an oscillation around an equilibrium" (393). The force of love is such that it can overwhelm and overpower the search for stability and control.

In his own private life, Valéry isolates two key events in his sentimental education—the infatuation for a married woman named Madame de R[ovira], which in part touched off the crisis of 1892, and his liaison with Catherine Pozzi, the "K" of the *Cahiers,* which was a passionate, although illicit, affair beginning in 1920.

As a result of the devastating "Genovese night" of October 1892, Valéry had decided to shun the world of emotions and love in favor of exploring and perfecting his intellect. He therefore looks at love during these years as an invention, a gigantic joke or a ridiculous literary fabrication (396). It disorganizes and disorients the whole organism, which is surprised to have transformed an absence into a presence, only to find the reality a bit less real and a bit less "delicious" than expected (398).

Sexuality is a cyclical activity that never reaches a goal but rather depends on repetition, therefore making it a less noble function (397). In its social and cultural context, it has become an artificial commodity that pushes people to folly and distorts or even destroys the acuity of their higher functions. Our culture has transformed a physiological phenomenon into a psychological necessity. "Love is a poor substitute for the knowledge that we cannot attain and we replace possession by a spasm. But this flash does not illuminate anything" (404). Although there can be some benefits from the sudden production of so much energy, most of the comments and analyses from these earlier years consider *éros* to be more destructive than productive.

The breadth and wealth of entries seem to change in 1920 with the appearance of "K" or "Karine" in his life, since she possessed both the emotional and intellectual ability to satisfy Valéry. While their liaison was often turbulent, it also provided Valéry with a range of insight into love that opened up greater comprehension and acceptance of the emotions he was capable of feeling. He recognizes immediately that to be loved and to feel that "obscure warmth of the soul" might be the greatest thing in the world (409). Comparable to religious faith, the worth of a veritable exchange with someone else becomes for Valéry not only possible but even desirable above all else (449).

This does not mean that he has changed his entire position and renounced his previous skepticism. It would seem rather that he has come to realize, as he put it in later life, that "the mixture of love and mind is the most intoxicating drink in the world" (510). Love is stronger than the intellect, perhaps explaining Valéry's distrust of a force that he might not be able to control.

He notes, in this context, that love affairs always have bad endings and that the greatness of love can be measured by the greatness of pain that is caused (467). This is about as close as Valéry comes to a *romantic* position. This imbalance stems from an internal contradiction in the way we desire, wanting both to give ourselves and keep ourselves while failing to recognize or accept that we are entirely made up of what we give (463).

Valéry remains aware that what often passes for love is also, to a great degree, a learned behavior that is more complicated than necessary for the perpetuation of the species. This "zoological and ethnographical comedy" results from the way in which civilization has made sexuality into a divine activity with mysterious, spiritual values (486).

Many of Valéry's comments on sexual behavior give a very scientific analysis of intercourse as a "physico-psycho-aesthetic" proceeding (487). The later entries are more typical of Valéry's broader preoccupations in that he attempts to gain insight into the possible relationship between *éros* and literature, especially insofar as the general awakening of the senses by erotic energies can have beneficial effects for the creative process (535).

Thêta (CII, 565–718)

Valéry explains at considerable length the reasons why he rejects religion, or rather, why he has found his own faith in the exercise of his intellect and his own calendar of saints in the illustrious thinkers who have preceded him. He objects to belief in anything that he has not witnessed or that he has not invented himself (573). One can only profess faith if one accepts to believe in the most unbelievable of concepts, an idea that goes against Valéry's entire system of values. Rather than explaining things, religious texts and leaders propose ready-made solutions to unsolvable problems (569) and then ask the faithful to believe in their edicts and dogmas.

For Valéry, what would be interesting to determine is the importance accorded the human being in a religious system: his individual destiny, feelings, acts, and value, instead of universal proclamations (612). Most religions appeal to our superstitious need for mystery, miracles, or other forms of stories that ground their present claims on past events that no one can verify. This did not, of course, keep the Romans from building a great civilization (610).

Valéry maintains that the question, "Does God exist?" has no meaning and cannot be answered since it implies that the notion of God is essentially linguistic and could not survive the suppression of its name (686). Valéry finds it impossible to believe in a god that chose to sacrifice his only son instead of talking clearly and reasonably to his people (594). The force of fear and intimidation that motivates much religious belief and practice leaves him cold. Valéry's self-directed pride leads him to declare that he needs nothing, thus making him unresponsive to the message of such a god (596).

Death is not a fact of ominous portent since life itself is due to chance or accident (574). Fear of death has been successfully directed at weaker individuals and used to direct their moral and emotional lives. Of the many unknown factors that religion pretends to address and solve, death is the most powerful one. Without it, religions would lose their *raison d'être*. Christianity has made a cornerstone out of pain instead of pleasure by giving it a sort of absolute value (589).

Valéry avows his own atheism (639) or agnosticism (667), convinced as he is that the very question of religious belief is unanswerable and therefore pointless. In that context, he cannot follow Pascal, who inspires terror and horror in the souls of believers and leaves them no alternative but to worship a cruel god (666). Such a perspective is hard to accept for someone like Valéry who does not believe in "metaphysical anguish," which he dismisses as an impure mixture of illegitimate questions and incoherent images (684).

Bios (CII, 721–74)

Valéry demonstrates both a literary and scientific interest in biology. In a semiserious definition that dates from 1900, he qualifies life as something that goes on between 8000 meters in altitude and 8000 meters in depth (721). During later deliberations for the French Academy's dictionary project, he recalls how he objected to the use of the word *organized* in the proposed definition of the word *Life* (760). His general world view extends here to biological life, which is a combination of spontaneity and organization in degrees that are practically impossible to determine. Life on earth is very much the result of a fortuitous set of circumstances, both biological and environmental.

Valéry expresses several times his wonder at the elaborate genetic codes that are inscribed in the smallest units of biological matter. This leads him in places to envision genetic manipulation, although one can only imagine what he might think of the strides taken by scientists since his day. In his view, each living organism contains such a complicated set of characteristics that we should despair at ever knowing or understanding them all.

The random, accidental nature of life causes Valéry to cast some doubts on the theory of evolution as well as on the presence of life in other parts of the universe (748). Life is made possible (although not necessary) by the numerous factors that coexist on the planet. It survives and proliferates, thanks to its ability to enact transformations on its environment and, conversely, to be transformed by that environment (748). The law of transformation combines with a principle of conservation to make life possible on earth (753, 768).

Valéry also notes at several points how we execute drastic transformations around us, killing to preserve life in a way that requires true genius to imagine that it is not a great work of folly (766). Contrary to many living forms that know strictly cyclical existences, nature seems to have endowed human beings with a greater degree of individuality (752); however, all of our efforts cannot escape the finality of death, which ultimately overcomes life. "Life is what can be abolished," according to Valéry in 1937 (765).

Mathématiques (CII, 777–830)

In the context of this section, we should remember that Valéry's first Parisian apartment had as an essential piece of furnishing a chalkboard on which he could carry out mathematical problems. Throughout his life, he frequented mathematicians with whom he could converse and exchange views. In 1896, Valéry envisioned the possibility of translating everything into mathematics (777).

His interest in mathematical systems comes from his admiration of their formal properties by which operations can be distinguished from the contents that they create (780). It is their form or structure that intrigues him more than some meaning that might be contrived from such an artificial language. Such systems are ideal creations of the mind and can thus provide insight into the functioning of thought processes. They represent mental operations in a way that no other art or science can. At one point, Valéry compares them to an "exercise," one of his favorite words when applied to poetry, and adds that they are comparable to dance (788).

Mathematics trains the mind to enlarge its potential to analyze and understand problems that are created by that same mind. Valéry insists on the arbitrary quality of mathematics, which is, for him, the "science of the arbitrary" (815). Mathematical systems rely on imagination and inventiveness in the search for solutions to highly complex problems. There is, however, little overlap between the pure realm of mathematics and the impure world of reality. Mathematics teaches the valuable lessons of what can and cannot be transformed within a given system (824). Their real value, however, is not to be found in mechanical applications in the outside world.

Valéry especially admires algebra and geometry, the former for its ability to combine unlimited variables and factors (787), the latter which he compares to "a temple erected to the gods of space by the god Speech" (792). The superior language of mathematics gives it a rigor and coherency that push the mind to its extreme limit.

Science (CII, 833–920)

Valéry here demonstrates his interest in science cultivated both through readings and through personal acquaintance with some of the premier scientific minds of his day—Albert Einstein, Jean Perrin, and Paul Langevin. He shows a broad knowledge of the history of science (849, 884–85) as well as of modern developments, especially in the realm of physics.

In keeping with his concept of cross-fertilization between disciplines, Valéry does not hesitate to comment or question ideas put forward by eminent specialists, feeling pleased that his point of view might be useful and unusual to them. He is particularly interested in the methods used by scientists in their explorations and experiments, even if the main objective is to define the problems more than to find answers to specific questions (833).

In order not to influence the observations by the very fact of observing, it is important to get a proper distance and perspective on whatever one is attempting to study. This does not mean that we know any more about such fundamental questions as time, movement, or space (888). Depending on the point of view of the observer, it is always possible to find some sort of explanation that may or may not be valid, that is, that can be repeated again and again with the same result.

Many great discoveries, such as those of Galileo, come from an individual's will to question common wisdom and even previous experiments that pretend to have solved a problem (843). Despite the great scientific advances seen in modern times, Valéry still maintains that this apparent increase in knowledge has not in any way threatened to diminish the mystery of the world. Quite to the contrary, we now have even more questions to address and problems to solve than before (870).

Art et esthétique (CII, 923–83)

Valéry shows himself to have been an avid student and admirer of a wide range of art forms, including music, painting, dance, and architecture. His tastes go resolutely to those artists who establish a necessary relationship between the formal and signifying elements of their work (968).

Despite careful and prolonged thought on the subject, Valéry also recognizes that a work of art will always remain somewhat obscure and unexplainable (944). In creating such a work, there must be conscious craft on the part of the artist, who then harmonizes the elements of his piece, enclosing them in a coherent group.

Every work of art produces a state of desire in the spectator, a state that it both creates and satisfies, forming a closed circle (963–64). A musical phrase, for instance, that succeeds in this communication does so by producing in the listener what enables that listener to produce in turn the "expression" by which he received knowledge (947).

Instead of relying on repetition or reproduction, such a process transforms the receiver into a producer capable of realizing a series of substitutions. Perfect harmony between the spectator and the performance allows that spectator to (re)produce indefinitely and with unlimited energy the beauty of a piece (941). The aesthetic source has been transferred from the producer to the spectator, who now becomes a producer. This is a capital notion in Valéry's aesthetic theory and can be applied to poetry as well as to other arts.

Music occupies the lion's share of Valéry's thoughts, perhaps as part of the heritage of symbolism, which aimed at restoring to music its letters of nobility. Its force and freedom give it a wider range of pure expression than literature (929). Music appeals directly to the nervous system of the listener and puts the listener back in touch with himself. Music is a "massage," he notes in 1914 to underscore the physical activity that is involved in music (934). It is the consummate art of exciting pure possibility since a single note can awaken the whole system of sounds that lies dormant in the psyche (974). Valéry, like many artists of his generation, holds Wagner in highest esteem since the German composer writes for the Self, playing on the whole breadth and depth of possibilities of the individual (956). He has applied the greatest possible force in order to achieve the greatest possible signification. His true orchestra is the organism's entire nervous system, connecting with complete control of all available resources in a way that can hardly be rivaled. Valéry also admires Bach, Mozart, and Gluck. He especially appreciates Bach's formal ability to achieve pure combinations (955, 979).

Valéry's tastes in the arts rarely extend to modern forms, which he dismisses for their reliance on tricks and their search for originality at all costs. He compares the adulterated compositions of modern art to decaffeinated coffee (976)! He deplores the decadence of modern painting with its lack of technique, thought, conception, or attention to detail, wondering if perhaps there is nothing left to paint (952). Alongside his appreciation for such classical masters as Leonardo, Rembrandt, and Velásquez, the only moderns whom Valéry seems to admire are Degas and Monet (948).

Architecture, one of Valéry's lifelong passions, occupies a privileged place in his thoughts for its plant-like ability to grow upward with modulations and modifications in every detail (937). His dialogue *Eupalinos* spells out that admiration in no uncertain terms. He deplores the way in which modern cities have ruined architecture. Skyscrapers do not demonstrate ideas, only confusion (958). The constructions are mass-produced instead of being actually built by human hands (983).

To the contrary, we find his admiration for many types of architecture and ornamentation—Gothic (981), Greek (939, 941), and Arabic (971)—as well as praise for Egyptian sculpture (961). They all have in common that they correspond to Valéry's conception of beauty as a perfect exchange between the spectator and the object, thereby forming an endless source of energy that conserves both parties (941).

The two sections in the Pléiade *Cahiers* devoted to Valéry's ideas on poetry, *Poïétique* (*CII,* 987–1056) and *Poésie* (*CII,* 1059–1142), have been incorporated into chapter 2, "Poetics."

Littérature (*CII,* 1145–1242)

Beyond the specific question of poetry, which I have treated elsewhere, Valéry's comments in this section include a broad range of topics such as the novel, specific writers or periods, and literary criticism. These entries should be read in conjunction with the published articles and conferences gathered in *Variété* ("Etudes littéraires," *ŒI,* 427–784), which cover many of the same topics in more organized fashion. Valéry notes that all of the great French writers have also been excellent critics (1191), able to analyze and judge the works of peers. The analytical approach in literature is most obviously exemplified by Poe and Mallarmé, two figures whom Valéry admires above all.

He suggests that the best place to begin the study of an author is by examining his vocabulary to determine which words occur with what frequency and which words do not occur at all (1210). This would be especially revealing in Racine where a very limited number of words (1800, according to Valéry, [*CII*, 1184]) can be combined in a wealth of ways to obtain concentrated effects of unrivaled intensity.

In contrast to Racine, Valéry criticizes Shakespeare's more or less direct appeal to the audience in order to move his spectators by whatever means seem necessary to achieve the desired effect (1185). The very richness of his plays becomes a drawback for Valéry. He most vividly criticizes Pascal and has little esteem for Molière or Gustave Flaubert. Besides Racine, his preferences go towards the eighteenth century or Stendhal.

On the other hand, there are no kind words for contemporary literature, which suffers, as Valéry wrote about Breton and the surrealists, from a desire to achieve the greatest scandal through the most facile means (1208). In his rather limited admiration for literature, Valéry expresses a marked preference for those writers that give him a sense of discovery (1150) and whose works aspire to the criteria of purity and consciousness that he valued above all.

The genre of the novel is a frequent target of criticism, qualified as both arbitrary and trivial, lacking in the constant rigor and high standards that characterize poetry (1172). His own disinterest in plot, character, and setting, could possibly stem from his inability to tell a story, which he attributes to his quick turn of mind. One must slow down to write a novel (1162). Unlike the poem, which demands the collaboration of its readers, a novel requires that we suspend our natural disbelief and agree to become credulous consumers of unlikely lore (1206). Valéry also holds novels in lesser esteem because they do not, he claims, require the same degree of personal work and investment to produce given the fact that even the writer himself does not believe in 85 percent of what he writes (1221). Fiction appeals, therefore, to our lower mental functions instead of challenging us to interact with it as is the case with a successful poem. The public's appetite for novels can be attributed in large part to the fact that people no longer take the trouble to read, content as they are to get the general sense of a message in as short a period of time as possible. The culprits in this trend are advertising and newspapers since they inundate the public with slogans and headlines that require little or no real thought or effort to be swallowed and digested.

Valéry also reserves some scathing comments for critics, who rarely take into account the aims of the work or the conditions under which it was conceived. His tongue-in-cheek list of phrases that critics might use show how much he disliked and distrusted professional critics as readers (1177–78). Their activity essentially consists of saying, "I like this work" and "I don't like that one" (1192), a job that almost anyone can perform.

Valéry recognizes, however, that an author does not have the prerogative of interpreting his own work once it has left his hands. His intention may very well have been his intention, but the reader also has the right to interpret it as he pleases (1191). A work that reaches the public is only the latest version of a given piece and should not be considered to be the definitive pronouncement of the author. The true value of a literary work remains to be determined by the readers, who, from generation to generation, will reinterpret and reevaluate it according to an evolving set of criteria.

Poèmes et PPA (CII, 1245–1306)

This section contains short fragments of poetry or prose poems; "PPA" signifies "Petits poèmes abstraits" (Short abstract poems) in Valéry's shorthand. Although not included in the collections as finished pieces, many of them found their way into one or another of the texts contained in *Tel Quel* or *Mélange*.

A complete study of this grouping would require a return to the full text of the *Cahiers* in the C.N.R.S. edition with variants and corrections. As presented here, they are interesting examples of some of Valéry's more spontaneous writings since most of them deliver isolated impressions, cursory sketches, or snippets of verse or prose to which he rarely returned with the intent of crafting them into more polished works. They confirm the role of the *Cahiers* as a sort of laboratory or sounding board for work in progress. In that respect, they are revealing of some of the ideas that Valéry picked up and abandoned at various points in his career, especially during the silent years of 1892–1917.

These pieces prove that Valéry was carrying on a rich, personal literary dialogue with himself and continuing to think about writing poetry even if his official production was practically nil. They rhyme in some cases, although few observe the fixed patterns that Valéry adopted for most of his published poetry. One might be surprised, however, to find a haiku (1300).

The subject matter is of some interest since they tend to be more personal and more concerned with the natural world and with outside sensations and observations. Quite a few of them deal with seasons and weather (1246, 1294), time and the universe (1249), dawn (1272, 1275, 1283), and awakening (1268, 1270–71). The wealth of sensations described in his 1915 evocation of a forest gives a sense of mystery and wonder that rarely transpires in his other poems (1262–63).

Another particularity that sets these "Poèmes et PPA" aside from either the published poems or the rest of the *Cahiers* is the anecdotal interest of many of the pieces. Rather than being the product of Valéry's early-morning musings in his Paris study, they include evocations of places as varied as Genoa (1256), Grasse (1299), Brittany (1269), or the seaside (1259). Once again, it is the presence in the *Cahiers* of such pieces and their absence in the more "official" collected works that gives this section its special flavor.

Sujets (CII, 1309–56)

This section contains sketches and notes for a number of projects or ideas that Valéry never executed, including plays, novels, short stories, a ballet, monologues, and dialogues. Certain passages shed light on other published works, such as *Faust* (especially 1342–53) or *Teste* (1326). There is even a hypothetical ending for the Narcissus poem of *Charmes* in which the "symmetry of death" appears in his reflection, leaving his soul present and his body absent (1327). We can only wonder at what might have become of his idea for a "Journal of the Body" (1323), or a poem about Einstein going to Zurich to learn differential calculus in order to be able to construct his theory of relativity (1324).

Perhaps of greater interest than any of the specific subjects that were jotted down here is the quantity of ideas for novels or short stories. Given Valéry's oft-proclaimed scorn for the genre, it is surprising to find him in 1901 sketching out the plot for a sort of moral police story or, in 1934, outlining a science fiction tale about a man made to live according to the rhythms of another planet (1336).

Likewise, many notes subsist for a projected drama on Tiberius or for a later tragedy on Stratonice: "I like to study this *Stratonice* that will never be written—that's the enjoyment" (1339). These and many other projects attest to the vivid and diversified mind of Valéry.

Homo (*CII*, 1359–1443)

Many of these pronouncements on human nature are of the kind that shed light not only on the object but also on the subject of the reflections. In this section, we find a Valéry much in the lineage of the seventeenth-century French *moralistes,* offering a cogent, often cutting, observation about fellow men—and sometimes women. It is no coincidence that many of the aphoristic sentences included here also appear in the published volumes, such as *Mélange, Choses tues,* or *Mauvaises pensées et autres* (contained in the *Œuvres* volumes). They are the type of pithy lessons that straddle both universal and personal concerns.

Valéry himself does not necessarily offer them as definitive judgments on human nature since any moralistic thought that has as its object such a vacillating, unstable entity as a human being must be approached with caution. A large group of these maxims aims at debunking the myth of deep thought and intellectual certitude that makes morality possible and truth attainable: "The superiority of mankind stems from his useless thoughts" (1365); "The world is interesting only in its extreme points but survives only by the middle ground" (1368); "Children see but know not. Adults know but see not" (1415).

This generally disparaging view of humankind can be attributed to the fact that the vast majority of people have not even a vague idea of their own selves since they have never developed their consciousness beyond a primitive level. The imperative of self-development remains vital for Valéry, who reproaches our tendency to identify ourselves with an image of what we believe ourselves to be rather than what we are (1440). True intellectual life should have as its goal the reconstruction of the self (1386), even striving for divine status (1387).

The image that we sometimes have of Valéry as an isolated thinker or one who sought refuge within himself belies the important fact that his self-awareness constituted for him the greatest of all possible adventures. One should only approach oneself "armed to the teeth" (1406) and with few illusions. This pride can turn to a veritable passion (1385) whereby the individual, like Robinson Crusoe, begins to imagine himself to be the only soul on earth. Only constant, lucid self-evaluation can avoid the pitfalls of a misdirected sense of self.

In addition, he recognizes here, as elsewhere, the need for others, without whom we can never become ourselves (1428). The truly dangerous persons are not those who seek overtly to do evil, but rather those who are weak and credulous enough to lend indifferent support to other evil minds (1416).

Whether in the political arena or the social sphere, Valéry shows himself to be very distrustful of the motives and motivations of those who reach high levels of power and prestige. They were, after all, placed in the spotlight by frail human beings who have, by and large, no clear idea of what they are doing. Our moral systems discourage us from being ourselves and seeking truth with passion, even at the risk of making mistakes along the way. Great men and stupid men alike are those who have trusted their own judgments (1403).

Histoire-Politique (CII, 1447–1552)

These excerpts from the *Cahiers* overlap in many areas with the published essays that have already been examined in the chapter on Valéry's critique of the modern world. He is particularly adamant about the weaknesses inherent to history as a field of study. Events of the past are no more important than waves of the ocean, which are the visible part hiding the vast depths that we cannot see (1479). Those who deal in history could best be compared to charlatans or magicians since they recount events that they could not possibly have witnessed themselves and even base predictions for future events on such misguided speculation. He goes on to lodge a familiar reproach, stating that history displays very little consciousness of itself and of the trade it undertakes (1527).

In the middle of the Second World War, Valéry adds to a long analysis of the stupidity of mankind the observation that history has been used to kindle old fires of hatred and animosity, thus contributing to conflicts in an indirect manner (1536). Instead of concentrating on events of the past, history should seek to discover more about those less perceptible facets that make up life in the present (1537).

Politics is the scourge of modern times, deriving its power largely from the passivity of the people (1456). Valéry finds democracy to be less satisfactory than a system based on merit since the majority of people are not able to make informed and intelligent decisions. This does not mean that he favors autocratic systems but rather shows his general distrust of all political systems. Politicians, not unlike historians, manipulate language with a total disregard for truth or the general welfare of the people they govern. They use modern media and advertising to spread their propaganda and to sway people by fabricating tastes.

Politics is particularly reprehensible because it attempts to make the people of a nation conform to a single preconceived model of the mind, whether it be "Nation," "State," or "People" (1522). This abstraction can then be manipulated and redefined through rhetoric and slogans to turn docile populations into fanatical believers. Unless the population is aware of these ruses and has developed its mind to think independently, politicians will continue their strategy of indoctrination and manipulation. In 1926–27, Valéry advocates a form of "global thinking" that will bypass the divisions of nationalism and turn towards the future instead of re-creating the past (1476).

France, of course, occupies a central position in his analysis of history and politics. In its official history, Napoleon stands out as an individual who had a uniquely personal vision and the intelligence and perseverance to pursue it (1449, 1490). Valéry sees France as a heterogeneous and undisciplined country in search of unity. The centralization of power is a result of that thrust (1477). Its unity is, however, more one of morals by the way in which French people interact, fight, and joke among themselves (1458). He comments that it is essentially a conservative country in the proper sense of the term ("that seeks to conserve"), as well as harboring many contradictory aims and directions (1511). Contrary to the Germans, who despise disorder, the French can only live in the disorder that they call "freedom" (1519).

Despite his often harsh criticism of his compatriots during the debacle in 1940, he refrains from assigning any direct blame that would only worsen the situation of France and Europe. Valéry notes that the country has inflicted this sad state upon itself and will have to redefine itself once the conflict is over (1506). Although he speaks loudly and clearly for a united Europe, he is also painfully aware of its capacity for self-destruction under the strong impulsion of science, technology, and money (1533).

Enseignement (CII, 1555–83)

This rubric on education and teaching was originally part of the preceding section on history and politics. In connection with his comments, it is useful to remember that Valéry, during his later years, held the chair of poetics at the Collège de France and was the first administrator of the

Centre Universitaire Méditerranéen at Nice (the proposed charter of this "open university" can be found in *Œuvres II*, 1128–44). His own memories of his school years show little sympathy or satisfaction with educational practices that do more to squelch learning than to promote it.

In order to teach effectively, the first step must be to kindle a student's interest in the subject; the rest will follow naturally (1556, 1558). It is also important to encourage questions, he states, adding that it is the student and not the teacher who should be asking them (1574).

Valéry insists on the fact that a bored teacher will only bore students and that natural curiosity will die in the face of boredom (1555). Most of the subjects taught in schools are taught by unqualified teachers who attempt to pass along knowledge about subjects that are of little or no interest to children. Our so-called humanistic education has made *Phèdre* into a bibliographic exercise, Virgil into a translation text, and mathematics into a form of punishment. Latin and Greek cannot be appreciated before the age of forty (1556), yet our schools ignore such important subjects as music, drawing, and dance.

Valéry is especially critical of the way in which poetry is taught without taking into account the musicality of verse (1560, 1565). Philosophy, one of the mainstays of French education, is also taught as a dry set of precepts and problems instead of being attached directly to life (1567). Rather than teaching French per se, Valéry suggests introducing ideas about language, which is the foundation for all future study of literature and philosophy (1568–69).

Learning is widely defined as accumulating generally worthless or irrelevant knowledge instead of cultivating our senses of observation and analysis. The French system of national examinations leads students and teachers to direct their efforts at success in obtaining a diploma or a job instead of at true learning (1570, 1580). Such a system rewards short-term performance and leads to laziness and inertia by encouraging people to settle into routines that are fatal to real inquiry and discovery.

Chapter Nine
Conclusion: Posterity and Heritage

The idea of concluding a study on Paul Valéry now might seem incongruous and paradoxical, given the French author's own incessant practice of rewriting, rereading, and revising his own work. The time comes, however, to close this presentation and, reluctantly, to conclude. Valéry's insights and observations speak for themselves. His example and accomplishment set the bar a notch higher for those who follow. As for the posterity of great men, he once wrote that they die twice—the first time as men, the second as great (*Œll*, 592).

While certain writers, like Baudelaire or Stendhal, wrote with the distinct feeling that they would only be appreciated by later generations, the opposite seems to have happened with Valéry. He was hailed as a renowned poet in his own lifetime, even by those who hardly read poetry, and now seems to have become the victim of that success. The general public, at least in France, has reduced him to a few poems learned in school, a quotation about which to write a composition, and a series of inscriptions on the Palais de Chaillot in Paris. This view seems so partial as to be false. Valéry remains to be discovered by the vast number of readers, even literate, who would benefit from contact with such a truly intelligent individual.

It is extremely refreshing to read someone of Valéry's caliber who refuses to take himself too seriously. He can be, at times, the most self-deprecating of men. For a writer who spent a lifetime exploring the sinuous paths of consciousness, knowledge, and language, his lesson remains surprisingly understated. Valéry himself refuses to conclude since that is a literary contrivance. Novels have conclusions; life does not.

This should not be interpreted to mean, as some have suggested, that the famous *système* was a failure. We should, to the contrary, appreciate Valéry's intellectual honesty in refusing to propose an airtight, infallible system based on a prearranged set of premises. Does he not point out in the *Cahier B 1910* that literature is full of people who have no idea of what to say, yet who persist in their urge to write (*Œll*, 575)?

His reticence to publish was the sign of a natural modesty and a self-imposed silence. But then, those who speak the most are not necessarily those who have the most to say. Valéry's greatest work, the *Cahiers,* is paradoxically the one that was born out of the silence of his daily meditations and not directly intended for the general public. One cannot help but marvel and wonder at the figure of a lone individual dialoguing every morning with himself, as if he were one of the rare people capable of understanding what Paul Valéry truly had to say. Valéry teaches us to listen to the words we utter, to speak the words we hear.

This does not mean that his public persona was not authentic, even if his term as the "unofficial poet of the Troisième République" brought him glory and paid the bills. He shows a very real human understanding that can come only from prolonged acquaintance with one's fellow human beings. The image of a Valéry smugly installed in his role as member of the Académie française or dining with heads of state and international celebrities should not obscure the reality of a man with rare insight into the inconsequential nature of human existence. Behind the *habit vert* that he donned for official ceremonies was a man who could perhaps be characterized as a conservative nihilist with a healthy dose of skeptical humor. T. S. Eliot, who was one of Valéry's foremost admirers outside of France, commented that "his modesty and his informality were the qualities of a man without illusions, who maintained no pretense about himself to himself, and found it idle to pretend to others."[1]

Despite his desire to translate into mathematical and scientific language the wealth of human knowledge, Valéry also knew that there are forces at play in the universe that will never submit to his dreams of a perfectly rigorous system. Perhaps taking a page from Mallarmé, who wondered if he was not mad to undertake such an impossible project as the "Coup de dés," Valéry might seem to have set his sights so high that he could never realistically hope to achieve his goal.

In retrospect, this might seem of secondary importance since the thoughts generated along the way in his quest for knowledge and understanding constitute the true victory of Valéry. We are fortunate that he shared the journey with us in a characteristic gesture of generosity. "Palme," the concluding poem in *Charmes,* shows how exertion does not lead to exhaustion where the mind is concerned, but rather generates more words, more thoughts, more gifts.

There are also those who would claim that Valéry left poetry in an impasse with no room to advance or retreat. Does he represent, as Eliot suggests, the last in a line of poets that began with Baudelaire and went extinct after Valéry's death? While it is true that he did not spawn a school or movement as was the case with the surrealists, it is also true that these are questions of modes and styles that change periodically. It seems likely that there has always been and will always be a place for a poet of his formal and musical qualities.

Indeed, it is necessary to state loud and clear that Valéry, for all of his intelligence, should not be painted with the brush of "intellectual poetry." Although less obvious than with some of his peers, Valéry depicts a drama of sensual life that has rarely been rivaled. Certain critics are beginning to see his work less as a mathematical problem to solve and more as a distinctly human expression of the complexities of the body and mind.

The posterity of Valéry has perhaps not yet occurred, although the attention paid him by structuralist and post-structuralist critics would nevertheless suggest the interest that can be kindled by his poetics, if not always by his poetry. As Roland Barthes notes about *Monsieur Teste,* the conventional style of Valéry's writing overshadows the marginality of his thought (*Magazine Littéraire,* 30).

The demanding nature of his intellect has given Valéry the reputation of being a "difficult" writer. Like most generalizations, this one contains a grain of truth since it is usually necessary to read and reread a poem before feeling comfortable in its presence. That explains the general decline in the readership for poetry. Valéry's prose and poetry are designed more to challenge the reader than to comfort him in his ways. With some patience and perseverance, the rewards can be many times the investment in time and effort. Once entered into the rich world of Paul Valéry, readers will discover that many other writers pale in comparison. The great Argentinean writer Jorge Luis Borges expresses his appreciation of Valéry in this way:

> To propose lucidity to men in a lowly romantic era, in the melancholy era of Nazism and dialectical materialism, of the augurs of Freudianism and the merchants of *surréalisme,* such is the noble mission Valéry fulfilled (and continues to fulfill).[2]

Such lessons deserve to be repeated and meditated upon by readers of every new generation who will find in the writings of a great author the expression of some of their own dilemmas and, it is hoped, the answers to some of their questions.

Notes and References

Preface

1. André Gide, 17 July 1941 *Journal 1939–1949: Souvenirs* (Paris: Gallimard "Bibliothèque de la Pléiade," 1954), 86.
2. *Cahiers,* vol. 1 (Paris: Gallimard "Bibliothèque de la Pléiade," 1973), 252; hereafter cited in text as *CI.*

Chapter One

1. This biographical introduction is indebted to the valuable information included in Agathe Rouart-Valéry's prefatory notes to the first volume of Paul Valéry's *Œuvres* (Paris: Gallimard "Bibliothèque de la Pléiade," 1957); hereafter cited in text as Rouart-Valéry when referring to the biographical introduction and as *ŒI* when referring to *Œuvres,* vol. 1.
2. *Cahiers,* vol. 2 (Paris: Gallimard "Bibliothèque de la Pléiade," 1974), 1555; hereafter cited in text as *CII.*
3. *Œuvres,* vol. 2 (Paris: Gallimard "Bibliothèque de la Pléiade," 1960), 1432–33; hereafter cited in text as *ŒII.*
4. André Gide–Paul Valéry, *Correspondance (1890–1942)* (Paris: Gallimard, 1955), 426; hereafter cited in text as *Corr. Gide–Valéry.*
5. Gustave Fourment–Paul Valéry, *Correspondance (1887–1933)* (Paris: Gallimard, 1957), 169; hereafter cited in text as *Corr. Fourment–Valéry.*
6. For an excellent discussion about this encounter between two exceptional individuals, readers are encouraged to consult Lawrence Joseph's *Catherine Pozzi: Une robe couleur du temps* (Paris: Editions de la Différence, 1988). Many of Catherine Pozzi's writings, including her poems and philosophical texts as well as a private journal, have been edited or reedited since the late 1980s.

Chapter Two

1. André Gide, 30 December 1922, *Journal 1889–1939* (Paris: Gallimard "Bibliothèque de la Pléiade," 1951), 749.
2. *Les Critiques de notre temps et Valéry,* ed. Jean Bellemin-Noël (Paris: Garnier Frères, 1971), 183.
3. Roland Barthes in "Paul Valéry," *Magazine littéraire* (October 1982), 26; hereafter cited in text as *Magazine littéraire.*

Chapter Three

1. For a detailed presentation of the history and chronology of each poem in the *Album,* interested readers can consult the Notice to the Pléiade edi-

tion of *Œuvres I*, Suzanne Nash's excellent book-length study of the *Album*, or the second chapter of Pierre-Olivier Walzer's useful and informative volume devoted to Valéry's poetry (see Selected Bibliography).

2.   Suzanne Nash, *Paul Valéry's "Album de vers Ancien": A Past Transfigured* (Princeton: Princeton University Press, 1982), 115–41; hereafter cited in text as Nash.

3.   For some discussion of this angle, see Robert W. Greene's "'La Fileuse' and/as Valéry's Philosophy of Composition," *French Literature Studies* XVIII (1991), 106.

Chapter Four

1.   One interesting exception is Elisabeth Howe's "An Intellectual Autobiography: *La Jeune Parque*," *French Literature Series* XVIII (1991), 94–104.

2.   Cf. Régine Pietra, *Valéry directions spatiales et parcours verbal* (Paris: Lettres Modernes, Minard, Bibliothèque Paul Valéry, 1981), 411; hereafter cited in the text as Pietra.

3.   Both Régine Pietra and Christine Crow have discussed this point in some detail (see Selected Bibliography).

Chapter Five

1.   The Chassang & Senninger, *Recueil de textes littéraires français: XXᵉ siècle* (Paris: Librairie Hachette, 1970) contains "Cantique des Colonnes," two excerpts from "Fragments du Narcisse," "L'Abeille," an excerpt from "Ebauche d'un serpent," "Les Grenades," "Le Cimetière marin" and "Palme." The Lagarde et Michard, *XXᵉ siècle* (Paris: Les Editions Bordas, 1968) contains "Les Pas," "Cantique des Colonnes," three excerpts from "Fragments du Narcisse," "Les Grenades," "Le vin perdu," three excerpts from "La Pythie," an excerpt from "Ebauche d'un serpent," "Le Cimetière marin" and "Palme." Another more recent French anthology, *La Poésie française du XXᵉ siècle*, edited by Daniel Bergez (Paris: Les Editions Bordas, 1986), contains "L'Abeille" and "Les Grenades." Robert Leggewie's *Anthologie de la littérature française* volume 2 (New York: Oxford University Press, 1990) contains "Cantique des colonnes" and "Le Cimetière marin."

2.   See James R. Lawler's *Lecture de Valéry. Une étude de "Charmes"* (Paris: Presses Universitaires de France, 1963), 66–70; hereafter cited in text as Lawler. Also Charles G. Whiting's *Charmes ou Poèmes* (London: Athlone Press, 1973), 84.

3.   Robert Sabatier, *La Poésie du vingtième siècle. Tradition et Evolution* (Paris: Albin Michel, 1982), 224.

4.   Pierre-Olivier Walzer, *La Poésie de Valéry* (Genève: Slatkine Reprints, 1966), 296; hereafter cited in text as Walzer.

5.   This line of interpretation is the only option available to the unin-

formed reader in the Classiques Larousse edition of *Charmes,* which places a colon after "corps impur" on line 220, page 79, thus leading to direct speech.

    6.   Christine M. Crow, *Paul Valéry and the Poetry of Voice* (Cambridge: Cambridge University Press, 1982), 174–75.

Chapter Six

    1.   According to Henry Grubbs, *Lust, la demoiselle de cristal* was performed in 1962, while *L'Idée fixe* was brought to the stage in 1966. The presence of the great French actor Pierre Fresnay contributed to their success. *Le Solitaire,* the second play in *Mon Faust,* was read at the Comédie-Française in the spring of 1945, not long before Valéry's death. See Henry Grubbs, *Paul Valéry* (Boston: Twayne Publishers, 1968), 136, n.10.

Chapter Eight

    1.   In order to avoid unnecessary repetition of *CI* and *CII,* page references are given in parentheses and correspond to the heading and volume unless otherwise indicated.

Chapter Nine

    1.   T. S. Eliot, "Leçon de Valéry" in *Paul Valéry vivant* (Marseilles: Cahiers du Sud, 1946), 74.

    2.   Jorge Luis Borges, "Valéry as Symbol" in *Labyrinths* (Middlesex, England: Penguin Modern Classics, 1970), 233.

Selected Bibliography

PRIMARY SOURCES

Collected Works

Cahiers. Edited by Judith Robinson-Valéry. Paris: Gallimard "Bibliothèque de la Pléiade," vol. 1: 1973; vol. 2: 1974. These volumes are organized by theme and cover over 30 different subjects from Valéry's *Cahiers,* presented in chronological order. Topics in volume 1: Les Cahiers, Ego, Ego scriptor, Gladiator, Langage, Philosophie, Système, Psychologie, Soma et CEM, Sensibilité, Mémoire, Temps. Topics in volume 2: Rêve, Conscience, Attention, Le Moi et la personnalité, Affectivité, Eros, Thêta, Bios, Mathématiques, Science, Art et esthétique, Poïétique, Poésie, Littérature, Poèmes et PPA, Sujets, Homo, Histoire-politique, Enseignement.

Cahiers. Centre National de la Recherche Scientifique, 29 vols., 1957–1961. A photographic reproduction of some 26,600 pages of notes and observations written by Valéry between 1894 and 1945.

Cahiers (1894–1914). Edited by Nicole Celeyrette-Pietri and Judith Robinson-Valéry. Paris: Gallimard, vol. 1: 1987; vol. 2: 1988, vol. 3: 1990. A "definitive" edition of Valéry's thoughts, covering a period of 20 years.

Œuvres. Edited by Jean Hytier. Paris: Gallimard "Bibliothèque de la Pléiade," vol. 1: 1957; vol. 2: 1960. These two volumes include all of Valéry's most important works as well as extremely useful notes, variants, excerpts, and rare or unpublished materials. The main contents of volume 1 are a biographical introduction by Agathe Rouart-Valéry, *Poésies, Mélange,* and *Variété* (each of these with numerous subheadings and sections as well as copious notes); volume 2 contains *Monsieur Teste, Dialogues, Histoires brisées, Tel Quel, Mauvaises Pensées et autres, Regards sur le monde actuel et autres essais,* and *Pièces sur l'art.* As in volume 1, many of these major groupings have several subdivisions, as well as excellent notes. Volume 2 also contains a bibliography through 1982.

Paperback Editions

It is still relatively easy to procure individual works in many of the reprinted Gallimard editions, including the "Collection blanche."

Charmes. Edited by Robert Monestier. Paris: Larousse "Classiques Larousse," 1975. Contains the poems of *Charmes* with notes and commentary, as

163

well as a judicious selection of texts concerning Valéry's poetic theory; it also has helpful critical appendices.

Eupalinos. L'Ame et la danse. Dialogue de l'Arbre. Paris: Gallimard "Poésie," 1945.

La Jeune Parque et poèmes en prose. Paris: Gallimard "Poésie," 1917–1974. Preface and commentary by Jean Levaillant. Contains *La Jeune Parque,* "L'Ange," "Agathe," and "Histoires brisées."

Monsieur Teste. Paris: Gallimard "Imaginaire," 1946.

Poésies. Paris: Gallimard "Poésie," 1929, 1958. Contains the *Album de vers anciens* and *Charmes,* as well as other assorted pieces.

Regards sur le monde actuel et autres essais. Paris: Gallimard "Folio essais," 1945.

Tel Quel I. Paris: Gallimard "Idées," 1941. Contains *Cahier B 1910, Moralités, Littérature,* and *Choses tues.*

Tel Quel II. Paris: Gallimard "Idées," 1943. Contains *Rhumbs, Autres rhumbs, Analecta,* and *Suite.*

English Language Editions

The Collected Works of Paul Valéry. Edited by Jackson Mathews. Princeton, N.J.: Princeton University Press (The Bollingen Series 45), 15 vols., 1956 and since. A very handsome and convenient collection that makes the range of Valéry's writings available to an English-speaking audience, often with facing French text and prefaces by such noted poets as T. S. Eliot, Wallace Stevens, and W. H. Auden. The general volume titles are: 1. *Poems*; 2. *Poems in the Rough*; 3. *Plays*; 4. *Dialogues*; 5. *Idée fixe*; 6. *Monsieur Teste*; 7. *The Art of Poetry*; 8. *Leonardo, Poe, Mallarmé*; 9. *Masters and Friends*; 10. *History and Politics*; 11. *Occasions*; 12. *Degas, Manet, Morisot*; 13. *Aesthetics*; 14. *Analects*; 15. *Moi.*

Paul Valéry. An Anthology. Selected and introduced by James R. Lawler. Princeton: Princeton University Press (The Bollingen Series 45: A), 1956 and since. An excellent selection of texts, both poetry and prose, with an introduction by one of the foremost specialists on Valéry.

Letters

Fourment, Gustave–Valéry, Paul. *Correspondance (1887–1933).* Introduction and notes by Octave Nadal. Paris: Gallimard, 1957. An exchange with one of his closest friends that shows a more private side to Valéry. Contains some earlier versions of poems.

Gide, André–Valéry, Paul. *Correspondance (1890–1942).* Preface and notes by Robert Mallet. Paris: Gallimard, 1955. One of the most interesting modern literary correspondences, especially during the crucial years of the late nineteenth century, when both men laid the foundations of their future careers. There exists an English-language selection of these letters, abridged and translated by June Guicharnaud, titled *Self-Portraits: The*

Gide/Valéry Letters (1890–1942) (Chicago and London: The University of Chicago Press, 1966).

Valéry, Paul. *Lettres à quelques-uns.* Paris: Gallimard, 1952. A selection of letters to a wide range of correspondents, some famous, some not.

SECONDARY SOURCES

Bibliographies

The "bibliographie" at the end of *Œuvres II* contains most of the important critical works published up to 1982, both in France and abroad. For more recent information, readers can consult Douglas Alden's *French XX Bibliography* (Susquehanna University Press), Otto Klapp's *Bibliographie de la littérature française,* Peter Hoy's "Carnet bibliographique" in the "Série Paul Valéry" of the *Revue des lettres modernes* (directed by Huguette Laurenti for Minard); or the regular bibliographical sections in the *Cahiers Paul Valéry* (Gallimard), or the *Bulletin trimestriel des études valéryennes* (Université Paul-Valéry de Montpellier).

Books and Parts of Books

Alain. *Paul Valéry. "La Jeune Parque" commentée par Alain.* Paris: Gallimard, 1953. Commentary and exegesis of this famous poem.
———. *Charmes. Poèmes de Paul Valéry commentés par Alain.* Paris: Gallimard, 1928. Commentary and exegesis of this collection to which Valéry responded in his "Commentaires de *Charmes.*"
Bellemin-Noël, Jean, ed. *Les Critiques de notre temps et Valéry.* Paris: Garnier Frères, 1971. A useful compendium of excerpts from noted scholars and writers, including Marcel Raymond, Jean Hytier, Judith Robinson, Walter Ince, Pierre-Olivier Walzer, Charles Du Bos, Jean Levaillant, Ned Bastet, Georges Poulet, Gilberte Aigrisse, Charles Mauron, Pierre Laurette, Albert Thibaudet, Alain, Octave Nadal, and Gérard Genette.
Bemol, Maurice. *La Méthode critique de Paul Valéry.* Paris: Nizet, 1960. Although somewhat dated, this classic study examines Valéry's critical positions vis-à-vis a number of other thinkers and writers.
Celeyrette-Pietri, Nicole. *"Agathe" ou "Le Manuscrit trouvé dans une cervelle" de Valéry.* Paris: Minard "Archives des lettres modernes," 1981. A noteworthy attempt at explaining one of Valéry's most fascinating but most enigmatic texts; not for uninformed readers.
Charpier, Jacques. *Paul Valéry.* Paris: Seghers "Poètes d'aujourd'hui," 1956. A general introduction to Valéry's life and works. Illustrated.

Cohen, Gustave. *Essai d'explication du "Cimetière marin."* Paris: Gallimard, 1933. An explication based on Professor Cohen's course given at the Sorbonne in 1928 that led to Valéry's essay, "Au sujet du 'Cimetière marin'."

Crow, Christine M. *Paul Valéry and the Poetry of Voice.* Cambridge: Cambridge University Press, 1982. A perceptive study of poetic voice in theoretical terms and as applied to *La Jeune Parque* and *Charmes.*

Duchesne-Guillemin, Jacques. *Etudes pour un Paul Valéry.* Neuchâtel: Editions de la Baconnière, 1964. Essays on a wide range of subjects by one of the foremost Valéry scholars.

Grubbs, Henry. *Paul Valéry.* New York: Twayne Publishers, 1968. The previous volume in the Twayne series devoted to Valéry.

Hytier, Jean. *La Poétique de Valéry.* Paris: Armand Colin, 1970. A systematic presentation of Valéry's poetic theory by the editor of the Pléiade volumes of *Œuvres.*

Joseph, Lawrence. *Catherine Pozzi: Une robe couleur du temps.* Paris: Editions de la Différence, 1988. A fascinating biography of the woman who captured both Valéry's heart and mind in the 1920s, relying on much unpublished or little-known information.

Lawler, James R. *Lecture de Valéry. Une étude de "Charmes."* Paris: Presses Universitaires de France, 1963. An essential study by a leading scholar that incorporates much background material into an exemplary commentary of each poem.

————. *Edgar Poe et les poètes français, suivi d'une conférence inédite de Paul Valéry.* Paris: Julliard, 1989. Two excellent lectures given at the Collège de France, one devoted particularly to Poe and Valéry, followed by the text of a 1922 lecture given by Valéry on Poe.

Lazarides, Alexandre. *Valéry: pour une poétique du dialogue.* Montréal: Presses Universitaires de Montréal, 1978. A valuable study of the *Dialogues,* even if given over at times to theoretical considerations that might prove beyond the tolerance of most inexperienced readers of Valéry and critical theory.

Lussy, Florence de. *La genèse de "La Jeune Parque" de Paul Valéry. Essai de chronologie.* Paris: Minard "Bibliothèque Paul Valéry," 1975. A detailed account of the genesis of *La Jeune Parque* by one of the leading specialists of Valéry's manuscripts.

Moutote, Daniel. *Maîtres livres de notre temps: Postérité du "Livre" de Mallarmé.* Paris: Librairie José Corti, 1988. Analyzes Valéry's debt to Mallarmé's conception of *Le Livre* in the *Cahiers*; other chapters devoted to Proust, Gide, and the "Nouveau roman" allow for interesting comparisons.

Nash, Suzanne. *Paul Valéry's "Album de vers anciens": A Past Transfigured.* Princeton, N.J.: Princeton University Press, 1983. The best and most complete treatment of Valéry's early poetry; history and exegesis.

Oster, Daniel. *Monsieur Valéry. Essai.* Paris: Editions du Seuil, 1981. A highly personal series of short reflections on Valéry, sometimes irritating, sometimes enlightening.

Pietra, Régine. *Valéry directions spatiales et parcours verbal.* Paris: Lettres Modernes, Minard, "Bibliothèque Paul Valéry," 1981. A rambling study that contains many insights, especially about Valéry's intellectual, philosophical, and ideological positions.

Poulet, Georges. "Valéry" in *Etudes sur le temps humain.* Paris: Plon, 1949, 350–63. A study of temporality across a wide range of texts by Valéry, carried out with brio by a leading proponent of the phenomenological approach to literature.

Robinson, Judith. *L'Analyse de l'esprit dans les "Cahiers" de Valéry.* Paris: Librairie José Corti, 1963. A ground-breaking book that has lost none of its relevance; essential reading for anyone engaged in the *Cahiers.*

Rouart-Valéry, Agathe. *Paul Valéry.* Paris: Gallimard, 1966. A very interesting photographic presentation by Valéry's daughter, showing Valéry both on official occasions and with family and friends.

Sabatier, Robert. *La Poésie du vingtième siècle. 1 - Tradition et Evolution.* Paris: Albin Michel, 1982, 213–37. A short but perceptive introduction with attention paid to the debate on "pure poetry."

Walzer, Pierre-Olivier. *La Poésie de Valéry.* Genève: Slatkine Reprints, 1966. A classic in Valéry studies, covering the range of poetry, with numerous early versions of poems and a piece-by-piece exegesis. For its scope and depth, it is probably the best general work to date on Valéry's poetry.

Whiting, Charles G. *Charmes ou Poèmes.* London: The Athlone Press, 1973. A very concise introduction on the themes of *préciosité,* sexuality, and the mind; followed by texts of the poems and notes and commentary.

———. *Paul Valéry.* London: The Athlone Press, 1978. A general overview of the man and his works with many insightful comments along the way.

Yeschua, Silvio. *Valéry, le roman et l'œuvre à faire.* Paris: Lettres Modernes, Minard, "Bibliothèque Paul Valéry," 1976. Examines, through Valéry's conception of the novel, his entire intellectual and artistic framework.

Articles

These volumes of collected articles contain numerous valuable contributions to Valéry scholarship and give some idea of past, present, and future directions.

Bulletin des études valéryennes. "Revue trimestrielle," published regularly since 1974 by the Centre d'Etudes Valéryennes of the Université Paul-Valéry (Montpellier).

Cahiers Paul Valéry. Published by Gallimard for the Amis de Paul Valéry. 1. "Poétique et poésie," 1975; 2. "Mes théâtres," 1977.

"Paul Valéry." *French Literature Series* 18 (1991), 77–113.

"Paul Valéry." *Magazine littéraire* 188 (October 1982), 14–58.

"Paul Valéry." *MLN* 87:4 (May 1972), 539–681.

"Paul Valéry: Poétique et communication." Proceedings from the Colloque international de Kiel held 19–21 October 1977. Edited by Karl-Alfred Blüher and Jürgen Schmidt-Radefeldt. *Cahiers du 20e siècle* 11 (1979), 5–261.

"Paul Valéry." *Yale French Studies* 44 (1970), 1–230.

Paul Valéry. Series published by Les Lettres modernes under the direction of Huguette Laurenti. 1. "Lectures de *Charmes*," 1975; 2. "Recherches sur 'La Jeune Parque'," 1977; 3. "Approches du 'système'," 1979; 4. "Le Pouvoir de l'esprit," 1981.

Paul Valéry vivant. Marseilles: Cahiers du Sud, 1946. Homage to Valéry from over 40 contributors, including Gide, Honegger, Rilke, and others.

For individual articles beyond those listed above, curious readers can consult any of the bibliographical sources listed at the beginning of this section. *French XX* is particularly complete and up-to-date. Among the myriad articles on Valéry, these three recent contributions seemed particularly interesting:

Goodkin, Richard E. "Zeno's Paradox: Mallarmé, Valéry, and the Symbolist 'Movement'." *Yale French Studies* 74 (1988), 133–56. Reexamines Zeno's paradox, linking it to notions of movement in "L'Après-midi d'un faune," "Le Cimetière marin," and theory of the symbolist "movement."

Pickering, Robert. "Valéry: les deux poétiques de *Charmes*." *Revue d'Histoire Littéraire de la France* 4–5 (1991), 573–90. A clear argument for the rereading of the poems of *Charmes* in light of Valéry's poetic theory.

Sirvent, Michel. "Chiffrement, déchiffrement: de Paul Valéry à Jean Ricardou." *French Review* 66:2 (December 1992), 255–66. Interesting, if sometimes obscure, comments on mathematics and writing, showing the connection between Valéry and more recent theoreticians.

Recordings

Pages choisies. One recording (on cassette) with excerpts from poems and prose works read by French actors (Hachette).

Poèmes. One recording of selected poems read by Jean Vilar (Ades).

Index

|

The Author

Walter Putnam is Associate Professor of French at the University of New Mexico. He was also invited to teach as a Visiting Professor of French and Comparative Literature at the Université de Paris X-Nanterre in 1990. A graduate of Duke University (B.A. English), he went on to carry out all of his French studies at the Université de Paris III-Sorbonne Nouvelle, where he received his doctorate in Comparative Literature in 1985. He has served as President of the Rocky Mountain Modern Language Association, member of the UNM Faculty Senate, chair of the UNM European Studies program, and as a regular member and contributor to the Association des Amis d'André Gide and to *French XX.* Among his publications are a book, *L'Aventure littéraire de Joseph Conrad et d'André Gide,* and a dozen articles that have appeared in the *Bulletin des Amis d'André Gide, Stanford French Review, Revue de littérature comparée, Conradiana,* and *Littérales.* He lives in Albuquerque with his wife and daughter.

The Editor

David O'Connell is Professor of French at Georgia State University. He received his Ph.D. in 1966 from Princeton University, where he was a National Woodrow Wilson Fellow, the Bergen Fellow in Romance Languages, and a National Woodrow Wilson Dissertation Fellow. He is the author of *The Teachings of Saint Louis: A Critical Text* (1972), *Les Propres de Saint Louis* (1974), *Louis-Ferdinand Céline* (1976), *The Instructions of Saint Louis: A Critical Text* (1979), *Michel de Saint Pierre: A Catholic Novelist at the Crossroads* (1990), and *François Mauriac Revisited* (1994). He is the editor of *Catholic Writers in France since 1945* (1983) and has served as review editor (1977–79) and managing editor (1987–90) of the *French Review*. He has edited more than 50 books in Twayne's World Authors series.

Gramley Library
Salem College
Winston-Salem, NC 27108